PERSONAL LIABILITY AND DISQUALIFICATION OF COMPANY DIRECTORS

PERSONAL LIABILITY AND DISQUALIFICATION OF COMPANY DIRECTORS

Stephen Griffin

LLB; Lecturer in Law, University of Wales, Aberystwyth

·HART·
PUBLISHING

OXFORD · PORTLAND
1999

Hart Publishing
Oxford and Portland, Oregon

Published in North America (US and Canada) by
Hart Publishing c/o
International Specialized Book Services
5804 NE Hassalo Street
Portland, Oregon
97213-3644
USA

Distributed in Netherlands, Belgium and Luxembourg by
Intersentia, Churchillaan 108
B2900 Schoten
Antwerpen
Belgium

Distributed in Australia and New Zealand by
Federation Press
John St
Leichhardt
NSW 2000

© Stephen Griffin **1999**

Hart Publishing is a specialist legal publisher based in Oxford, England. To order further
copies of this book or to request a list of other publications please write to:

Hart Publishing, 19 Whitehouse Road, Oxford, OX1 4PA
Telephone: +44 (0) 1865 434459 Fax: +44 (0) 1865 794882
email: hartpub@janep.demon.co.uk

British Library Cataloging in Publication Data
Data Available

ISBN 1 84113-075-3 (cloth)

Typeset in 11/13pt Sabon by C.K.M. Typesetting, Salisbury, Wiltshire
Printed and bound in Great Britain by Bookcraft (Bath) Ltd, Midsomer Norton, Somerset

CONTENTS

FOREWORD

The Hon Mrs Justice Arden DBE

The publication of this book is to be welcomed. It focuses readers' attention on the liabilities that can arise when the company of which he or she is a director becomes insolvent. These liabilities are the sanctions for the responsibilities which the law imposes on directors. Directors need information about the consequences of insolvency, and anyone who advises directors should be fully conversant with those consequences.

Many directors are also major shareholders in their company. In that situation they often do not fully appreciate that the company is a separate legal person, and that they owe it a duty to act in good faith in what they consider to be the best interests of the company and not their own interests. A director should always keep this point in the forefront of his or her mind in deciding how to act as a director.

The responsibilities which company and insolvency law impose on directors are far-reaching. One of the subjects covered in this book is wrongful trading. Section 214 of the *Insolvency Act 1986* was highly innovative: never before had a director's conduct been subject to both a subjective and an objective test. Section 214 is relatively new territory for the courts, and deserves careful study by all. It has already led to important developments in the law of negligence which raise the standard of care to be expected of directors and thus the risk of personal liability in damages for negligence.

Another mechanism for making directors accountable is the procedure for disqualification of persons as directors where the court is satisfied that their conduct as directors makes them unfit to be concerned in company management. The law is explained clearly and in detail in this book. More cases are now being investigated and pursued. The experience of many has shown that risk of disqualification is a real one.

Proposals for further legislative changes have been discussed over several years, and some new legislation may be anticipated.

All in all, this is a work to be highly commended.

Royal Courts of Justice
Strand
London WC2A 2LL

PREFACE

Underpinning the regulation of corporate law in the UK and other common law jurisdictions is the principle that a registered company is a separate legal entity, an entity which possesses rights and which is subject to duties and obligations in a manner akin to a natural person. Although the directors of a company are ultimately responsible for guiding the will of the corporate enterprise, a director, as an agent of the company, is generally divorced of any responsibility in respect of the liabilities and debts of the principal.

While the general law recognises and vigorously defends the separate legal identity of the corporate entity, the ability to facilitate an efficient commercial order deems that the interests of corporate creditors should also be protected. Accordingly, where a company's affairs have been mismanaged to the extent that the company is trading in an insolvent state, legislative provisions have been enacted to protect the interests of corporate creditors by deeming that directors contribute to the repayment of corporate debts. The protection of the public interest is also exercised in respect of the courts' ability, under the Company Directors Disqualification Act 1986, to disqualify culpable directors from participating in the future management of a company.

The first part of this book undertakes a thorough examination of the statutory provisions which impose personal liability on directors of insolvent companies. The second part of the book is concerned with a comprehensive analysis of the law governing the disqualification of company directors. The subject matter of each chapter of this book commences with a brief historical account of the provision under consideration. The majority of the provisions have been greatly influenced by the recommendations of the Cork Report (1982) and where relevant, emphasis is placed on the significance and influence of the Report's recommendations. There is an obvious connection between Part 1 and Part 2 of this book in so far as the exposition of factors considered in Part 1 may often be relevant to the determination of matters pertinent to disqualification.

It is hoped that the subject matter of this book will be of interest to corporate lawyers, accountants, academics, students, corporate creditors and, of course, company directors. My aim in writing this work has been to provide a detailed and thorough recital of the law governing the personal liability and disqualification of directors. I have also endeavoured to present the subject matter of the book in a clear and interesting manner.

In writing this book I have been aided by the kindness of a number of people. First I would like to thank The Honourable Mrs Justice Arden D.B.E. for writing the foreword to this book. My former colleague, Professor Michael Hirst, now of the University of De Montfort, deserves a very special mention in so far as he was kind enough to comment upon draft chapters of the work. I would also like to thank my former publishing editor, Susie Hamblin, for the encouragement and enthusiasm which she constantly provided during the various stages of writing the book. Further, my thanks to Daden Hunt and all the staff of John Wiley who aided in the preparation of this work and of course to Hart Publishing for producing the final version of the book. I express particular thanks to Richart Hart for acquiring the publication rights to this title. I am delighted to be involved with such a committed and resourceful publishing team and sincerely hope that Richard's great faith and confidence in this work will be rewarded. My final vote of thanks is reserved for my wife Donna, who, in addition to looking after our two infant daughters, Vicky and Emily, has, throughout, been a tower of strength and patience.

I have endeavoured to state the law as of 1st October 1998.

Stephen Griffin.

TABLE OF CASES

TABLE OF STATUTES

AUSTRALIA

TABLE OF STATUTORY INSTRUMENTS

Part I

PERSONAL LIABILITY OF COMPANY DIRECTORS

Chapter 1

INTRODUCTION

1.1 Directors of insolvent companies

The objective of this chapter is to prepare the stage for Part 1 of this book wherein the author will discuss the effect of the companies legislation in respect of the imposition of personal liability as against directors involved in the management of insolvent companies. This introductory chapter discusses the characteristics attributable to the identification of both a company director and an insolvent company. In addition, the chapter will undertake a brief analysis of the duties expected of directors in the context of the management of insolvent companies. While Part 1 of this book is dominated by a consideration of the personal liability of directors, as determined by the companies legislation, this chapter also provides a summary of the circumstances whereby directors may be made personally liable for the debts and liabilities of an insolvent company under common law and in accordance with equitable principles.

1.1.1 *Identifying the characteristics of a company director*

The appointment of a company director will ordinarily take place by the passing of an ordinary resolution[1] or in a manner which otherwise complies with the terms of a company's articles. A formally appointed director is referred to as a *de jure* director. A *de jure* director may be classed as either an executive or non-executive director.[2] An executive director is a salaried employee of the company, his functions in the management of the company will be delegated to him by the board of directors.

In accordance with the standard Table A articles, the board may appoint one or more of its number to hold office as an executive director.[3] By contrast,

---

[1] See Table A, art. 78, Companies (Tables A to F) Regulations 1985 (hereafter referred to as Table A).

[2] In accordance with the Companies Act 1985 (CA 1985), s.282(1) a public company registered on or after 1 November 1929 is obliged to have at least two directors. All private companies are obliged to have one director.

[3] See Table A, art. 84.

a non-executive director is not a salaried employee of the company and his managerial tasks will normally be of a less arduous nature than those expected of an executive director. Persons who hold office as non-executive directors are quite often appointed because of an expertise or public recognition in a particular field.[4] Although a non-executive director may be expected to play a subsidiary role in the managerial affairs of a company, the duties and obligations imposed by the companies legislation in relation to a non-executive director are indistinguishable from those applicable to executive directors, albeit in practice the standard of proficiency expected of an executive director will, because of the office holder's more intense involvement in a company's affairs, normally give rise to a greater expectation of competence.

In addition to a formally appointed director, a person will also be deemed to be a director of a company where, in accordance with section 741 of the Companies Act 1985, that person occupies the position of director, by whatever name called. Accordingly, the identification of an occupant of the managerial structure of a company is not necessarily dependent upon a formal appointment to a directorship. Notwithstanding the absence of any formal appointment, a person may be deemed to be a company director where that person performs managerial tasks properly associated with the office of a director.[5] In such circumstances that person will be classed as a *de facto* director. The provisions of the companies legislation which seek to impose personal liability against *de jure* directors, will be also applicable in relation to persons who hold office as a *de facto* director.

In evaluating whether a person acted as a *de facto* director, the court will be required to consider the degree of involvement and control which that person exerted over the conduct of a company's affairs. In cases where the affairs of a company are, *prima facie*, under the guardianship of a validly appointed and active board of directors, the evaluation of the control which is necessary to equate a person's activities with those of a *de facto* director may be especially difficult. This difficulty may be particularly prevalent in cases where a person is appointed in a professional capacity to advise on matters connected with the internal and/or external management of the company.

---

[4] The Cadbury Report (1992), the Greenbury Report (1995) and more recently the Hampel Report (1998) considered that non-executive directors should play an important role in maintaining a degree of independence in relation to the constitution of a company's board of directors.

[5] Although a person's position in a company may be described as that of a director, for the person to be properly construed as an office holder in accordance with CA 1985, s.741, the tasks performed by that person must exceed those of a mere employee, they must extend to an authority in matters related to the administration of the company's affairs, see, for example, *Secretary of State v. Tjolle* [1998] BCC 282.

Although the perception of whether a person acted as a *de facto* director will always be a question of fact, determined on a case to case basis, the courts have sought to offer guidance in these matters. However, the guidance offered has not always been of a uniform character. For example, in *Re Hydrodam (Corby) Ltd*,[6] Millet J considered that a person would act as a *de facto* director[7] when he was held out as a director by the company, although never actually or validly appointed to hold office. Whereas, in *Re Richborough Furniture*,[8] Timothy Lloyd QC, sitting as a deputy High Court judge, described a *de facto* director, not in terms of whether he had been held out as occupying the office of a director, but rather, as a person who would act on an equal footing with persons formally appointed to hold office as directors of the company.[9]

Although a person may fall outside the definition of a director as provided by section 741(1), that person may still be identified as a "shadow director". The statutory provisions which affect the personal liability of *de jure* and *de facto* directors of insolvent companies are also applicable to shadow directors. Section 741(2) of the Companies Act 1985 defines a shadow director as,

"A person in accordance with whose directions or instructions the directors of a company are accustomed to act ... a person is not deemed a shadow director by reason only that the directors act on advice given by him in a professional capacity".

A person will act as a shadow director where that person is responsible for engineering and directing corporate activity through a "puppet" board of directors. In contrast to a *de facto* director, a shadow director will not be held out as a director of the company. The shadow director will, in effect, instruct the company's *de jure* and *de facto* directors in relation to the management of the company's affairs. The shadow director will be obeyed in those instructions. Although section 741(2) would appear to expressly exempt a person from being construed as a shadow director when acting in a professional capacity, the exemption will not cover a situation in which, for example, a professional offers advice beyond the reasonable scope of the

---

[6] [1994] 2 BCLC 180.

[7] This case was concerned with determining whether a director of a holding company could be identified as either a *de facto* or a shadow director of the holding company's subsidiary. On the facts of the case, it was held that he could not be. However, the holding company was found to have acted in the capacity of a shadow director.

[8] [1996] 1 BCLC 507.

[9] The identification of a *de facto* director is discussed further in Chapter 8, at p.154 *et seq.*

advice one would normally expect from a person occupying a position of a similar professional status.[10]

1.2 Identifying an insolvent company

The majority of corporate failures are caused by the employment of poor management practices. The management practices most likely to be at fault relate to the production process of a product, the marketing of the product, the financial management of the business and the ability to alternate business practices to accommodate changing economic or market conditions. Although in a strict sense, a company may be properly viewed as insolvent when its liabilities exceed its assets[11] (balance sheet insolvency), a company may, for the purposes of a winding up petition, be viewed as insolvent where it can no longer pay its debts as they fall due (cash flow insolvency).[12] It is therefore possible for a company to be insolvent, calculated on the cash flow basis, but nevertheless solvent in the sense that its assets may still exceed its liabilities (the balance sheet test). It must also be noted that for the purposes of a disqualification order made under section 6 of the Company Directors Disqualification Act 1986 (CDDA 1986), a director of an insolvent company is defined in broad terms to not only include a director of a company which is in liquidation at a time when its assets are insufficient for the payment of its debts (and other liabilities and the expenses of winding up)[13] but also to include a situation where an administrative receiver has been appointed to the company or where an administration order has been made in relation to the company.[14]

---

[10] See, for example, the comments of the members of the Court of Appeal in *Re Tasiban Ltd (No. 3)* [1992] BCC 358, and the judgment of Knox J in *Re a Company (No. 005009 of 1987)* (1988) 4 BCC 424; here the learned judge refused to hold, on a preliminary point of law, that a bank was incapable of acting as the company's shadow director.

[11] Insolvency Act 1986 (IA 1986), s.123(2). Under this test, contingent and prospective liabilities are also taken into account.

[12] Section 123(1) provides that a company will be deemed to be unable to pay its debts and, accordingly, may be subject to winding up proceedings where it is unwilling or unable to discharge a debt to the value of £750 or more. The failure to pay such a debt is considered conclusive evidence of the company's insolvent state, see, for example, *Cornhill Insurance plc v. Improvement Services Ltd* [1986] 1 WLR 114.

[13] See, *Official Receiver v. Moore. Re Gower Enterprises* [1995] BCC 293.

[14] CDDA 1986, s.6(2).

1.3 The duties owed to creditors by directors of insolvent companies

Fiduciary, and common law duties have evolved to prevent an abuse of directors' corporate powers. Traditionally, company directors were exclusively considered to owe such duties to the commercial entity in which they held office.[15] However, in reality, such a perception was artificial because it failed to recognise that a corporate entity was comprised of various interest groups without which it would have no practical existence. Accordingly, directors' duties may be said to be owed to the "company as a whole", an expression which not only encompasses the company as a commercial entity but also the interests of the general body of shareholders, company employees[16] and corporate creditors. The ability to determine the nature and extent of a director's duty to one or more of the aforementioned groups will obviously depend on the circumstances of any given case, although in respect of a director's duty to consider the interests of corporate creditors, this duty will essentially operate where a company is trading in an insolvent state.

1.3.1 *Fiduciary duties*

The scope of a individual director's fiduciary duty will, in part, depend upon the director's role in the management of the company's affairs. The nature of a director's fiduciary duty may be compared to a trust or agency relationship. For example, in relation to the management of corporate funds, a director will act in the capacity of a trustee and, accordingly, may be held personally liable to account for any misapplication of such funds.[17] However, in relation to plotting and implementing corporate strategy, the position of a company director may be more appropriately described as one of agency. A director of a company will be required to exercise reasonable commercial judgment in acting on behalf of his principal but, unlike a trustee he will be permitted to commit the company to transactions which may involve a commercial risk.

Whether as a trustee or an agent, a director stands in a fiduciary relationship to the company in which he holds office. A director who is in breach of a fiduciary duty may be held liable to account for the consequences of the breach. Where a company is in liquidation, the company's liquidator

---

[15] See, for example, *Percival v. Wright* [1902] 2 Ch 421.

[16] In accordance with CA 1985, s.309(1), directors must have regard to the interests of company employees, albeit that this obligation is, in any given instance, only enforceable by the shareholders in general meeting.

[17] See, for example, the judgment of Lindley LJ in *Re Lands Allotment Co* [1884] 1 Ch 616, at p.631.

may enforce a breach of fiduciary duty by commencing proceedings under section 212 of the Insolvency Act 1986.[18]

In a theoretical sense, there are two specific fiduciary duties. The first provides that a director must act *bona fide* for the benefit of the company as a whole and not for some other collateral purpose.[19] The test to determine whether a director is in breach of the *bona fide* duty is a subjective one. However, notwithstanding that a director may have subjectively believed that the pursuit of a course of conduct was for the benefit of the company, he may nevertheless be held to be in breach of a fiduciary duty if the purpose of the transaction was objectively considered to be an abuse of the director's allocated powers. This second fiduciary duty, namely that a director must act for a proper purpose, overrides the first duty. The overriding nature of the duty to act for a proper purpose was alluded to by Hoffmann LJ in *Bishopsgate Investment Management Ltd v. Maxwell*.[20] Hoffmann LJ stated that,

"If a director chooses to participate in the management of a company and exercises powers on its behalf, he owes a duty to act bona fide in the interests of the company. He must exercise the power solely for the purpose for which it was conferred. To exercise the power for another purpose is a breach of his fiduciary duty".[21]

1.3.2 *The conflict of interest rule*

The conflict of interest rule is closely related, as a rule of equity, to the fiduciary duties owed by a director of a company. The rule may be stated as one which prohibits a director from exploiting a corporate opportunity.[22] Although a transaction which results in a conflict of interest may be beneficial to the interests of a company, it may, except in circumstances where the

---

[18] Discussed further in Chapter 2.

[19] See, for example, *Re Smith Fawcett Ltd* [1942] Ch 304.

[20] [1993] BCC 120. Also see, *Howard Smith Ltd v. Ampol Petroleum Ltd* [1974] AC 821, *Mutual Life Insurance Co v. The Rank Organisation Ltd* [1985] BCLC 11.

[21] *Ibid.*, at p.140.

[22] Where a director has an interest in a contract to which the company is a party, CA 1985, s.317 requires the director to disclose that interest to a meeting of the full board of directors, albeit that the degree of disclosure required is of a general as opposed to a specific nature. A director who fails to notify a meeting of the board of directors of such an interest is liable to be fined in accordance with CA 1985, s.317(7). As a breach of s.317 constitutes a criminal as opposed to a civil wrong, a director may comply with s.317, but may still be subject to the conflict of interest rule, see for example, *Guinness plc v. Saunders* [1990] 2 AC 663, *Cowan de Groot Properties Ltd v. Eagle Trust plc* [1991] BCLC 1045.

articles otherwise provide,[23] be set aside by the company in general meeting.[24] A director who acts in breach of the conflict of interest rule will be liable to compensate the company for any personal benefit gained, or loss sustained to the company, as a consequence of the transaction. Where a company is in liquidation, the company's liquidator may enforce the conflict of interest rule by commencing proceedings under section 212 of the Insolvency Act 1986.[25]

1.3.3 *Duty of care*

A director of a company may, in the performance of his managerial tasks, be called upon to enter into business transactions which carry a potential element of risk. The nature of commercial reality dictates that a commercial gamble may be necessary to secure economic stability or growth. Accordingly, the duties of care and skill of a company director are, in relation to entering business transactions, far less onerous than those in a trustee-beneficiary relationship. Nevertheless, a director is expected to exhibit reasonable care in the general conduct of a company's affairs. The standard of care required is not, however, measured in terms of a professional standard applicable to directors as a class. Mere errors of judgement or acts of imprudence will not necessarily constitute a breach of duty, although directors qualified in a particular business related area will be expected to exhibit a reasonable standard of skill appropriate to their area of expertise.

The duty of care expected from executive directors will, in accordance with their active involvement in the management of a company, normally be more extensive than for non-executive directors. However, where non-executive directors are entrusted with business matters in which they have a personal expertise, they too must exhibit a reasonable standard of care which is appropriate to their level of expertise. For example, in *Dorchester Finance*

---

[23] A company may waive the conflict of interest rule by including within its articles a provision which corresponds to the form adopted by Table A, art. 85. At first sight, Table A, art. 85 would seem to conflict with CA 1985, s.310, which precludes a company from including a provision within its articles, or in any contract with a director, whereby the director is exempted from liability in respect of a breach of duty. The potential discrepancy between s.310 and Table A, art. 85 was considered by Vinelott J in *Movitex Ltd v. Bulfield & Ors* (1986) 2 BCC 99,403. Vinelott J concluded that the conflict of interest rule was an overriding rule of equity, a distinct rule of equity, a breach of which would not necessarily cause harm to a company or result in a breach of duty.

[24] See, for example, *Aberdeen Railway Co v. Blaikie Bros* (1854) 1 Macq 461. The nature of the conflict which may give rise to the application of the rule must involve more than a trivial interest, see, for example, *Boulting v. ACTAT* [1963] 2 QB 606. For a recent case analysis of the conflict of interest rule see, *Framlington Group plc v. Anderson* [1995] BCC 611.

[25] Discussed in Chapter 2.

Co Ltd v. Stebbing[26] a company successfully brought an action against two non-executive directors who were in breach of their duty of care. One of the said directors was a chartered accountant while the other had considerable accounting experience. The company's action was commenced because the two directors had been in the practice of signing blank cheques which were to be drawn on the company's bank account. As experienced accountants, the directors should have known better, their actions clearly amounted to a breach of their duty.

In order to comply with the duty of care, a director must pay diligent attention to the business affairs of the company in which he holds office. A director's non performance of an act which it is his duty to perform may result in a breach of duty. For example, in *Re Duomatic,*[27] a director who failed to seek specialist help or guidance (in this case from the general body of shareholders), when it was reasonable in the circumstances for him to have done so, was found to be in breach of his duty of care to the company.

The test to determine the duty of care expected of a director[28] may be expressed as a standard whereby a director need not exhibit in the performance of his duties any greater degree of skill than could reasonably be expected from a person occupying a similar position. In considering whether a breach has occurred, the general knowledge, skill and experience which may be reasonably expected of a person holding the office in question must be taken into account, albeit that in appropriate circumstances the knowledge, skill and experience of the particular director accused of acting in breach of the duty, must also be considered.[29] A director who is in breach of a duty of care may be held liable by the company in general meeting, to account for the consequences of the breach. Where a company is in liquidation, the company's liquidator may enforce a breach of fiduciary duty by commencing proceedings under section 212 of the Insolvency Act 1986.[30]

1.3.4 *Directors' duties in respect of insolvent companies*

In considering the exercise of directors' duties, it may be said that while a company is solvent, the interests of the shareholding body will outweigh considerations relating to the interests of corporate creditors. However, where a company continues to trade at a time when its liabilities exceed its

---

[26] [1989] BCLC 498.

[27] [1969] 2 Ch 365.

[28] Discussed further in Chapter 2.

[29] The test is, therefore, comparable to the one used to determine wrongful trading under IA 1986, s.214. See Chapter 4, at p.64 *et seq.*

[30] *Supra*, n.27.

assets,[31] the interests of corporate creditors will supersede the interests of shareholders.[32] In such a situation, the dominance of creditor interests is logical in the sense that when a company is insolvent its creditors will take priority over shareholders in the expected realisation of corporate assets, should the company's insolvency develop into receivership or liquidation.[33]

The decision of the Court of Appeal in *West Mercia Safetywear Ltd v. Dodd*[34] provides a lucid example of the courts' acceptance of the afore-mentioned "insolvency qualification". The case concerned a subsidiary company which was in debt to its holding company to the sum of approximately £30,000. D, a director of both the holding company and its subsidiary, authorised the payment of £4,000 from the account of the subsidiary for the purpose of repaying part of its debt to the holding company. However, following the liquidation of the subsidiary, the liquidator sought the recovery of the £4,000 on the premise that the payment constituted a breach of duty (and preference) to the subsidiary company. The Court of Appeal, in reversing the first instance judgment of Ward J, held that the director, in authorising the payment of £4,000 to the holding company, had failed to take into account the interests of the subsidiary's creditors. As the subsidiary had been insolvent at the time of the payment of the £4,000, the director had acted in breach of his duty in not considering the interests of the subsidiary's creditors. D was made personally liable to account for the £4,000.

A more exceptional example of the court's ability to protect the interests of corporate creditors is to be found in *Standard Chartered Bank v. Walker*.[35] In this case, the court granted an injunction to restrain a director of an insolvent company from exercising his right to vote, *qua* shareholder, on a motion

---

[31] As defined by the IA 1986, s.123.

[32] It should be noted that employee interests may, in exceptional cases, supersede those of corporate creditors. For example, in *Re Welfab Engineers Ltd* [1990] BCLC 833, in the course of misfeasance proceedings, the directors of a company which had been trading in an insolvent state were held to be entitled to sell the company as a going concern, albeit that the sale was at an undervalue. The sale of the company as a going concern was sanctioned in so far as it protected the employment prospects of the company's workforce.

[33] The recognition of creditors' interests owes much to the Australian High Court's decision in *Walker v. Wimbourne* (1976) 137 CLR 1. In the UK, one of the earliest cases to discuss the company's interest being construed in terms of creditor interests was the Court of Appeal's decision in *Re Horsley Weight Ltd* [1982] Ch 442. Subsequent case law has confirmed that creditor interests may displace those of the general body of shareholders in circumstances where a company has declined into a state of insolvency, see, for example, *Brady v. Brady* [1989] AC 755. See, Grantham — "The Judicial Extension of Directors' Duties to Creditors" [1991] JBL 1.

[34] [1988] BCLC 250.

[35] [1992] BCLC 603.

which had two purposes. The first purpose was to enable a consortium of banks to instigate a rescue package on behalf of the company. The second purpose was one which sought to remove the director from holding office in the company. As the director could have used (and indeed would have used) his votes to block the ordinary resolution required to pass the two part motion (to maintain his directorship of the company), the court granted the injunction; without the injunction the company's position would have been perilous. The court's action served to protect the very existence of the company, and more specifically the interests of the company's major creditors. In analysing this case, it may be said that had the director exercised his votes to block the resolution, then his actions (albeit *qua* shareholder) would not have been for a proper purpose in so far as they would have been prejudicial to the interests of the company as a whole.[36] It should be noted that the action, in so far as it had the effect of indirectly enforcing the director's fiduciary duty, was unusual in the sense that the action sought to prevent a breach of duty as opposed to correcting an executed breach. Further, the proper plaintiff to such an action should, under the principles of law enunciated in *Foss v. Harbottle*,[37] have been the company, and not a consortium of the company's creditors.[38]

Notwithstanding that the consideration of directors' duties in relation to creditor interests is normally triggered by a company's insolvent state, there is judicial support for the view that the duty to consider creditor interests should also be applicable where a company is solvent. The arguments in support of this contention[39] are based on the premise that the collection of interests which comprise the concept of the corporate enterprise (the "company as whole") and which include the interests of corporate creditors, are operative interests irrespective of whether a company is in a solvent or insolvent state. In *Winkorth v. Edward Baron Development Co Ltd*,[40] Templeman LJ remarked that,

> "... a company owes a duty to its creditors, present and future. The company is not bound to pay off every debt as soon as it is incurred and the company is not obliged to avoid all ventures which involve an element of risk, but the company owes a duty to its creditors to keep its property

---

[36] Note that it is difficult to reconcile this decision with the principles enunciated in *Pender v. Lushington* (1870) 6 Ch D 70.

[37] (1843) 2 Hare 461.

[38] In addition, it must be observed that creditors have no right to pursue a derivative action.

[39] See, for example, Sappideen — "Fiduciary Obligations to Corporate Creditors" [1991] JBL 365.

[40] [1987] 1 All ER 114.

inviolate and available for the repayment of its debts ... A duty is owed by the directors to the company and to the creditors of the company to ensure that the affairs of the company are properly administered and that its property is not dissipated or exploited for the benefit of the directors themselves to the prejudice of creditors".[41]

In one sense, the words of Templeman LJ expound a common-sense logic in respect of a company's ability to manage its business affairs, affairs which will obviously include the repayment of corporate debts. The failure to repay a debt or to maintain the payment of instalments due to a creditor may be prejudicial to the very existence of the corporate enterprise. However, the contention advanced by Templeman J that directors of solvent companies should owe specific duties to corporate creditors is, with respect, misplaced and unnecessary. Although a corporate creditor takes a risk in advancing credit, that risk will be compensated for by interest payments and the creditor's ability to take security over the company's assets. A corporate creditor is an outsider in the internal management of a solvent company and as such should not be allowed to enforce that outsider right *via* the internal mechanisms of the company, mechanisms which are designed to regulate the duties of company directors in respect of their relationship with the company's shareholders.

1.4 The general presumption against a director's personal liability for the debts and other liabilities of an insolvent company

The recognition of a corporate entity's legal independence[42] creates what is commonly referred to as the "corporate veil". The corporate veil is "drawn" between the corporate entity and the membership and management of a company to separate the company's independent legal existence from that of its human constituents. Further, as the majority of registered companies are incorporated with a share capital and a limited liability status, the members of such companies will cease to incur any liability to contribute to the debts of the company following the payment of the nominal value of their shares.[43] It should be noted that although a director of a company will not ordinarily be compelled to become a member of the company in which he

---

[41] *Ibid.*, at p.118.
[42] The CA 1985, s.13(3) provides that a company registered in accordance with the provisions of the companies legislation is, as from the date of its incorporation, a body corporate.
[43] *Salomon v. A Salomon & Co Ltd* [1897] AC 22.

holds office,[44] in the vast majority of cases, a director of a company will also be a member of that company. Indeed, in a private limited company, it is commonplace for the directors of the company to hold the vast majority, if not all of the company's shares.

As a business form, the advantage of forming a limited liability company is patently obvious, because should the company's enterprise fail, the members and directors of the company will ordinarily be shielded against the incursion of personal liability. Additionally, in incorporating a business enterprise, it may also be possible for a founding member/director of the company to protect his personal investment in the company by taking a security interest over the corporate assets.

Although the separate legal identity of a limited liability company ordinarily divorces the company's interests and responsibilities from those of the company's membership and management, the corporate veil will, in exceptional circumstances, be disturbed, to impose personal liability on a member or/and directors of the company. The disturbance of the corporate veil may take place in accordance with the specific terms of a statutory provision or, at common law, where the formation of a company is considered to be contrary to the national interest,[45] where its formation constitutes a fraud[46] or facade,[47] or, alternatively, in a holding company-subsidiary relationship, where the two entities are deemed to constitute a single economic entity.[48] Further, the independence of a subsidiary company may be ignored on the premise that it is viewed as but an agent of its holding company.[49]

---

[44] The terms of a company's articles may compel a director to become a shareholder of the company in which he is to hold office, in such a case and in accordance with the CA 1985, s.291, the director must acquire his share qualification within two months after his appointment.

[45] See, for example, *Daimler v. Continental Tyre & Rubber Co* [1916] 2 AC 307.

[46] For example, where the underlying motive for the incorporation of the company was to enable its controllers to impugn an existing obligation, see, *Gilford Motor Co v. Horne* [1933] Ch 935.

[47] The motive behind a company's incorporation may be highly relevant to the determination of whether a member/director of the company can be made personally liable for an act purportedly entered into on behalf of the company, see, *Hare v. Commissioners of Custom & Excise* (1996) *The Times* 29 February. However, it should be noted that in relation to a holding company-subsidiary relationship, the Court of Appeal in *Adams v. Cape Industries* [1990] Ch 433 could find no legal objection where the corporate structure of a group of companies had been used to ensure that any future legal liability, which might be attached to the group enterprise, fell on a subsidiary of the holding company, rather than on the holding company itself.

[48] See, for example, *DHN Food Distributors v. Tower Hamlets LBC* [1976] 1 WLR 852.

[49] See, for example, *Smith Stone & Knight v. Birmingham Corporation* [1939] 4 All ER 116.

Where a statutory provision seeks to disturb the corporate veil its effect will not normally be to deny the existence of the corporate entity but will primarily be aimed at penalising company directors for some form of corporate malpractice. The said malpractice will inevitably be concerned with the activities of directors of insolvent companies. A detailed discussion of the relevant statutory provisions will form the basis of the following chapters in Part 1 of this book.

Whilst at common law the judiciary have generally sought to restrict the disturbance of the corporate veil to instances of fraud or facade, in some cases the justification for imposing personal liability on a member/director of a company has been extended to take account of equitable principles, with the purpose of preventing injustice and a perversion of the corporate form. Indeed, Lord Denning advocated that a court's power to lift the corporate veil should be viewed as a discretionary power as opposed to a tool which could only be employed in specific and well defined circumstances.[50] Nevertheless, more recently in *Adams v. Cape Industries plc,*[51] the Court of Appeal forcefully denied that the disturbance of the corporate veil should be advanced on the premise of considering issues relevant to the justice of a case. The Court of Appeal resolved that a justice qualification was an unstable and imprecise measure against which an issue of such fundamental importance should be decided.[52]

---

[50] See, for example, the judgment of Lord Denning in *Littlewoods Mail Order Stores Ltd v. IRC* [1969] 1 WLR 1241, at p.1254. Also see the judgment of Cumming Bruce LJ in *Re a Company* (1985) 1 BCC 99,421, at p.99,425.

[51] [1990] Ch 433.

[52] It should be noted that while in *Adams v. Cape Industries* the Court of Appeal unequivocally denied that issues of justice could form the basis of a decision to dislodge the corporate veil, the first instance judgment of Richard Southwell QC, sitting as a deputy High Court judge in *Creasey v. Beachwood Motors Ltd* (1992) BCC 639, reasserted the belief that the underlying justification for lifting the corporate veil may, in appropriate circumstances, be couched in terms of equitable considerations and as such the decision in *Adams v. Cape Industries* should not be viewed to have been written in stone. However, in *Re Polly Peck International plc (No. 3)* [1996] 1 BCLC 428, Robert Walker J supported the approach taken by the Court of Appeal and insisted that the lower courts should not seek to expound the concept of justice as a means by which the corporate veil could be disturbed. Indeed, the recent decision of the Court of Appeal in *Ord v. Belhaven Pubs.* [1998] BCC 607 expressly approved the decision in *Adams v. Cape Industries* and in doing so held that the decision in *Creasey v. Beachwood Motors* should be considered to be overruled.

1.5 The liability of a director for personal undertakings

Although the corporate veil will generally shield a director from the incursion of personal liability in a situation where the director acted in his capacity as an agent of the company, a director's immunity from the imposition of personal liability will not be safeguarded where he undertakes a collateral and personal obligation on behalf of the company; notwithstanding that the undertaking was instigated to benefit the company.

1.5.1 *Personal liability in contract*

In circumstances where the assets of a company may be insufficient to secure corporate liabilities, a director may be obliged to enter into a contractual obligation to personally guarantee the repayment of the company's debts. A binding contractual agreement to guarantee a corporate debt may also be found in the guise of a letter of comfort.[53] A letter of comfort may take the form of a personal assurance from a director of a company whereby he personally promises that a corporate debt will be met. Where, in reliance on the terms of the letter, its recipient alters his position in respect of a right to enforce the debt, that reliance may amount to consideration, thereby in law substantiating the creditor's right to enforce the director's assurance that the debt will be paid.

Therefore, the director's assurance, albeit that it may take the form of a letter of comfort as opposed to a formal guarantee, may be construed as a contractual promise to repay the debt.[54] In determining whether the terms of a comfort letter provide evidence of the existence of a contractual promise, it is to be observed that where the words in the letter are construed to amount to a mere statement of corporate policy, then it is unlikely that such words will be given any legal effect. Accordingly, where, for example, a director writes, "It is our policy to ensure that the company's business is at all times in a position to meet its liabilities to you under the loan facility agreements", then following the decision of the Court of Appeal in *Kleinwort Benson Ltd v. Malaysia Mining Corp Bhd,*[55] it is unlikely that the said statement of

---

[53] See Milman, "Personal Liability and Disqualification of Company Directors: Something Old, Something New" (1992) 43 NILQ 1.

[54] Following the case of *Edwards v. Skyways* [1964] 1 All ER 494, a promise made for consideration is intended to have contractual effect unless the contrary is shown. The party seeking to deny legal relations has a heavy onus of establishing his case and will not escape his legal responsibility by merely heading a letter "comfort letter".

[55] [1989] 1 WLR 379, see also, *Re Atlantic Computers plc (in administration). National Australia Bank Ltd v. Soden* [1995] BCC 696.

corporate policy will be regarded as a contractual promise. Evidence which supports the fact that a comfort letter was not intended as a contractual promise may also be found where a creditor made unsuccessful attempts to persuade the director(s) to personally guarantee the debt or where, for example, as a consequence of the comfort letter, a creditor sought to charge the company a higher rate of interest in recognition of the fact that the comfort letter did in fact contain no formal guarantee in respect of the repayment of the debt.

1.5.2 *Personal liability for pre-incorporation contracts*

A director of a company will be personally liable on any contract which he entered into on behalf of the company at a time prior to the company's incorporation.[56] Although a pre-incorporation contract may be for the future benefit of the company, until a company is incorporated, the company has no legal existence and therefore cannot be bound by contracts made in its name or on its behalf.[57] Even after its incorporation, a company cannot expressly, or by conduct, retrospectively ratify or adopt a contract made in its name or on its behalf.[58]

1.5.3 *Personal liability in tort*

Where an officer of a limited liability company, acting within the scope of his delegated or ostensible authority, causes the company to commit a tort, the normal presumption of liability will be against the company and not the individual officer.[59] The said presumption expounds the principle that, in law, an incorporated company is a separate entity, an entity which is distinct from its human constituents. Accordingly, where the performance of a wrongful act is committed in the company's name, liability should properly rest with the company. However, in exceptional circumstances a director may (in addition to the company's incursion of liability for the commission of the tort) incur personal liability for the ordinance of the tort.

The extent of a director's personal liability for a tort which was committed in the name of the company will be dependent upon whether the director

---

[56] See, CA 1985, s.36C.
[57] See, for example, *Natal Land & Colonisation Co v. Pauline Colliery Syndicate* [1904] AC 120.
[58] See, for example, *Re Northumberland Avenue Hotel Co* (1886) 33 Ch D 16.
[59] See, for example, *Rainham Chemical Works Ltd v. Belvedere Fish Guano Ltd* [1921] 2 AC 465.

exhibited a personal responsibility in directing or procuring the commission of the tort.[60] To incur liability, a director must have acted in a manner which goes beyond his authority as an officer of the company by expressly or impliedly ordering or procuring the commission of the tort. Liability will also be dependent upon whether the tort imposed a standard of strict liability, or required proof of the defendant's mental state or knowledge.[61]

In considering the nature of a director's personal involvement in the commission of a tort, it must be emphasised that his involvement should not be assumed on the premise that the director held a prominent position in a company.[62] To hold otherwise would amount to a clear failure to recognise the nature and implications of corporate personality. Accordingly, the court must find cogent evidence to displace the presumption of the director having acted otherwise than as the company's instrument. In effect, the director must, through his actions and dealings with the injured party, have impliedly or expressly represented a personal involvement in the affairs of the company, a representation which goes beyond the routine involvement of a company director in the management of the affairs of a company. The director must have accepted a personal commitment as distinct from involving himself in a corporate obligation. The evidence to displace corporate responsibility must be overwhelming.

A case which is most pertinent and instructive of the determination of a

---

[60] See, for example, *Performing Right Society Ltd v. Ciryl Theatrical Syndicate Ltd* [1924] 1 KB.

[61] See, for example, *C Evans & Sons Ltd v. Spritebrand Ltd and Sullivan* [1985] 1 WLR 317. At one time, the courts, in following a decision of the Federal Court of Appeal of Canada in *Mentore Manufacturing Co Ltd v. National Merchandising Manufacturing Co Ltd* (1978) 89 DLR (3d) 195, moved away from the test applied in *Performing Right Society Ltd v. Ciryl Theatrical Syndicate Ltd* and sought to apply a far more restrictive test to determine liability for a tort of strict liability. This test would render a director liable only in circumstances where the director had directed or procured the tortious act in a reckless or deliberate manner. Indeed, in *White Horse Distillers Ltd v. Gregson Associates Ltd* [1984] RPC 61, Nourse J, in following the lead of the Federal Court of Appeal, considered that a director's liability for any type of tort would need to be established where, in addition to directing the tortious act, the director had acted deliberately or recklessly so as to make the wrongful act his own, as distinct from the act or conduct of the company. Nevertheless, following the Court of Appeal's decision in *Spritebrand*, the interpretation of the *Mentore* case was seriously doubted. The Court of Appeal in reaffirming earlier authorities such as *Performing Right Society Ltd v. Ciryl Theatrical Syndicate Ltd* and *Wah Tat Bank Ltd v. Chan Cheng Kum* [1924] 1 KB 1, held that accountability for a tort of strict liability could be established solely on the premise of a director's personal involvement in the commission of the tort and without further investigation into whether the act had been performed in a reckless or deliberate manner.

[62] This consideration will be especially relevant in a situation where the company is controlled by one person, see, for example, *Trevor Ivory v. Anderson* [1992] 2 NZLR 517.

director's personal liability in tort is the recent decision of the House of Lords in *Williams v. Natural Life Health Ltd*.[63] In *Williams v. Natural Life Health Ltd*, the House of Lords was called upon to determine whether the managing director (M) of Natural Life Health Ltd (the company) who held the vast majority of the company's shares (his wife held a nominal holding) could be held personally liable to the plaintiffs for negligent misstatements made on behalf of the company; such statements were alleged to have induced the plaintiffs to enter into a franchise agreement with the company. The franchise agreement, which related to the sale and supply of the company's health food products, was entered into on 1 May 1987. The company, originally the sole defendant to the action, was wound up in 1992. Thereafter, M was joined as the second defendant.

Prior to considering entering into a franchise arrangement, the plaintiffs had sought advice from R, an independent advisor. R approved the plaintiff's choice of site but advised them that due to a lack of capital, their interests would be better served if they entered into a franchise agreement with the defendant company. It is to be noted that R was paid a commission by the company for the introduction. In the brochure sent to the plaintiffs, the company described itself as a proven concept and stated that it offered expertise to potential franchisees in site and shop selection, and other financial matters related to operating a franchise. The negligent misstatements which formed the subject matter of the plaintiff's claim concerned projections of the expected turnover for the franchise during the first two years of its existence. The projections were prepared by P, the company's franchise director. Prior to the date of the actual franchise agreement, the projections had been upwardly amended on three occasions. The final projections forecasted a turnover in year 1 of £237,250, giving a surplus for the year of approximately £15,250, and in year 2, a turnover of £388,000, giving a surplus of nearly £41,000. However, in reality, the franchise agreement proved itself to be a most unsuccessful venture. Its existence was short-lived, spanning but an eighteen month period during which the plaintiffs made a loss totalling £38,600; instead of a projected profit of some £30,000. The plaintiffs net capital loss in investing in the business totalled £84,641.

The projections had been purportedly based upon figures calculated from the sales figures of businesses operating similar franchise agreements with the company. While, prior to its agreement with the plaintiffs, the company had entered into four other franchise agreements, the said agreements had all been undertaken within a year or less of the agreement entered into with the plaintiffs and as such, the projections relied upon by the plaintiffs could not

---

[63] [1998] 1 BCLC 689.

have been based upon the working figures of the four other businesses. Although M had previously operated a successful health food business, a business which was highlighted in glowing terms[64] in the company's sales brochure, (with photographs) M's business was an independent concern and as such was, in law, unrelated to the business activities of the company.[65]

At first instance, Langley J[66] found in favour of the plaintiffs, a decision which was subsequently confirmed by a majority of the Court of Appeal.[67] In analysing the legal principles relevant to the case, the Court of Appeal examined the principles laid down in *Hedley Byrne v. Heller & Partners Ltd*[68] and concluded that where a reasonable man was asked to furnish information or advice knowing that he was being trusted or that his skill and judgement was being relied upon, and he gave such advice or information without qualification, then in such circumstances he must be held to have accepted some responsibility for the accuracy of his answer or, alternatively, he must have accepted a relationship with the enquirer which required him to exercise such care as the circumstances required. Therefore, as a pre-requisite to establishing liability for the tort of negligent misstatement it was necessary to establish that the defendant had assumed responsibility for the misstatement and that the plaintiff had sought to rely on the defendant's assumption of responsibility.[69]

In relation to determining M's personal liability, Hirst LJ, in delivering the leading judgment of the court, considered that to safeguard commercial adventure, a director would, save in special and exceptional circumstances, rarely be deemed to have a responsibility for the commission of a tort where that act was executed for the benefit of the company. His lordship stated that if liability was to be imposed, the special and exceptional circumstances would require the director to have assumed a personal responsibility for the commission of the tort. Hirst LJ concluded that the special circumstances would not necessarily require any form of personal dealings between the parties but would, however, require the director to have played an instru-

---

[64] The store was described as a pilot unit for the Natural Life franchise network, a leader in the trade which, in 1983, had been awarded the title "Retailer of the Year".

[65] The brochure was misleading in other respects, for example, it had falsely described the concept as proven, the Natural Life name as "well known" and the business method ascribed to Natural Health as tried and well tested.

[66] [1996] 1 BCLC 288, [1996] BCC 376.

[67] [1997] 1 BCLC 131.

[68] [1964] AC 465, at p.486.

[69] These principles were re-affirmed by the House of Lords in *Henderson v. Merret Syndicates Ltd* [1995] 2 AC 145. Further, the House of Lords held that the assumption of responsibility principle enunciated in *Hedley Byrne* was not to be confined to statements but could also apply to any assumption of responsibility for the provision of the services.

mental role which indicated that the director's involvement in the tort was in a personal capacity as opposed to in his capacity *qua* director.

In assessing M's liability, Hirst LJ found that although M's role in the franchise agreement had been of an indirect nature, the involvement had nevertheless been a considerable one. Crucial to the finding of M's personal liability was the fact that the company's own purported expertise in franchising health food shops had been exclusively based upon M's own personal experience of the franchise business. The plaintiffs had impliedly relied upon M's business experience rather than company's experience in such matters. The projections had been solely based upon M's personal proficiency in the franchise business. Accordingly, there had, on M's part, been an assumption of personal responsibility, a responsibility which extended beyond his activities as a director of the company.

In the dissenting judgment of Sir Patrick Russell, his lordship considered that M's involvement in the franchise project had not been exceptionally different from the involvement one would normally expect from a director of a company of a small company. Although M was portrayed as the experienced expert, Sir Patrick Russell opined that the managing director of a small one man company would almost inevitably be possessed of qualities essential to the functioning of the company, indeed he would often be expected to be an expert in matters pertinent to the company's business affairs. Accordingly, in his lordship's view, M never stepped outside the performance of his functions as the company's managing director.

The case proceeded to the House of Lords where the decision of the majority of the Court of Appeal was reversed. The House of Lords concluded that although it was patently evident that the projections had been negligently prepared, the majority of the Court of Appeal had nevertheless failed to give effect to the correct interpretation of the principles enunciated in *Hedley Byrne & Co v. Heller & Partners Ltd* and *Henderson v. Merrett Syndicates Ltd*.[70] Lord Steyn, in giving the leading judgment of the House, observed that the crucial question to ask was whether the defendant, or anybody on his behalf, conveyed directly or indirectly to the prospective franchisees that he, the defendant, was to assume personal responsibility towards the prospective franchisees.

The House of Lords found that M had held himself out at all times as the managing director of a limited company and, accordingly, never assumed to involve himself in the franchise agreement in a personal capacity. Although the company relied almost exclusively on M's personal expertise, that expertise was never marketed or advanced otherwise than under the

---

[70] *Ibid.*

company's corporate umbrella.[71] While M viewed and impliedly approved the financial projections for P's franchise business, M never played an active role in their preparation nor had he ever expressly held himself out as having done so. Accordingly, as M never assumed any direct responsibility for the preparation of the projections, it was impossible to conclude that he had ever assumed a personal responsibility to the plaintiffs. Further, the plaintiffs' dealings with the company had, at all times, been with the company as a distinct legal entity, they had relied on the company's projections and not, for example, sought to identify the defendant other than as a part of the company. Therefore, the House of Lords concluded that there was never any positive or direct evidence which indicated that M had acted otherwise than in his capacity as the company's managing director. As such, he was devoid of any personal responsibility in respect of the commission of the tort.

---

[71] By contrast, see, *Fairline Shipping Corp v. Adamson* [1975] 2 QB 180. In this case, the director made personal assurances to the plaintiff in respect of the safe storage of the plaintiff's goods. The products were damaged due the company's negligence in storing the goods. The director was held to be personally liable for the plaintiff's loss on the premise that he had personally assumed responsibility for the safe storage of the goods.

Chapter 2

MISFEASANCE PROCEEDINGS

2.1 Introduction

This chapter considers the extent and nature of a director's personal liability under section 212 of the Insolvency Act 1986. Section 212, commonly referred to as the "misfeasance provision",[1] is a procedural device and as such does not purport to create any new form of liability.[2] The provision, which is only applicable at a time when a company is in liquidation, provides an expeditious means by way of a summary remedy whereby persons who prior to the company's liquidation were involved in the management of the company may be held accountable for any breach of duty, or other act of misfeasance.

Prior to the introduction of section 212, misfeasance proceedings were regulated by section 631 of the Companies Act 1985. Section 631 provided a remedy for any misfeasance or breach of trust. Although the courts construed section 631, and its statutory predecessors,[3] in wide terms, so that misfeasance proceedings were deemed to be appropriate in circumstances involving any breach of fiduciary duty[4] resulting in a misapplication of

---

[1] In law, the term "misfeasance" does not describe any specific wrongful act, instead it is employed in a generic sense. The use of the term describes conduct which results in any breach of duty, conflict of interest, or breach of trust, in circumstances where the consequences of the wrongful act result in an improper application of the company's assets or property.

[2] Although s.212 does not create any distinct form of liability, it is interesting to note that there are procedural differences which distinguish cases heard under s.212 from those actions which are commenced prior to a company's liquidation and which involve a breach of duty or other act of misfeasance. For example, under s.212, a respondent will be unable to apply for third party proceedings, see, for example, *Re B Johnson & Co (Builders) Ltd* [1955] Ch 634. It is also notable that in commencing proceedings under s.212, the liquidator will not (unlike in actions commenced prior to liquidation) ordinarily be asked to provide security for costs, despite the fact that the company's lack of assets may result in the liquidator being deemed personally liable for costs, see, for example, *Re Strand Wood Co Ltd* [1904] 2 Ch 1.

[3] The legislative history of s.212 may be traced back to the Companies Act 1862, s.165. Prior to CA 1985, s.631, misfeasance proceedings were regulated by CA 1948, s.333(1), a provision which was drafted in identical terms to CA 1985, s.631.

[4] The fiduciary duties of directors are discussed in Chapter 1.

corporate funds or property,[5] the precise scope of the type of conduct which could give rise to proceedings was nevertheless obscured by the vagueness of the statutory provision. The uncertainty as to the scope of the misfeasance provision was especially prevalent in cases involving a negligent breach of duty.[6] However, following its re-drafting,[7] the provision was clarified to the extent that it is now applicable to conduct arising from any breach of duty.[8]

Proceedings under section 212 may only be pursued where, prior to a company's liquidation, the misconduct which formed the subject matter of the misfeasance claim could have been made the subject of an action by the company.[9] Accordingly, the wrong which forms the basis of the proceedings, must have been perpetrated against the company and not in violation of the interests of an individual shareholder or individual corporate creditor.[10]

Further, as a pre-requisite to successfully pursuing a misfeasance claim, the applicant must establish that the breach of duty or other act of misfeasance resulted in a pecuniary loss to the company. Pecuniary loss is, however, defined in terms, to the extent that misfeasance proceedings may still be

[5] For example, misfeasance proceedings have been successfully brought in respect of the following types of misconduct (the examples provided are by no means exhaustive of the type of misconduct which may give rise to misfeasance proceedings): (a) an improper and self serving use of corporate assets by a director in the form of gifts or unwarranted levels of remuneration, see, for example, *Re George Newman & Co* [1895] 1 Ch 674; (b) the unnecessary expenditure of corporate funds by a director, see, for example, *Re Purpoint Ltd* [1991] BCLC 491; (c) the failure of a director to disclose an interest in a transaction involving the company, see, for example, *Re Hanley Theatres of Varieties Ltd* [1902] 2 Ch 809; (d) in cases where shares or debentures have been improperly issued to a director at a discount or undervalue, see, for example, *Hirsche v. Sims* [1894] AC 654; and (e) the receipt by a director of corporate money as a preference, see, for example, *West Mercia Safetywear Ltd v. Dodd & Anor* (1988) 4 BCC 30.

[6] Prior to s.212, the authorities were inconsistent in respect of whether the term "misfeasance" would incorporate negligent conduct. For example, in *Re Kingston Cotton Mill Co* [1896] 2 Ch 283, the Court of Appeal held that an auditor's liability could be established on the premise that he had failed to exercise reasonable care and skill in the valuation of corporate assets. However, in *Re B Johnson & Co (Builders)* [1955] Ch 634, the Court of Appeal held that a claim based exclusively on common law negligence could not form the subject matter of a misfeasance claim.

[7] The re-drafting of the provision was first recommended by the Jenkins Committee Report 1961 (Cmnd. 1749, para. 503(d)).

[8] However, it must be noted that, even in its amended form, misfeasance proceedings will not be appropriate where the wrong in question is unconnected to an act (or omission to act) performed by a director in his capacity as an officer of the company. Accordingly, proceedings under IA 1986, s.212 will not be applicable in a case where the company seeks to recover a contractual debt, see, for example, *Re Etic Ltd* [1928] 1 Ch 861.

[9] See, for example, the comments of James LJ in *Re Canadian Land Reclaiming & Colonizing Company* (1880) 14 Ch D 660, at p.669.

[10] See, for example, *Re Hills Waterfall Estate & Gold Mining Co* [1896] 1 Ch 947.

sustained notwithstanding that a company's financial loss is of a hypothetical as opposed to a quantifiable nature. For example, although a company may have suffered no accountable financial loss in a situation where a director exploits his fiduciary position to obtain a secret profit, misfeasance proceedings may still be invoked against the director. In such a case, the secret profit will be recoverable on the premise that, in equity, it belongs to the company.[11]

Nevertheless, the decision of the Court of Appeal in *Re Derek Randall Enterprises Ltd*[12] may afford some flexibility to the otherwise rigid acceptance of a company's ability to recover a secret profit in the course of misfeasance proceedings. In this case, a director improperly obtained secret commissions in respect of transactions which were entered into on behalf of the company. The secret commissions were paid into the director's personal bank account. The sum of the director's personal bank account, which was in excess of the total amount of the secret commissions was, however, subsequently used to guarantee the company's overdraft. Following a decline in the company's fortunes, the company's bankers demanded the repayment of the overdraft and called in the sum guaranteed. Although the retention of the commissions amounted to an abuse of the director's fiduciary position, the Court of Appeal (by a majority) held that the director was not liable to compensate the company. As the company had benefited from the funds represented by the sum of the director's guarantee, the Court of Appeal found that the company had, albeit indirectly, recovered the sum of money representing the amount of the secret commissions. Accordingly, the company had suffered no loss and as such was not, in respect of the misfeasance proceedings, entitled to any compensation from the director.

Whilst the company may have gained an unjust windfall if the director had been ordered to pay compensation in respect of the act of misfeasance, in another sense, the outcome of this case is difficult to comprehend, because, underpinning the Court of Appeal's decision was its finding that the company had a proprietary claim to the secret commissions,[13] that is, the company was considered to have a right to regard the money derived from the secret commissions as property to which it had a legal right of ownership. The rationale of the decision is therefore confusing because although the company had a claim over the money, in the form of an equitable debt, it had no right to regard the money held in the director's account as its own money. Indeed,

---

[11] See, for example, *Regal Hastings Ltd v. Gulliver* [1942] 1 All ER 378, [1967] 2 AC 134.

[12] [1990] BCC 749.

[13] See, for example, the comments of Stocker LJ, *ibid.*, at p.760. For a detailed and lucid criticism of this case see, Oditah "Misfeasance Proceedings Against Company Directors" [1992] LCLQR 207, at p.222.

had that right existed, it is logical to assume that the director would have been guilty of theft.

2.2 Section 212 of the Insolvency Act 1986

In accordance with section 212, the court may examine the conduct of any person who is, or who acted as a promoter, officer,[14] liquidator, administrator or administrative receiver of a company which is in the course of being wound up,[15] where it is suspected that the said person misapplied or retained, or became accountable for, any money or other property of the company, or was guilty of any misfeasance or breach of any fiduciary or other duty in relation to the company.[16] An application under section 212[17] may be made by the official receiver, liquidator or any creditor or contributory[18] of the company. In circumstances where a person's liability is established, the court may compel[19] that person to:

(a) repay, restore or account for the money or property or any part of it, with interest at such rate as the court thinks just; or

---

[14] The CA 1985, s.744 provides that an officer includes a director, manager or secretary. It has also been held that an auditor may be an officer for the purposes of a misfeasance action, see *Re London and General Bank* [1895] 2 Ch 166. Any person exercising a supervisory or a controlling managerial function in relation to the general policy or administration of a company may also be properly regarded as an officer of the company, see, for example, *Re a Company* [1980] 1 All ER 284. Accordingly, both a *de facto* director and a shadow director will fall within the ambit of s.212. However, a person will not fall within the ambit of s.212 in circumstances where his position as an employee of the company was devoid of any active management functions, see *Re Clasper Group Services Ltd* (1988) 4 BCC 673, *Secretary of State v. Tjolle* [1998] BCC 282.

[15] Section 212 applies irrespective of whether the company is being wound up voluntarily or by the court.

[16] See IA 1986, s.212(1). In accordance with IA 1986, s.212(2), the reference to any misfeasance or breach of any fiduciary or other duty in relation to the company includes, in the case of a person who has acted as liquidator or administrator of the company, any misfeasance or breach of any fiduciary or other duty in connection with the carrying out of his functions as liquidator or administrator of the company. The power to make an application in relation to a person who acted as liquidator or administrator of the company is not permitted, except with the leave of the court, after that person has had his release, see IA 1986, s.212(4).

[17] Proceedings under s.212 will be by way of summons under an application in the form laid down by the Insolvency Rules 1986 (IR 1986), see IR 1986, Chp. 1.

[18] Except with the leave of the court, the power of a contributory to make an application is not permitted, however it will not be defeated on the basis that the contributory would not benefit from any order that the court made, see IA 1986, s.212(5).

[19] See IA 1986, s.212(3).

26

(b) to contribute such a sum to the company's assets by way of compensation in respect of the misfeasance or breach of fiduciary or other duty as the court thinks just.[20]

2.3 Claims based upon negligent conduct

Under section 212, misfeasance proceedings may be commenced in circumstances where a director is in breach of any of his corporate duties. In accordance with the decision of Hoffmann LJ in *Re D'Jan of London Ltd*,[21] the term "any duty" is indicative of the provision's applicability to both a breach of fiduciary duty and a breach of a director's duty of care.

Historically, the test to determine a breach of a director's common law duty of care was, until recently, based upon the test advanced by Romer J in *Re City Equitable Fire Insurance Co*.[22] This test provided that a director was not expected to exhibit in the performance of his duties, any greater degree of skill than could reasonably be expected from a person of his knowledge and experience. The test was predominantly subjective in its nature, in so far as it was driven by a consideration of the director's own personal knowledge and experience in relation to the performance of corporate duties. Accordingly, a director could evade liability on the premise that he was unskilled in the matters which gave rise to an allegation of negligent conduct, notwithstanding the fact that had the conduct been measured against the skill and experience of a reasonable businessman, it may have been construed to have been both negligent and culpable conduct.

However, in the 1980s, a time which witnessed an increased willingness on the part of the general public to become a part of an expanding shareholding society, the standard of skill and care which was to be expected of company directors was revised to reflect a more professional model. For example, in *Re D'Jan of London Ltd*,[23] Hoffmann LJ, in assessing whether the respondent director's conduct was in breach of his duty of care to the company, considered that the duty of care owed by a director at common law was

---

[20] Where more than one director is found to be responsible for a breach of duty or other act of misfeasance, liability may be divided in a manner which the court deems appropriate. In determining the extent of a director's liability the court will take into account the nature of his corporate responsibility and the degree of culpability in respect of the performance of the wrongful act, see, for example, *Re Morecambe Bowling Ltd* [1969] 1 All ER 753, *Re Alexandra Palace Co* (1882) 21 Ch D 149.

[21] [1993] BCC 646 (Hoffmann LJ heard the proceedings as an additional judge of the Chancery Division).

[22] [1925] Ch 407.

[23] *Supra*, n.21.

accurately represented by section 214(4) of the Insolvency Act 1986.[24] Accordingly, the director's conduct was to be measured against the conduct of "... a reasonably diligent person having both:

(a) the general knowledge, skill and experience that may reasonably be expected of a person carrying out the same functions as are carried out by that director in relation to the company; and
(b) the general knowledge, skill and experience that director has".

In *Re D'Jan of London Ltd*, a director (D) held 99% of the company's issued share capital, the remaining 1% of share capital was held by his wife. D was negligent in authorising the contents of an insurance form in so far as he allowed his insurance agent to complete the form in a manner which contained a misrepresentation appertaining to D's past experience as a director of another company. D signed the completed insurance form without having confirmed its contents. Following a fire at the company's premises, in which stock to the value of £174,000 was destroyed, the insurance company, as a consequence of the said misrepresentation, refused to indemnify the company's losses. In the course of the company's liquidation, the liquidator commenced proceedings under section 212, on the premise that D's negligent conduct had precluded the company from recovering a loss which it may otherwise have been entitled to recover. Hoffmann LJ observed that in relation to D's conduct,

"People often take risks in circumstances in which it was not necessary or reasonable to do so. If the risk materialises, they may have to pay a penalty. I do not say that a director must always read the whole of every document which he signs. If he signs an agreement running to 60 pages of turgid legal prose on the assurance of his solicitor that it accurately reflects the board's instructions, he may well be excused from reading it himself. But this was an extremely simple document asking a few questions which D was the best

---

[24] In *Norman v. Theodore Goddard* [1991] BCLC 1028, a case which was also heard by Hoffmann J, the s.214(4) test was accepted to be applicable to the determination of a breach of the common law duty of care. In this case, the learned judge found that there had been no breach of duty on the basis that the respondent, who was alleged to have acted negligently in investing corporate funds, had, in so investing the funds, been entitled to place his trust in advice received from the representative of the company's sole shareholder (B). The respondent would have been expected to have trusted B until such a time as that trust was exposed to have been misplaced. In this case, B had advised the respondent to transfer the company's funds to a company controlled by B. B on receiving the funds had in fact used them for his own purposes. The learned judge found that the respondent had been unaware of B's fraudulent activities.

person to answer. By signing the form he accepted that he was the person who should take responsibility for its contents".[25]

Hoffmann LJ concluded that on the basis of the section 214(4) test, D had not shown reasonable diligence in signing the insurance form. He was therefore in breach of his duty of care to the company and liable under section 212.[26]

Notwithstanding that the section 214(4) test sets a stricter standard against which a director's liability for a breach of the common law duty of care is to be measured, it is to be observed that while the test may more readily facilitate a finding of a breach of duty in instances of internal maladministration, it may, nevertheless, have little effect in respect of matters relating to issues of negligent conduct relating to the commercial viability of business decisions. Historically, other than in cases involving self-serving negligence, the courts have been most reluctant to interfere with management decisions concerning the validity of commercial transactions. In many ways, the reluctance is understandable, given that a director will often in the context of commercial realities, be required to enter into speculative transactions which, by their very nature, carry a potential element of risk. Accordingly, it is submitted that other than where a director's conduct amounts to gross negligence, mere errors of judgment or acts of imprudence in respect of a decision to enter into a commercial transaction will rarely constitute grounds for finding that a director acted in breach of his common law duty of care.[27]

2.4 Ratification

A potential difficulty in implementing section 212 may arise in circumstances where, prior to the company's liquidation, a breach of duty or other act of misfeasance had been ratified by the company's general meeting. Other than where the director's wrongful act results in a fraud on the company,[28]

---

[25] *Supra,* n.21, at p.648.

[26] D's potential liability under s.212 was partly excused by his ability to advance the defence represented by CA 1985, s.727, discussed *infra,* at p.31.

[27] By analogy, under CA 1985, s.459, other than for acts of gross negligence or self serving negligence, a petitioning member of a company will not be able to obtain relief for unfairly prejudicial conduct in circumstances where the subject matter of the complaint is based upon an allegation that the management of the company was negligent in pursing a particular transaction, see, for example, *Re Eligindata Ltd* [1991] BCLC 959. An action under CA 1985, s.459 will, however, be sustainable where the negligent conduct relates to the administration of a company's affairs, see *Re Macro (Ipswich) Ltd* [1994] 2 BCLC 354.

[28] Whereby, as an exception to the rule in *Foss v. Harbottle* (1843) 2 Hare 461, the corporate wrong may be pursued by way of a derivative action.

ratification will ordinarily absolve the delinquent director from the incursion of any personal liability incurred as a consequence of the wrongful act. Indeed as section 212 is a procedural device, and does not create any new form of liability, the implementation of section 212 would, *prima facie*, appear to be inappropriate in circumstances where the alleged misfeasance had previously been ratified by the general meeting. Certainly, it would appear logical to assume that the ratification of a breach of duty or other act of misfeasance, at a time when the company was solvent, would, other than in a case involving a fraud on the company, negate the possibility of an action under section 212.[29] The said assumption may be made on the premise that while the company is solvent, the company's creditors have no legitimate interest in the internal management of the company's affairs.

However, in a situation where the ratification of the breach of duty or other act of misfeasance occurred at a time when the company was insolvent, that is, at a time when creditor interests were paramount, the effectiveness of ratification would appear questionable. Where a company is insolvent, the interests of the company's creditors will effectively override the interests of its shareholders in so far as the latter's financial interest in the company will be superseded by the former's expectation of participating in the liquidation of the company's assets.[30] The effectiveness of the ratification of a wrongful act will be particularly dubious in a situation where the company's liquidation was an inescapable certainty.[31]

Indeed, and in accordance with the decision of the Court of Appeal in *West Mercia Safetywear Ltd v. Dodd*,[32] it would seem inappropriate for the shareholders of an insolvent company, *qua* shareholders, to have any legitimate authority to ratify a breach of duty or other act of misfeasance in circumstances where, shortly after the ratification of the wrongful act, the insolvent company is placed into liquidation. In *West Mercia Safetywear Ltd v. Dodd*, Dillon LJ, giving the leading judgment of the court, approved[33]

---

[29] See, for example, the decision of the Court of Appeal in *Multinational Gas & Petrochemical Co v. Multinational Gas & Petrochemical Services Ltd* [1983] Ch 258.

[30] Had the recommendations of the Cork Report (Cmnd. 8558, para. 1973) been implemented, a misfeasance would have been actionable, notwithstanding that the alleged wrong had been ratified, in circumstances where the misfeasance or breach of duty occurred within two years before the commencement of winding up and in circumstances where it was established that the company was insolvent immediately after the alleged misfeasance or breach.

[31] Despite the fact that a director who committed a breach of duty may hold all, or virtually all, of the company's voting shares, the ratification of a breach of duty cannot be presumed to have taken place without some formal or informal affirmation, see, *Re D'Jan of London* (*supra* n.21).

[32] [1988] BCLC 250.

[33] *Ibid.*, at pp.252-3.

the following statement taken from the judgment of Street CJ in *Kinsela v. Russell Kinsela Pty Ltd (in liq)*:[34]

"In a solvent company the proprietary interests of the shareholders entitle them as a general body to be regarded as the company when questions of the duty of directors arise. If, as a general body, they authorise or ratify a particular action of the directors, there can be no challenge to the validity of what the directors have done. But where a company is insolvent the interests of the creditors intrude. They become prospectively entitled, through the mechanism of liquidation, to displace the power of the shareholders and directors to deal with the company's assets. It is in a practical sense their assets and not the shareholders assets that, through the medium of the company, are under the management of the directors pending either liquidation, return to solvency, or the imposition of some alternative administration".

2.5 The section 727 defence

Section 727(1) of the Companies Act 1985 provides that:

"If in any proceedings for negligence, default, breach of duty or breach of trust against an officer of a company or a person employed by a company as auditor (whether he is or is not an officer of the company) it appears to the court hearing the case that officer or person is or may be liable in respect of the negligence, default, breach of duty or breach of trust, but that he has acted honestly and reasonably, and that having regard to all the circumstances of the case (including those connected with his appointment) he ought fairly to be excused for the negligence, default, breach of duty or breach of trust, that court may relieve him, either wholly or partly, from his liability on such terms as it thinks fit".

Although section 727 may be an inappropriate defence to actions commenced under sections 213 and 214 of the Insolvency Act 1986,[35] its applicability in respect of section 212 proceedings is a more tangible prospect. In relation to section 212 proceedings, the ability of a director to successfully bring himself within the ambit of the section 727 defence[36] will depend upon his capacity to convince the court that, notwithstanding that his conduct may have resulted in a breach of duty or other act of misfeasance, the instigation of the course of

---

[34] (1986) 4 NSWLR 722, at p.730.

[35] Discussed in Chapter 4, at p.77.

[36] The defence need not be specifically pleaded, it may be raised in the course of proceedings, see *Re Kirby's Coaches Ltd* [1991] BCC 130.

conduct was not intended to cause prejudice to the interests of the company as a whole. Accordingly, the director must establish that he acted honestly in pursing a course of conduct; clearly the conduct must not have been undertaken with a view to benefiting the director's own interests or the interests of some other third party.[37] Nevertheless, notwithstanding that a director may have genuinely believed his actions to have been in the best interests of the company as a whole, he will not succeed in establishing the section 727 defence where, in relation to all the circumstances of a case, his conduct is viewed to have been of an unreasonable nature.

Following the decision of Hoffmann LJ in *Re D'Jan of London*,[38] section 727 may even prove to be an appropriate defence to misfeasance proceedings involving a negligent breach of duty. In *Re D'Jan of London*, Hoffmann LJ held that, although objectively, the respondent's conduct was unreasonable, thereby justifying the court in finding that he was liable for the negligent breach of duty, such conduct could, for the purposes of section 727, still be viewed to be both honest and reasonable. This decision was reached on the basis that section 727 lent itself to a subjective consideration of the director's conduct and as such the director's error of judgment was of a type which could happen to any busy man. Further, Hoffmann LJ opined that as the company's share capital was wholly owned by the director and his wife (the director held 99% of the share capital) and given the fact that the company was solvent at the relevant time, the economic realities of the case dictated that the only persons whose interests the director could foreseeably have put at risk, were those of himself and his wife.

However, in analysing the judgment of Hoffmann LJ, it is suggested that the ability to apply the section 727 defence to a case involving a negligent breach of duty, must be viewed with some caution. It must be remembered that the section 727 defence is not construed by an entirely subjective standard, that is, it will only apply in circumstances where the director acted in both an honest *and reasonable way*. Whilst it is true that the terms of

---

[37] An example of the type of conduct which may, in relation to misfeasance proceedings, give rise to the deployment of the s.727 defence, was alluded to by Hoffmann J in *Re Welfab Engineers Ltd*. In this case, the directors of a financially troubled company sought to accept the lowest of two competing bids for the company's undertaking, on the premise that, the lowest bid was made on the understanding that the company would be maintained as a going concern. Although Hoffmann J concluded that in this particular case the acceptance of the lowest bid did not amount to a breach of the directors' fiduciary duty, he noted that even if the sale had constituted a breach of duty (in so far as it could have potentially prejudiced the interests of corporate creditors) the breach would have been excusable in accordance with s.727, because the intention of the directors in accepting the lowest offer was driven by an honest and reasonable desire to protect the company as a business unit.

[38] *Supra*, n.21.

section 727 confirm that the defence may be applicable to cases involving a negligent breach of duty, it is nevertheless difficult to justify the utilisation of the defence in this manner, because where a director's conduct is adjudged to have been negligent, the conduct must, by its very nature, have been of an unreasonable standard.

Given that the section 214(4) test seeks to establish "reasonableness" by the application of both an objective and subjective test, it would seem illogical to conclude that, if, in accordance with the section 214(4) test, a director's conduct is viewed to be unreasonable, the director, nevertheless, should still be capable of being excused from the whole or a part of his liability, in accordance with section 727. Indeed, if he was to be so excused, it would be on the premise that the unreasonable conduct (found in accordance with the application of the section 214(4) test) was, in some other respects, of a reasonable nature in relation to section 727. Indeed, Hoffmann LJ, conceded that,

"It may seem odd that a person found to have been guilty of negligence which involves failing to take reasonable care, can ever satisfy a court that he acted reasonably".[39]

Accordingly, although the section 214(4) test is predominantly determined in accordance with an objective test, whereas the test to establish the section 727 defence is more subjective in character, the concept of reasonableness must, in relation to its inclusion in section 727, also be measured on an objective basis. Further, it must be noted that if the reasoning adopted in *Re D'Jan of London* is to be accepted, it would seem logical to assume that section 727 may also be applicable to cases involving section 214. The fact that section 727 is, following *Re D'Jan of London*, apparently applicable to cases involving a negligent breach of duty but not applicable to actions commenced under section 214, would appear to represent a contradictory and confusing state of affairs. It is suggested that the section 727 defence should be inapplicable in both instances.

2.6 Set-off claims

For over a century, it has been an established principle of law that a director will be unable to set off any liability, imposed by the court in the course of misfeasance proceedings, against any outstanding debt which the company

---

[39] *Supra*, n.21, at p.649.

may have owed to him.[40] However, it is also to be noted that until the recent case of *Manson v. Smith*,[41] the Court of Appeal had never been called upon to adjudicate on the correctness of this principle of law, a principle which is also applicable to actions commenced under sections 213 and 214 of the Insolvency Act 1986.

In *Manson v. Smith*, the respondent director alleged that a sum of £27,000, representing the extent of his liability under section 212, should be set off against a sum of £109,000, which represented the outstanding amount of a loan, advanced to the company by the director. The director's breach of duty comprised a false claim for expenses (£7,000), and an improper withdrawal of an interest payment from the loan account (£20,000). The director contended that he should be allowed to set off his liability under section 212 on the premise that his case fell within Rule 4.90 of the Insolvency Rules;[42] a rule which regulates set off claims in insolvency proceedings. Rule 4.90 applies in a situation where, prior to the company's liquidation, there had been mutual credits, mutual debts or other mutual dealings between the company and any creditor of the company proving or claiming to prove for a debt in the liquidation.

In dismissing the director's claim, the Court of Appeal held that it was impossible to equate a director's misappropriation of corporate assets with the concept of the director having dealt with the company. Accordingly, the director's contention that there had been mutual dealings between himself and the company could not be sustained. Further, in relation to the director's claim that there had been a mutual debt, the court held that, as the emphasis of Rule 4.90 was targeted at mutual dealings at a time prior to the company's liquidation, the rule could not be applicable to proceedings under section 212, insofar as any liability which was incurred under section 212 (the debt owed by the director to the company as a result of the misfeasance proceedings) would not have existed at a time prior to the company's liquidation.[43]

---

[40] This principle of law was established in *Re Anglo French Co-operative Society* (1882) 21 Ch D 492. The principle applies, notwithstanding that a set off claim would have been permissible in circumstances where, prior to its liquidation, the company had sued the director.

[41] [1997] 2 BCLC 163.

[42] SI 1986/1925.

[43] However, as s.212 does not create any new right of action, but is merely a procedural remedy, surely the debt would have been in existence at a time prior to the company's liquidation, albeit the debt would not have been recoverable in accordance with s.212 proceedings.

2.7 The extent and nature of a director's liability

Although, in the course of misfeasance proceedings, an applicant may be successful in establishing a director's breach of duty or other act of misfeasance, the court, in accordance with section 212(3), will not be compelled to make an order against the director to account for, to return, or to compensate the company in respect of property or moneys which were misapplied as a result of the misfeasance. Section 213 (3) provides that,

> "The court may, on the application of the official receiver or the liquidator, or of any creditor or contributory, examine into the conduct of the person falling within subsection (1) and compel him—
>
> (a) to repay, restore or account for the money or property or any part of it, with interest at such rate as the court thinks just, or
> (b) to contribute such sum to the company's assets by way of compensation in respect of the misfeasance or breach of fiduciary or other duty as the court thinks just".

While the court may exercise its discretion in favour of not compelling a director to make some form of restitution for a breach of duty or other act of misfeasance, in the majority of cases, it is unlikely that the court's discretion will be applied in this manner. However, a possible example of where the discretion could be employed, so as to absolve a director's responsibility, would be in a situation where a restitutionary order would have the effect of affording the company an unjust or undeserved benefit.[44]

In accordance with section 212(3), where a director is ordered to restore or account for money or property, or to contribute to the company's assets, the extent of the director's liability may not necessarily correspond with the extent of the actual loss sustained by the company. Following the company's liquidation, the calculation of the director's liability may, in part, depend upon the company's liability to its corporate creditors. For example, where a director's potential liability for the misfeasance is of a greater monetary value than the company's debt to its creditors, then the section 212(3) order may reflect this fact, to the extent that the amount of the order, while of a sufficient level to compensate creditor interests, may be of a sum which falls short of the actual loss sustained by the company.[45]

However, while it may appear logical to assume that an order under section

---

[44] The court's discretion, although not expressly alluded to, was applied in *Re Derek Randall Enterprises Ltd* (*supra*, n.12). See also, *Re Sunlight Gas Lamp Co* (1900) 16 LTR 535.
[45] See, for example, *Re VGM Holdings Ltd* [1942] Ch 235.

212(3) should not exceed a sum which satisfies the totality of corporate debts, on the other hand, an order of this type would appear somewhat generous to the perpetrator of the misfeasance. Indeed, although the interests of corporate creditors are considered paramount in a situation where a company is in liquidation, it must be remembered that the shareholders of the company may still have a legitimate interest in the company's assets in circumstances where, after the full payment of the company's creditors, a surplus exists. Accordingly, it may appear unjust to the interests of shareholders to limit the amount of an order to a level which is but sufficient to satisfy the company's creditors. Nevertheless, in some instances an order of this type may be justified on the premise that it would be inequitable for the shareholders to take the benefit of the order. For example, in *Re Home & Colonial Insurance Co Ltd*,[46] a liquidator mistakenly believed that he was legally obliged to settle an insurance claim made against the company. A misfeasance action was commenced seeking restitution for the sum of the said claim. The court found the liquidator to have been negligent in settling the claim and ordered him liable for an amount which would enable the company's creditors to be paid in full, with interest at 5%. However, this sum was less than the totality of the loss which the company had suffered as a consequence of the liquidator's negligence. The court held that the liquidator was not obliged to compensate the company for the full amount, on the premise that the company's shareholders had themselves resolved to put the company into liquidation, that is the shareholders also feared that the company would have been made liable on the insurance policy.

2.8 The distribution of the proceeds recovered in misfeasance proceedings

As the purpose for pursuing proceedings under section 212 is to enforce a pre-existing right of the company, it follows that the ability to pursue misfeasance proceedings is a property right of the company and that any proceeds obtained as a consequence of the proceedings will form part of the company's general assets.[47] Accordingly, the ability of the company's unsecured creditors to participate in the fruits of the section 212 proceedings will be subject to the prior claims of the holder of any floating charge[48] where the charge is capable, on crystallisation, of attaching itself to the company's

---

[46] [1930] 1 Ch 102.

[47] As a property right, it is perfectly permissible for the cause of action in the misfeasance proceedings to be legally assigned, see, for example, *Re Park Gate Waggon Works Co* (1881) 17 Ch D 234.

[48] See, for example, *Re Anglo-Austrian Printing & Publishing Co* [1895] 2 Ch 891.

general assets.[49] Therefore, in respect of misfeasance proceedings, an unsecured creditor's expectation to participate in a share of the proceeds of the action will be less favourable than in actions commenced under either section 213 or 214 of the Insolvency Act 1986. In accordance with the decision of the Court of Appeal in *Re Oasis Merchandising Services Ltd*,[50] the fruits of a section 213 or 214 action, cannot, at any stage, be regarded as a part of the property of the company and cannot, therefore, be subject to a floating charge.

2.9 The overlap between section 212 and section 214

In a situation where the evidence of a director's delinquent activities are sufficient to establish an action under section 214, the liquidator may, in a theoretical, if not practical sense, be faced with a dilemma as to whether to proceed under section 214, section 212, or alternatively, under both provisions. The dilemma exists because the evidence to substantiate a successful action under section 214 will also justify a finding that the director's conduct constituted a breach of duty. Although the wording of section 214 is devoid of any specific requirement to establish a specific breach of duty, the ability to establish a director's liability will, given the court's interpretation of section 214(4),[51] inevitably require proof of the fact that the director's conduct amounted to a breach of his duty of care to the company.

Although the evidence against a director may be sufficient to warrant the commencement of proceedings under section 214 or section 212, one would ordinarily expect the liquidator to proceed under the former provision. A successful action under section 214 will generally serve the interests of the general pool of corporate creditors in a more efficient manner than an action under section 212, in so far as the proceeds of any misfeasance proceedings may be limited by the prior claim of a floating charge(s). However, in some cases the liquidator may be compelled by the company's dire financial circumstances to favour an action under section 212, because, unlike the costs involved in a section 214 action, it is clear that the costs incurred in respect of

---

[49] For example, where the floating charge was expressed to have been taken over the company's undertaking. Also, given that the ability to commence a misfeasance action emanates in the enforcement of a property right, it follows that it would be possible for a company to expressly create a charge over the proceeds of any misfeasance proceedings.

[50] [1997] 1 WLR 764. This case, together with a discussion of an unsecured creditor's ability to participate in the fruits of an action commenced under IA 1986, s.214, is discussed further in Chapter 4, at p.84 *et seq.*

[51] See, for example, *Re D'Jan of London Ltd, supra*, n.21. Section 214 is discussed in Chapter 4.

section 212 proceedings will be payable out of the company's assets in priority to all other claims.[52] Therefore, in considering the plausibility of a section 214 action, the liquidator may calculate that after the prior payment of corporate debts, the company's position would be such that it had insufficient assets to pursue the action.

Where the evidence of a case is sufficient to substantiate an action under section 212 or section 214, it may, *prima facie*, appear logical for the liquidator to proceed under both provisions. However, in circumstances where dual proceedings are instigated in respect of the same alleged instance of misconduct, there would appear to be no benefit in such a course of action.[53] For example, where dual proceedings are commenced, it would be most unlikely that the court would ever consider penalising the director twice over. Further, the costs involved in a dual action would probably exceed those involved in a single action under either section 212 or 214.

Finally, a practical problem to the commencement of dual proceedings would be in relation to the priority aspects of the court's order. Other than where the court was required to perform the cumbersome task of attributing a specific amount of the total order in respect of each part of the dual action, it is probable that confusion could arise in relation to the rights of creditors to participate in the distribution of the proceeds of the order. The confusion would exist, in so far as under section 212, a holder of a floating charge would have priority in respect of the proceeds of the order, whereas, under section 214, that priority would not exist.

---

[52] See IA 1986, s.115. For a more extensive discussion of this provision see Chapter 4, at p.85.

[53] A dual action was commenced in *Re DKG Contractors Ltd* [1990] BCC 903. This case is discussed further in the context of IA 1986, s.214, in Chapter 4, at p.91.

Chapter 3

FRAUDULENT TRADING

3.1 Introduction

This chapter is concerned with the liability of persons who are a party to the fraudulent trading of companies. Although fraudulent trading constitutes a breach of the civil law, it is also punishable as a distinct criminal offence. The constituent elements of liability for fraudulent trading, under both civil law and criminal law, are virtually identical. Accordingly, in writing this chapter it has been necessary, in seeking to analyse the civil law's regulation of fraudulent trading, to also consider the criminal offence of fraudulent trading.[1]

3.2 The historical development of the prohibition against fraudulent trading

Legal controls, specifically designed to protect corporate creditors and the public interest from the fraudulent trading activities of company directors, were first introduced by section 75 of the Companies Act 1928.[2] This provision was subsequently re-enacted as section 275 of the Companies Act 1929. Under section 275, civil or criminal liability could be imposed against

---

[1] Although a person who is a party to the fraudulent trading of a company may be potentially liable under both the civil and criminal law, in the majority of cases, the nature of a person's liability will often fall to be determined on the basis of whether, under the civil law, the respondent, if found liable, would have been capable of discharging his civil liability, namely, contributing to the company's assets in accordance with the terms of the court's order. See, for example, the comments of Henry J, in giving the judgment of the Court of Appeal (Criminal Division) in *R v. Kemp* [1988] QB 645, at p.648.

[2] The legal controls were introduced following the recommendations of the Greene Committee Report 1926 (Cmnd. 2657). The report, chaired by Sir William Greene KC, sought specifically to preclude a person who held a floating charge over a private company and who was also in control of the company, from exploiting his knowledge that the company was insolvent and close to liquidation. The exploitation would frequently take the form of the said person appointing a receiver after he had obtained further goods on credit to enhance the worth of the company's assets, so as to increase the effectiveness of his floating charge. See, for example, *Re William C Leitch Bros Ltd* [1932] 2 Ch 71.

any present or past director of a company where, in the course of the winding up of a company, the director had knowingly been a party to the carrying on of the company's business for a fraudulent purpose or with an intent to defraud creditors of the company, or creditors of any other person. The constituent elements of liability in both civil and criminal law were identical. As the provision included a penal sanction, it was construed strictly, and the applicable burden of proof under both the civil and criminal parts of the provision was one whereby the respondent's fraudulent conduct had to be established beyond reasonable doubt.[3]

Section 275 of the Companies Act 1929 was subsequently replaced by section 332 of the Companies Act 1948.[4] However, the terms of section 332 remained consistent with its statutory predecessor, save that under section 332, liability was no longer confined to the past or present directors of a company, but was applicable to any person who had been a party to a company's fraudulent trading. As under the 1929 Act, an application under section 332, in respect of civil liability, could be made by the Official Receiver, liquidator or any creditor or contributory of the company. The court could, pursuant to section 332(1), declare that any person in breach of the fraudulent trading provision be made personally liable (to the extent that the court directed), without any limitation of liability, for all or any of the debts or other liabilities of the company. In accordance with section 332(3), criminal liability took the form of either a term of imprisonment, for a maximum period of two years, and/or a fine. Following the implementation of the Companies Act 1980, the maximum penalty for fraudulent trading was increased to seven years' imprisonment.[5]

In 1982, the Cork Report proposed that substantive reforms should be made to the fraudulent trading provisions.[6] The principal reform sought by the Cork Committee was for the removal of the provision's dual liability in both civil and criminal law. In cases of fraudulent trading involving an allegation of the respondent's dishonesty, the Cork Report proposed that the respondent should only be subject to criminal liability. In relation to a respondent's civil liability, the Cork Report proposed the creation of a new wrongful trading provision.[7]

---

[3] See, for example, the comments of Pennycuick V-C in *Re Maidstone Buildings Ltd* [1971] 1 WLR 1085, at p.1094.

[4] The CA 1948, s.332 was, in respect of the civil liability contained therein, replaced by the CA 1985, s.630 and then, subsequently, by the IA 1986, s.213.

[5] The maximum penalty is still seven years, see CA 1985, Sch. 24.

[6] Cmnd. 8558 paras 1775-1780.

[7] The inadequacies of the fraudulent trading provision, which led the Cork Report to call for the creation of the wrongful trading provision, are dealt with in Chapter 4 at p.57 *et seq*.

Although subsequently, the Insolvency Act 1986 sought to create a civil form of liability in the guise of a wrongful trading provision (section 214 of the Insolvency Act 1986), it did not, contrary to the recommendations of the Cork Report, remove civil liability from the ambit of the fraudulent trading provision. However, unlike section 332 of the Companies Act 1948, the two forms of liability were separated within distinct provisions of the companies legislation.[8] Accordingly, civil liability for fraudulent trading is now to be found in section 213 of the Insolvency Act 1986, whereas criminal liability is contained within section 458 of the Companies Act 1985. Section 213 of the Insolvency Act provides,

(1) "If in the course of the winding up of a company it appears that any business of the company has been carried on with intent to defraud creditors of the company or creditors of any other person, or for any fraudulent purpose, the following has effect.

(2) The court, on the application of the liquidator may declare that any persons who were knowingly parties to the carrying on of the business in the manner above-mentioned are to be liable to make such contributions (if any) to the company's assets as the court thinks proper".

Section 458 of the Companies Act 1985 provides,

"If any business of a company is carried on with intent to defraud creditors of the company or creditors of any other person, or for any fraudulent purpose, every person who was knowingly a party to the carrying on of the business in that manner is liable to imprisonment or a fine, or both. This applies whether or not the company has been, or is in the course of being, wound up".

By analogy to section 332 of the Companies Act 1948, the constituent elements of both provisions have remained virtually identical. Indeed, the distinction between the civil law and criminal law provisions are primarily of a procedural nature. The procedural differences are as follows:

(1) As the civil and criminal elements of the former provision (CA 1948, s.332) have been separated into distinct provisions, the civil provision is now untouched by any penal element. Therefore, the burden of proof in civil proceedings should, as with any other civil provision, be

---

[8] Prior to the passing of the IA 1986, s.213, it is to be observed that the civil provision was separated from the criminal provision. The civil provision, was contained in the CA 1985, s.630.

established on a balance of probabilities. However, in reality, given that section 213 embraces an allegation of fraud, the standard of proof may be adjudged to be more akin to the criminal standard of proof.[9]

(2) A criminal prosecution, unlike a civil action, may be commenced irrespective of whether a company has been put into liquidation.[10]

(3) Finally, in a civil action, the only party who is allowed to make an application to commence proceedings is the company's liquidator.[11] In criminal proceedings, the applicant will be the Crown.[12]

3.3 The protection provided by the fraudulent trading provisions

Both section 213 of the Insolvency Act and section 458 of the Companies Act 1985 are applicable in circumstances where a person knowingly participated in the carrying on of a company's business with an intent to defraud creditors of the company or creditors of any other person, or for any fraudulent purpose. The carrying on of a business may include a single transaction designed to defraud a single creditor.[13] Although the fraudulent trading provisions are primarily aimed at protecting the interests of corporate creditors, the carrying on of a company's business "for any fraudulent purpose" would appear to extend the provision to cover a fraudulent act committed against persons other than creditors of a company.

In *Re Cyona Distributors Ltd*,[14] Lord Denning commented that the words

---

[9] By analogy, consider the attitude of the courts in relation to the application of the civil standard of proof in disqualification cases (see Chapter 9 at p.222). Under CA 1948, s.332, the criminal standard of proof was applicable in so far as the fraudulent trading provision contained both a civil and criminal sanction.

[10] This distinction was first introduced by CA 1981, s.96. Prior to CA 1981, s.96, other than where a company was being wound up, there was some controversy as to whether a criminal prosecution could be brought. In *R v. Schildkamp* [1971] AC 1, the House of Lords, by a majority of 3-2, ruled that it could not.

[11] The liquidator may himself give evidence or call witnesses on the hearing of the application.

[12] Where a person is liable under IA 1986, s.213, that person may be subjected to a disqualification order under CDDA 1986, s.10 (see Chapter 7 at p.146), or, alternatively, evidence of fraudulent trading may be used to pursue a disqualification order under CDDA 1986, s.6 (see Chapter 8 at p.169). Where pursuant to CA 1985, s.458, the evidence of a case is indicative of a person's liability for fraudulent trading (whether he has been convicted or not), that person may be subjected to a disqualification order under CDDA 1986, s.4 (see Chapter 7 at p.143).

[13] See, for example, *Re Gerald Cooper Chemicals Ltd* [1978] Ch 262, *R v. Lockwood* (1986) BCC 93,347.

[14] [1967] Ch 889, at p.902.

"for any fraudulent purpose" were composed in deliberately wide terms to enable the court to bring fraudulent persons to book, and that they should be given their full width. The most probable class of person who is likely to be protected by the term "for any fraudulent purpose" is a customer of a company. However, following a number of decided cases,[15] a customer may be classed as a creditor of the company, notwithstanding that in a strict legal sense a customer cannot properly attain the status of a creditor without first having obtained a judgment order.[16] In effect, the courts in construing the fraudulent trading provisions, have extended the conventional definition of a creditor, namely, a person who is entitled to the immediate repayment of a debt, by allowing a customer, as a potential/contingent creditor, to be viewed as an established creditor.[17] A potential/contingent creditor may be defined as a person with an existing right to the payment of a debt at some future date.[18] However, it is respectfully submitted that the need to label a customer as having the status of a creditor for the purpose of placing him within the protective ambit of the fraudulent trading provision is unnecessary.[19]

---

[15] See, for example, *R v. Sellion* [1982] Crim LR 676.

[16] See, for example, *R v. Inman* [1966] 3 All ER 414, *R v. Burgess* (8th July 1994 unreported).

[17] However, in *Re Gerald Cooper Chemicals Ltd* [1978] Ch 262, Templeman J considered that a customer is not always to be regarded as a creditor of the company. According to the learned judge, a customer would not, for the purposes of the fraudulent trading provisions, be deemed a creditor of a company in circumstances where the customer, on becoming a judgment creditor, was able to recover his debt. Where, however, it would have been impossible for the customer, on becoming a judgment creditor, to recover his debt, then in this situation, the customer would be viewed as a creditor of the company.

[18] However, it is to be noted that in *Re Sarfax Ltd* [1979] 1 Ch 592, Oliver J treated a customer as a potential creditor of the company notwithstanding that the customer had no legal entitlement to be paid during the relevant trading period. Also note that in *R v. Grantham* [1984] QB 675, the Court of Appeal upheld a conviction for fraudulent trading which had occurred over a 28-day period, despite the fact that the goods which were the subject of the fraud were delivered on credit terms which extended the due date for their payment for a further 28 days. Therefore, the court accepted that a customer who would not have been entitled to sue the company during the alleged 28-day period of fraudulent trading could still, for the purposes of the fraudulent trading provisions, be classed as a creditor of the company.

[19] The only logical explanation for this state of affairs would seem to be that the judicial uncertainty concerning the exact ambit of the term "for any fraudulent purpose", coupled with the extended meaning given to the term "creditor", has hitherto meant that the former term is regarded as superfluous in respect of its application to a customer of a company. However, it is interesting to note that in *R v. Kemp* [1988] QB 645, the Court of Appeal interpreted the term "for any fraudulent purpose", as being applicable to potential creditors of a company, i.e. customers of the company. In *R v. Burgess* (July 8 1997, unreported), it was doubted whether the "potential creditor test" should be applicable to the determination of a creditor in accordance with the first limb of CA 1985, s.458. (This reasoning would also apply to the first limb of IA 1986, s.213.)

Unfortunately, it would appear that the construction of the fraudulent trading provision has generally been founded on the misconception that it is only applicable in a situation where the fraudulent act was perpetrated against a creditor of a company, this is despite the potential width of the term "for any fraudulent purpose" and the ease with which it could, in the context of the fraudulent trading provision, be applied, to bring a customer of a company within its ambit.[20]

3.4 Establishing whether a person participated in the fraudulent trading activities of a company

For a person to incur liability for fraudulent trading, it must first be established that he was knowingly a party to the carrying on of the company's business. The courts have construed this requirement as indicative of a person's active involvement in the commission of an act of fraudulent trading.[21] Although, fraudulent trading may be committed by any person who was actively involved in the commission of the fraud, in practice, liability will ordinarily fall on a person who is construed to have been a part of a company's directing mind.[22] As a person who acts as a part of a company's directing mind will normally be actively involved in the management of a company's affairs, persons who have a responsibility for the formulation and

---

[20] The courts have persisted in seeking to extend the term "creditor" to include customers in their guise as potential creditors of a company. For a recent example, see the Court of Appeal's judgment in *R v. Smith* [1996] 2 BCLC 109, at pp.119-122.

[21] See, for example, the comments of Pennycuick V-C in *Re Maidstone Buildings Ltd* [1971] 1 WLR 1085, at p.1092.

[22] See, for example, *R v. Miles* [1992] Cr LR 657. To establish whether a person was a part of the company's directing mind it is necessary to examine a company's management structure and chain of command. Such an examination will aid the determination of whether an officer or servant's wrongful act was directly attributable to the company, i.e. whether the officer or servant had, or was delegated, an authority to act as part of the company's directing mind, or held a position in the corporate structure which could be construed as being a part of the company's directing mind. As such, the question as to whether an officer or servant was a part of a company's directing mind cannot be resolved by the application of a simple set of rules, the question may only be resolved on a case to case basis by analysing the nature of the officer or servant's act and the position which that officer or servant occupied in the corporate structure. For recent case examples which have sought to examine the meaning of the term "directing mind", see, *El Anjou v. Dollar Land Holdings plc* [1994] BCLC 143, *Re Supply of Ready Mixed Concrete (No. 2)* [1995] 1 AC 456, *Meridian Global Funds Management Asia Ltd v. Securities Commission* [1995] BCC 942.

implementation of corporate policy, such as executive directors (and/or shadow directors) will be the most probable candidates to incur liability for acts of fraudulent trading.

Although one would expect liability for fraudulent trading to be restricted to persons who are involved in the internal management of a company, following the decision of Templeman J in *Re Gerald Cooper Chemicals Ltd*,[23] liability may, however, fall on a person who was not involved as an officer or employee of the company. In *Re Gerald Cooper Chemicals Ltd*, a company owed a considerable debt to one of its creditors (X). The company was undercapitalised and trading in an insolvent state. Unable to discharge the debt, the company obtained an advance payment for goods which it had in turn promised to supply to one of its customers. At the time of accepting the payment, the company realised that it would be unable to supply the goods in question. The funds obtained from the advance payment were used to discharge part of the debt, which the company owed to X. Clearly, the trading activities of the company were of a fraudulent nature. In respect of the payment made to X, Templeman J held that if X had been aware that the funds had been obtained as a consequence of a fraud on the company's customer, then X would be potentially liable as a party to the fraudulent trading.

However, in so far as the requirement that liability for fraudulent trading should only be incurred in circumstances where a party actively participated in the fraudulent activities of a company, it is submitted that the decision in *Re Gerald Cooper Chemicals Ltd* should be viewed with caution. Although, from the facts of the case, X may, as a constructive trustee, have been liable to account for the moneys paid to it by the company (as these funds properly belonged to the customer), X was nevertheless a passive and not an active party to the fraudulent trading. Other than in a situation where a creditor actively encourages a company to defraud a customer, it is difficult to accept that the creditor, albeit that he knowingly accepted the benefit of a fraudulent transaction, could, on the basis of his indifference to the manner in which that benefit was received, be classed as an active party to the fraudulent act.

The decision in *Re Gerald Cooper Chemicals Ltd* would appear even more problematic when compared with the judgment of Pennycuick V-C in *Re Maidstone Buildings Ltd*.[24] In this case, the administrative tasks of a company secretary were held not to be comparable with a person's active involvement in the fraudulent affairs of a company. Further, and more pertinent to

---

[23] [1978] Ch 262.
[24] [1971] 1 WLR 1085. See also, *Re Augustus Barnett & Son Ltd* (1986) 2 BCC 98,905.

criticism of the decision in *Re Gerald Cooper Ltd*, it was held that liability for fraudulent trading would not be incurred by an officer of a company where, despite having been in breach of his duty of care and aware of the company's insolvent state, he nevertheless failed to take positive steps to prevent the company's incursion of further trade debts.[25] The judgment of Pennycuick V-C affirmed the view that liability for fraudulent trading would only arise where a person's participation in a company's trading activities was of a dominant and significant nature, a participation which was directly related to the physical commission of the fraudulent act.

Although the approach taken by Pennycuick J in *Re Maidstone Buildings Ltd*, would appear to be inconsistent with the one portrayed in *Re Gerald Cooper Chemicals Ltd*, the decision in *Re Maidstone Ltd* should however, be treated with some caution, because in so far as the company secretary also acted as the company's financial advisor, he was in a position, within the internal management structure of the company, to have prevented the company's fraudulent trading. It is perhaps difficult to understand why the secretary/financial advisor was allowed to evade liability when, being aware of the company's insolvent state, he must have appreciated that the company would, in incurring further liabilities, have been trading in a fraudulent manner. The secretary had the opportunity and indeed responsibility, as an officer of the company, to attempt to prevent the company's fraudulent trading. The secretary's failure to act was an integral and important contribution to the company's subsequent act of fraudulent trading.

3.4.1 *The liability of a holding company*

For a holding company to be liable as a party to the fraudulent trading of its subsidiary company, it must have been an active participant in the subsidiary's business affairs. The extent of the holding company's participation must be substantial. The difficulty in establishing a holding company's liability will be more arduous in that the subsidiary will be clothed with its own separate legal identity (as with all registered companies) and, accordingly, will in law be deemed to be responsible for its own actions. Although a holding company may be found to have actively encouraged its

---

[25] In *Re Maidstone Building Provisions Ltd*, the respondent acted in a dual capacity, as the company's secretary and its financial advisor. Although the respondent failed to take steps to correct the company's financial position by, for example, advising its directors of the company's insolvent state, the respondent's omission to act was not construed as constituting an active and positive involvement in the fraudulent trading activities of the company.

subsidiary to trade in a fraudulent manner, an act of encouragement, as opposed to a positive act of participation, may not be sufficient for the purpose of establishing the holding company's liability.

Indeed, to justify a holding company's liability as a party to the fraudulent trading of its subsidiary, it is probably necessary to prove that the holding company was responsible for directing the subsidiary's affairs. In effect, the control which the holding company must exert over its subsidiary will be tantamount to a finding that the subsidiary's separate legal identity had been discarded to the extent that the subsidiary was but a division of its holding company, thereby creating a single economic entity. However, following the decision of the Court of Appeal in *Adams v. Cape Industries*,[26] it would appear that the identification of a holding company/subsidiary relationship as one which constitutes an economic entity, will be a rare and improbable occurrence.[27]

The case of *Re Augustus Barnett & Son Ltd*[28] provides an example of an unsuccessful attempt to render a holding company liable for the alleged fraudulent trading of its subsidiary company. This case involved a holding company (H) which had given assurances to the creditors of its subsidiary (S) to the effect that it intended to continue to offer financial support to S's failing business. The creditors accepted H's informal pledge of support for S. However, six months after H gave the last of its assurances, S was put into creditors' voluntary liquidation. The liquidator alleged that H had given the assurances at a time when it was fully aware that S was trading in an insolvent state. It was further alleged that H, at the time of giving the final assurances, had been aware that S had no reasonable prospect of trading itself out of its difficulties. The liquidator claimed that H had exhibited an obvious indifference to the repayment of S's creditors, an indifference which amounted to evidence of an intention to defraud.

The liquidator's argument was rejected by Hoffmann J on two counts. First, the directors of S, in allowing the company to continue to trade, had genuinely believed that H would come to its rescue. Therefore, S's business had not been carried on with an intention to defraud its creditors. The logical result of this finding was that H could not be liable for a non-existent act of fraudulent trading. Secondly, Hoffmann J found that even if S had traded in a fraudulent manner, the liquidator had not established that H had intended to defraud S's creditors. H's indifference to the plight of S's creditors, was, in

---

[26] [1990] Ch 433.
[27] An economic entity may be found where the subsidiary company was incorporated as a fraud or facade. These issues are discussed further in Chapter 1.
[28] (1986) 2 BCC 98,905.

substance, an insufficient state of mind,[29] from which H's intention to defraud, could be inferred.[30]

3.5 Identifying fraudulent conduct

Evidence which is indicative of a company's involvement in fraudulent trading will, *prima facie*, be found where the company incurs a liability in the knowledge that it has no reasonable prospect of being able to discharge the debt. In addition to the non-payment of trade creditors, a company's evasion of Crown debts, for example, the non-payment of corporation tax, value added tax and national insurance contributions, may also be tantamount to a presumption of fraudulent trading.[31]

In determining whether a company has been privy to an act of fraudulent trading the court will assess the nature and degree of the alleged fraudulent conduct in respect of the company's present and potential capacity to repay its debts. In civil cases, the most obvious example of allowing a company to trade fraudulently will be where the company continues to trade and incur liabilities when, in a state of insolvency, it has little or no prospect of avoiding liquidation. In *Re William C Leitch Bros Ltd*,[32] Maugham J stated that,

> "If a company continues to carry on business and to incur debts at a time when there is to the knowledge of the directors no reasonable prospect of the creditors ever receiving payment of those debts, it is, in general, a proper inference that the company is carrying on business with intent to defraud".[33]

---

[29] However, by contrast, compare the decision of the Court of Appeal in *R v. Grantham* [1984] QB 675, *infra*.

[30] The liquidator sought to strengthen his case, in respect of establishing the holding company's intention to defraud, by introducing an argument which had not been contained in the original pleadings. The argument was that the holding company had obviously withdrawn its assurances to the subsidiary's creditors, without informing the creditors of its intention to do so. Therefore, the creditors were left with a false belief that the holding company would continue to support its subsidiary at a time when the holding company had decided to withdraw that support. Hoffmann J considered the argument to be a conceptual possibility, but refused to allow the original pleadings to be altered, see the comments of Hoffmann J, *supra*, n.28, at p.99,909.

[31] See, for example, *Re L Todd (Swanscombe) Ltd* [1990] BCLC 454. For a discussion of the significance of Crown debts in respect of disqualification orders, see Chapter 8, at p.176.

[32] [1932] 2 Ch 71.

[33] *Ibid*., at p.77.

3.5.1 *The type of business activity caught by the fraudulent trading provisions*

To establish that a company is carrying on its business in a fraudulent manner, it is unnecessary to prove that the fraudulent conduct is synonymous with an active pursuit of the company's trading activities. For example, a company which ceases to trade but continues to exist for the purpose of collecting and distributing its assets, will be deemed to be carrying on its business, and may, in the pursuit of that business, be liable for fraudulent trading.[34] Similarly, where, for example, a company fraudulently obtains a licence to operate its business, the fraudulent act, although unrelated to the company's physical trading activities, will, in so far as it affects the company's capacity to "carry on its business",[35] give rise to a potential liability for fraudulent trading.

In accordance with the judgment of Oliver J in *Re Sarfax Ltd*,[36] it is highly unlikely that a company will be privy to an act of fraudulent trading where, in repaying its debts, it makes preferential payments to specific creditors. Therefore, preferential payments are unlikely to amount to fraudulent conduct even though the decision to repay one creditor in preference to another may have been taken with the intentional objective of benefiting a specific creditor at the expense and prejudice of another. In *Re Sarfax Ltd*,[37] Oliver J contended that although a preferential payment may have a discriminatory effect, a company is nevertheless entitled (other than where it was contractually prohibited from doing so) to discharge its liabilities as it sees fit. Accordingly, a decision to repay one creditor in preference to another would be unlikely to form the substance of a fraudulent act. Although an intentional decision to repay one creditor in full, without even discharging a part of a debt owed to another creditor, may be an inequitable business practice, and

---

[34] See, for example, *Re Sarfax Ltd* [1979] 1 Ch 592.
[35] See, for example, *R v. Philippou* (1989) 89 Cr App R 290.
[36] *Supra*, n.34.
[37] Sarfax Ltd ceased trading in 1971. Prior to its liquidation (the company was wound up in 1973), it sought to sell its assets to realise funds out of which corporate creditors would be paid. The company's principal creditor was its holding company (F Ltd). F Ltd and other established trade creditors were paid in preference to an Italian company which, having being supplied with faulty goods in 1966, had sought damages in the sum of £80,000. The claim for damages was commenced prior to the decision taken by Sarfax Ltd to cease trading and the respondents were well aware that there was no substantial defence to the claim. The Italian court entered judgment against Sarfax in 1973, shortly after which the company's liquidator accepted the judgment as proof of the debt. Sarfax Ltd was unable to meet the debt, having failed to take account of the Italian company's claim when collecting in and distributing its assets.

one which is contrary to sections 238-241 of the Insolvency Act 1986, it will not, ordinarily, be viewed as a dishonest business transaction. On the basis of the decision in *Re Sarfax Ltd*, it is suggested that for a preferential payment to be capable of being classed as a fraudulent act, the preference will need to be unwarranted in relation to the extent of the actual liability, which was owed by the company to the preferred creditor.

3.6 Establishing an intention to defraud

The ability to establish that a person was a party to a company's fraudulent trading is dependent upon proof that the person knowingly participated in the carrying on of a company's business with an intention to defraud creditors of the company or creditors of any other person, or for any fraudulent purpose. In seeking to prove that a person intended to commit the fraudulent act, it is unnecessary to establish that, as a consequence of the fraud, the object of the fraudulent trading suffered any actual economic loss.[38] The essential requirement of the provision is, quite simply, to establish that there was an intention to perpetrate the fraudulent act.

3.6.1 *Dishonesty*

In determining whether a person intended to participate in the fraudulent trading activities of a company, it must be established that he acted dishonestly.[39] The need to substantiate a person's dishonesty is an essential constituent of establishing any type of fraudulent conduct.[40] In accordance with section 213 of the Insolvency Act 1986, a person's dishonesty will be measured according to the notions of ordinary decent business people. In *Re Patrick Lyon Ltd*,[41] Maugham J commented that the words "defraud" and "fraudulent purpose" were words which,

"connote actual dishonesty involving, according to current notions of fair trading among commercial men, real moral blame".[42]

---

[38] See, for example, *Welham v. DPP* [1961] AC 103, *R v. Grantham* [1984] QB 675, at pp.683-4.

[39] *Re Patrick Lyon* [1933] 1 Ch 786.

[40] For example, in *R v. Cox & Hodges* (1982) 75 Cr App R 291, a case heard under CA 1948, s.332, it was held that the trial judge had misdirected the jury in stating that dishonesty was not an essential ingredient of s.332. The jury had found the defendant guilty of fraudulent trading. As a result of this misdirection, the guilty verdict was held to be unsafe.

[41] [1933] Ch 786. This requirement is common to all offences whereby it is necessary to establish an intention to commit a fraudulent act, see, for example, the comments of the House of Lords in *Welham v. DPP* [1961] AC 103.

[42] *Ibid.*, at p.790.

In respect of a person's criminal liability for fraudulent trading, dishonesty may, in so far as it is a question to be determined by a jury, be more aptly measured against the moral standards of ordinary and honest people.[43]

A person's dishonesty will be ascertained on the basis of whether, at the time of the incursion of a corporate debt, he was aware that the debt would not be met on the date it was due, or shortly after that date.[44] It should be noted that the requirement that the debt will be met, when due or shortly after that time, is at variance with some of the earlier authorities which, stretching back to the decision of Maugham J in *Re William C Leitch Bros Ltd*,[45] and exemplified by the decision of Buckley J in *Re White & Osmond (Parkstone) Ltd*,[46] had suggested that the directors of an insolvent company would not act in a dishonest manner where, notwithstanding the fact that they realised the company was trading in an insolvent state, they continued to incur further debts in the genuine belief that the company would be capable of recovering a solvent standing at some date in the future. For example, in *Re White & Osmond (Parkstone) Ltd*, Buckley J stated that,

"In my judgment, there is nothing wrong in the fact that directors incur credit at a time when to their knowledge, the company is not able to meet all its liabilities as they fall due. What is manifestly wrong is if directors allow a company to incur credit at a time when the business is being carried on in such circumstances that it is clear that the company will never be able to satisfy its creditors. However, there is nothing to say that directors who genuinely believe that the clouds will roll away and the sunshine of prosperity will shine upon them again and disperse the fog of their depression are not entitled to incur credit to help them get over the bad time".

The substance of this comment, namely that liability could be evaded in circumstances where a director held a genuine belief of the company's ability to trade itself out of an insolvent state at some time in the future, was clearly favourable to a respondent who was fully aware that the debt would not be discharged at the time when it was due. This "future date" test was finally discarded by the Court of Appeal in *R v. Grantham*.[47] In *R v. Grantham*, the Lord Chief Justice, in referring to the judgment of Buckley J in *Re White & Osmond (Parkstone) Ltd*, remarked that,

---

[43] This test was applied in *R v. Lockwood* (1985) 2 BCC 99,333.

[44] See, *R v. Grantham* [1984] QB 675.

[45] [1932] 2 Ch 71.

[46] 30 June 1960, unreported.

[47] *Supra*, n.44.

"In so far as Buckley J was saying that it is never dishonest or fraudulent for directors to incur credit at a time when, to their knowledge, the company is not able to meet all its liabilities as they fall due, we would respectfully disagree".

3.6.2 *Ascertaining a person's intention to defraud*

In ascertaining whether a person's participation in the fraudulent trading activities of a company was of an intentional nature, the courts will employ a subjective test to determine the state of mind of the respondent at the time of the alleged fraudulent trading.[48] Although a person's culpability for fraudulent trading will be dependent upon whether he formed an intention to commit the fraudulent act, the definition of an intention to defraud has been stretched to the point whereby, in reality, it resembles a test based upon recklessness; albeit that recklessness will be measured in a subjective as opposed to an objective sense. For example, in *R v. Grantham*,[49] the Court of Appeal refused to accept that an intention to defraud had to be defined in terms whereby a person must have known, at the time of incurring a debt, that it would not be paid. Instead, the court approved a test put forward in *R v. Sinclair*,[50] namely,

"It is fraud if it is proved that there was the taking of a risk which there was no right to take which would cause detriment or prejudice to another ... you have to be sure that it was deliberate dishonesty".

Therefore, in accordance with the decision of the Court of Appeal in *R v. Grantham*, it is possible to infer that a person may have been a party to the fraudulent trading of a company where, upon the company's incursion of a debt, he foresaw the strong possibility (as opposed to being actually aware) of the company's inability to discharge the liability. Indeed, by comparison, it is interesting to note that under the civil law of deceit, a tort which inevitably

---

[48] However, it is to be noted that in *Re Gerald Cooper* [1978] Ch 262, Templeman J held that the word "intent" was used in the sense that "a man must be taken to intend the natural or foreseen consequences of his act". This objective test was surely misplaced. In relation to criminal offences which require proof of the defendant's intention, it had been abolished by the Criminal Justice Act 1967, s.8(a).

[49] [1984] QB 675.

[50] [1968] 1 WLR 1246, at p.1249.

requires proof of a person's dishonesty,[51] the proof of a person's deceit may be comprised of either a reckless indifference to truth or falsity, as well as the deliberate making of false statements.[52]

3.6.3 *Objective considerations*

Although the court's perception of a whether a person intended to defraud will be measured by a subjective test, it would be misleading to suggest that objective considerations are completely ignored in the court's assessment. Realistically, a person's subjective perception of having not been aware that he actively participated in a company's fraudulent trading must be viewed in the light of the circumstances surrounding the alleged acts of fraudulent trading. For example, although a person, who is accused of fraudulent trading, may genuinely believe that the company, in which he was involved, would soon escape from its insolvent state, that belief may be without any reasonable foundation. Accordingly, where a company is privy to fraudulent trading, it would be most difficult to discount a person's active involvement in the perpetration of the fraudulent conduct unless he honestly **and** reasonably believed that he was not participating in the fraudulent conduct.

The case of *Re Augustus Barnett & Son Ltd* [53] provides an example of the manner in which the court will consider whether a person's genuinely held belief of having not participated in fraudulent trading, was of a reasonable nature. The respondents, the directors of the company, held a belief that the company would be rescued by its holding company. This belief was construed to be of a reasonable nature because throughout the period of the alleged fraudulent trading, the holding company had been in the habit of providing the subsidiary with financial assistance. Further, the holding company had made statements to the creditors of the subsidiary (via letters of comfort) to the effect that it would continue to support its subsidiary. In effect, the respondents' conduct and the perception of whether they genuinely believed that the subsidiary company would be rescued by its holding company, was measured, not only in terms of their own subjective expectations, but also by the court's objective consideration of whether such expectations were reasonably held.

---

[51] However, it is to be noted that the comparison between the civil law of deceit and fraud, as used in a criminal context, was doubted by the House of Lords in *Welham v. DPP* [1961] AC 103. Here, it was said that the elements of the civil law of deceit were not necessarily part of an intent to defraud, although it was clear that dishonesty was an integral part of the offence.

[52] See, *Derry v. Peek* (1899) 14 App Cas 337.

[53] [1986] BCLC 170.

3.7 The nature and extent of the liability

Where a person is found to be liable for fraudulent trading under section 213 of the Insolvency Act 1986, that person may be made to make such contributions (if any) to the company's assets as the court thinks proper.[54] The court's declaration will primarily be of a compensatory nature and will take account of the company's trading loss during the period of fraudulent trading. In some cases, the declaration may also include a punitive element and, accordingly, the contribution may exceed the totality of debts owed to those creditors who were affected during the period of the company's fraudulent trading.[55] In calculating whether the declaration should include a punitive element, the courts will consider matters such as the length of the duration of the fraudulent trading, whether there was some inadequacy in the company's accounting procedures, whether the levels of directors remuneration were excessive, and the priority in which the company sought to discharge its debts.[56] In accordance with section 215(2) of the Insolvency Act 1986,[57] the court may also provide that the liability of a person should also incorporate a charge on any debt or obligation which is due to that person from the company, or on any mortgage or charge on any of the company's assets which that person or an assignee holds, or which an agent holds on his behalf.

Notwithstanding that the fraudulent trading activities of a company may have predominantly caused damage to an individual creditor, any contribution which the court orders to be paid will be allocated to discharge the collective debts of the company's unsecured creditors. The fairness of this approach may be doubted. Why should corporate creditors who were untouched by the fraudulent acts of a company benefit from the distribution of funds pursuant to a successful application under section 213? Previously, under section 332 of the Companies Act 1948, an individual creditor could apply to the court and on such an application it would be possible for the court to direct that the creditor be paid in priority to the company's other

---

[54] The court's declaration should specify a particular sum of money and should not be in general terms, see *Re William C Leitch Bros Ltd* [1932] 2 Ch 71, at pp.77-79.

[55] See, for example, *Re a Company (No. 001418 of 1988)* [1991] BCLC 197. However, it should be noted that this case involved the application of CA 1985, s.630, the statutory predecessor to IA 1986 s.213.

[56] For example, in *Re a Company (No. 001418 of 1988)* [1991] BCLC 197, the company in question purchased a caravan which was to be paid for by instalments; the purchase was unrelated to its trading activities. The said instalments were paid in priority to the company's trade creditors.

[57] This provision is also applicable to proceedings under IA 1986, s.214.

unsecured creditors.[58] However, under the Insolvency Act 1986, only a liquidator may apply to instigate civil proceedings under section 213. The reasoning for excluding applications from individual creditors was to prevent the possibility of multiple actions in individual cases. However, in practice, this reasoning is difficult to understand, especially in those cases where the fraudulent trading activities of a company are concentrated around a single or small group of creditors. Further, the cost of commencing proceedings under section 213 would clearly discourage a swarm of individual applications under the provision.

---

[58] To this effect, see, for example, the comments of Lord Denning in *Re Cyona* [1967] Ch 889 at 902, also see the judgment of Templeman J in *Re Gerald Cooper Chemicals Ltd* [1978] Ch 262. However, in *Re Esal (Commodities) Ltd* [1997] 1 BCLC 705 (a case heard in 1993), the Court of Appeal doubted whether an individual creditor had, as of right, an ability to directly recover any payment made pursuant to an order under s.332. According to the Court of Appeal, assets recovered under s.332 had to be made in favour of the company's liquidator who would then distribute the assets for the benefit of the company's general pool of creditors.

Chapter 4

WRONGFUL TRADING

4.1 Introduction

4.1.1 *The Cork Report*

Section 214 of the Insolvency Act 1986, which is commonly referred to as the wrongful trading provision, was introduced following the recommendations of the report by the review committee into insolvency law and practice (The Cork Report).[1] The Cork Report's proposal for a wrongful trading provision was intended to replace section 332 of the 1948 Companies Act,[2] with a more efficient and accessible mechanism by which directors of insolvent companies could be held accountable for conduct which was prejudicial to the interests of corporate creditors. The Report's underlying criticism of section 332 was focused on that provision's failure to provide an effective means of penalising and discouraging the culpable behaviour of irresponsible directors involved in the management of insolvent companies. The Cork Report identified the limitations of section 332 as follows:[3]

(1) Under section 332, liability was dependent upon the arduous task of having to establish that a person intentionally sought to defraud creditors or that the person had intentionally acted for some other fraudulent purpose.[4]

(2) As the fraudulent trading provision comprised both a penal and civil sanction, section 332 was construed strictly, so that even in civil proceedings the burden of proof was deemed to be set in accordance with the criminal standard.[5]

---

[1] Cmnd. 8558. The report was chaired by Sir Kenneth Cork.

[2] For a detailed discussion of CA 1948, s.332, see Chapter 3.

[3] Cmnd. 8558, paras. 1776-1780. It should be noted that the Jenkins Committee Report of 1962 (Cmnd. 1749) had recommended a reform to CA 1948, s.332, the effect of which would have been to impose liability on directors who acted recklessly or incompetently in relation to the affairs of a company.

[4] Discussed in Chapter 3, at p.50.

[5] *Ibid.*, at p.39.

(3) The Cork Report doubted the effectiveness of the fraudulent trading provision in so far as its jurisdiction was limited to instances whereby a company was in liquidation.[6]

(4) Liquidators of companies were frequently inhibited from commencing civil proceedings for fraudulent trading because of the imminence or currency of criminal proceedings under section 332.[7]

Accordingly, although the Cork Report approved the retention of the criminal offence of fraudulent trading, it recommended that section 332 should be reformed in a manner which precluded a person from being subject to civil liability. As a matter of urgency, the Report concluded that civil liability should only be incurred where a person had been a party to a company's wrongful trading, a liability which would not necessarily be dependent upon proving the person's dishonest conduct.[8] The Cork Report proposed[9] that a company would trade in a wrongful manner where,

(a) the company had traded in a fraudulent manner, or

(b) in a situation where the company was insolvent,[10] the company had continued to incur further debts without having a reasonable prospect of discharging them.

The Cork Report envisaged that an action for wrongful trading action would be available where a company was in liquidation, receivership, or subject to an administration order. In addition to applications being made by, a liquidator (when the company was in liquidation), a receiver (when the company was in receivership) or an administrator of a company, (when the company had been made subject to an administration order) the Report concluded that an application for wrongful trading should also be open to any creditor or contributory of a company which was in liquidation, receivership or subject to an administration order.

Under the terms of the Cork Report, it was proposed that where an insolvent company's business had been carried on in a wrongful manner, any

---

[6] *Ibid.*

[7] *Ibid.*

[8] Cmnd. 8558, paras 1781-1806.

[9] The Cork Report's proposals were incorporated into a proposed draft clause (at para. 1806). The draft clause was the report's suggested blueprint for a legislative provision to cover wrongful trading.

[10] Insolvency was defined to include both balance sheet insolvency and cash flow insolvency, see Chapter 1, at p.6.

person who had knowingly been a party to the carrying on of that business,[11] would, in accordance with the court's directions, be made personally liable (without any limitation of liability) for all the debts and other liabilities of the company.[12] Additionally, where an officer of the company had been party to an act of wrongful trading, the Cork Report suggested that the officer should be made personally liable in circumstances where he ought to have known that the company's trading was wrongful.[13]

In determining a person's liability for wrongful trading, the Report endorsed the application of an objective test, under which the respondent's conduct would be measured against the standards expected of an ordinary businessman. Further, the Cork Report recommended that directors of a company would ordinarily incur civil liability where, having failed to take immediate steps to place the company in receivership, administration or liquidation, they had allowed the company to continue to trade at a time when it had become insolvent.[14] In respect of the sums recovered by the court in an action for wrongful trading, the Cork Report submitted that such sums should be paid to such persons or classes of persons, in such proportions as the court directed.[15] The Report considered that in some cases it would be necessary to draw a distinction between debts incurred at different times, or, perhaps, between the competing interests of creditors. For example, a creditor who dealt with a company knowing it to be in an insolvent state would be expected to be treated less favourably, in respect of the amount of his share of any contribution order, than, for example, a creditor who, at the time of trading with the company, had been induced into believing that the company was in a solvent state. The Report also suggested that where a creditor had, at his own expense and risk, successfully brought proceedings for wrongful trading, then such a creditor should, ordinarily, be afforded a priority over the recovered sums.

While the Cork Report recognised that the inception and growth of businesses should be encouraged, rather than curtailed by placing any unnecessary legal restraints upon a company's capacity to trade, the Report emphasised an urgent need to protect the interests of unsecured creditors in a more effective manner. Further, the Report considered that a provision which

---

[11] A person would require actual knowledge of the fact that the company was trading while insolvent or was unable to pay its debts as they fell due. However, a person would be deemed to have actual knowledge where he shut his eyes to the obvious, or where he deliberately refrained from asking obvious questions, for fear that he might learn the truth.

[12] See, the Cork Report's "Proposed Draft Clause", Cmnd. 8558, para. 1806.

[13] An officer of the company would include a shadow director of the company.

[14] Cmnd. 8558, para. 1786.

[15] Ibid., para. 1797.

was geared to prohibiting the wrongful trading activities of a company would encourage directors to ensure that their companies were adequately capitalised, and that the concept of wrongful trading would therefore, in one sense, compensate for the absence of any requirement in the companies legislation to provide an obligation on all trading companies to have a statutory prescribed minimum paid-up share capital.

In addition to defining the ambit of the proposed wrongful trading provision, it is also interesting to note that the Cork Report favoured the introduction of a statutory anticipatory declaration. The purpose of the anticipatory declaration would have been to allow an application to the court in chambers, whereupon, the court would determine whether the company's present or proposed trading activities were of a wrongful nature. The application would have been open to companies or any person who was interested in becoming a party to the company's business. Under the terms of the anticipatory declaration, the court, if it concluded that a company's present or proposed trading activities were not of a wrongful nature, would have been permitted to make a declaration to that effect (subject to any terms or conditions imposed by the court).[16] The objective of the declaration would have been to assure the company, its directors and creditors, that the specified trading activities referred to in the declaration were not of a wrongful nature. In addition, providing the terms of the declaration were followed, the directors of the company, or any other person who was a party to the company's business, would, in respect of the matters mentioned therein, be provided with an absolute defence in respect of any subsequent wrongful trading action.[17]

4.1.2 *The White Paper*

In 1984, two years after the publication of the Cork Report, the Department of Trade and Industry issued a White Paper entitled "A Revised Framework

---

[16] The Report (*ibid.*, at para. 1798) gave a number of examples of the type of declaration that could be made. The examples given, were as follows: (a) that trading for a specified period should not be wrongful; (b) that unless or until a certain level of borrowing had been reached trading should not be wrongful; (c) that trading with a view to completing certain existing or prospective contracts, should not be wrongful; (d) that trading, provided that the directors or others postponed loans or other accounts owing to them, should not be wrongful; (e) that trading on a cash basis should not be wrongful; and (f) that if agents were under instructions to effect a sale of the company's premises, then trading pending that sale, should not be wrongful.

[17] It was proposed that hefty penalties should be imposed where the terms of the declaration were not followed, or where the declaration had been obtained by wilfully or recklessly made depositions.

for Insolvency Law".[18] The White Paper represented the government's response to the recommendations of the Cork Report. In respect of the Cork Report's proposal for the creation of a wrongful trading provision, the White Paper confirmed the need for stricter controls to curb the reckless trading activities of persons involved in the management of insolvent companies, albeit that it proposed that liability for wrongful trading should be restricted to a situation where a company was being wound up. The White Paper recommended that liability for wrongful trading should be incurred where,

"... a company is allowed to continue trading, with the result that the position of existing creditors is worsened and/or additional liabilities are incurred which are not paid and the directors (including shadow directors) knew or ought to have known that there was no reasonable prospect of avoiding the situation".[19]

In comparison to the detailed proposals of the Cork Report, the White Paper's recommendations, in respect of the creation of a wrongful trading provision, were remarkably thin, lacking both depth and substance. Further, and most unfortunately, the White Paper failed, in impliedly rejecting many of the proposals contained in the Cork Report, to explain or justify the reasons by which such proposals had been discarded.

In December 1984, less than two months after the publication of the White Paper, the Insolvency Bill was introduced into the House of Lords. The resulting legislation, the Insolvency Act 1985, sought, amongst other matters, to regulate wrongful trading.[20] Following the consolidation of insolvency laws into the Insolvency Act 1986, the wrongful trading provision was incorporated into section 214 of the 1986 Act.

4.2 Section 214 of the Insolvency Act 1986

In accordance with the spirit of the recommendations contained in the Cork Report,[21] section 214 of the Insolvency Act 1986 aims to curb and deter the irresponsible conduct of directors who have prejudiced the interests of corporate creditors in a manner which abuses the privilege of limited liability.

---

[18] Cmnd. 9175.

[19] *Ibid.*, at para. 52.

[20] IA 1985, s.15.

[21] It is to be observed that the Cork Report's proposals were more closely reproduced in the Irish legislation, where under s.297 of the Companies Act 1963 (as amended by the Companies Act 1990), any officer of a company may be liable for all or part of the company's debts where it appears that, as an officer of the company, he was knowingly a party to the

The essential requirements for determining a person's liability for wrongful trading are contained in sections 214(1) to 214(3) of the Insolvency Act 1986. The remaining sections of the wrongful trading provision, namely, sections 214(4) to 214(8), are relevant to the interpretation of sections 214(1) to 214(3). Section 214(1) provides that:

"Subject to subsection (3) below, if in the course of the winding up of a company it appears that subsection (2) of this section applies in relation to a person who is or has been a director of the company, the court, on the application of the liquidator, may declare that person is to be liable to make such contribution (if any) to the company's assets as the court thinks proper".

Section 214(2), applies in relation to a person if —

"(a) the company has gone into insolvent liquidation,
 (b) at some time before the commencement of the winding up of the company, that person knew or ought to have concluded that there was no reasonable prospect that the company would avoid going into insolvent liquidation, and
 (c) that person was a director of the company at that time;
     but the court shall not make a declaration under this section in any case where the time mentioned in paragraph (b) above was before 28th April 1986".

Section 214(3) limits the ability of the court to make a declaration in the following circumstances:

"The court shall not make a declaration under this section with respect to any person if it is satisfied that after the condition specified in subsection (2)(b) was first satisfied in relation to him that person took every step with

---

carrying on of the company's business in a reckless manner. Reckless trading is established where the officer was a party to the carrying on of the company's business and, having regard to the general knowledge, skill and experience that might reasonably be expected of a person in his position, he ought to have known that his actions or those of the company would cause loss to the creditors. Alternatively, reckless trading may be established where the officer was a party to the contracting of a debt by the company and did not honestly believe on reasonable grounds that the company would be able to pay the debt when it fell due for payment as well as its other debts (taking into account contingent and prospective liabilities). It should be noted that the Irish courts have the power to relieve a person of his liability in whole or in part, in circumstances where he is viewed to have acted honestly and reasonably.

a view to minimising the potential loss to the company's creditors as (assuming him to have known that there was no reasonable prospect that the company would avoid going into insolvent liquidation) he ought to have taken".

Therefore, in accordance with sections 214(1) and 214(2), liability under the wrongful trading provision will arise in circumstances where a company is in insolvent liquidation[22] and where a person who was acting or who had previously acted as a director of the company, knew, or ought to have concluded at some time before the commencement of the winding up of the company,[23] that there was no reasonable prospect that the company would avoid going into insolvent liquidation.[24] For the purposes of section 214, a company goes into insolvent liquidation if it goes into liquidation at a time when its assets are insufficient for the payment of its debts and other liabilities and the expenses of winding up.[25]

On hearing an application under section 214, the court may declare (other than where the section 214(3) defence applies) that a director is to be made liable to make such a contribution (if any) to the company's assets, as the court thinks proper.

4.3 Conduct giving rise to an action under section 214

Section 214 is commonly referred to as the wrongful trading provision, notwithstanding that save for its appearance in the marginal note, the phrase "wrongful trading" is absent from the language of the provision. Indeed,

---

[22] The requirement that s.214 will only apply where a company is in insolvent liquidation runs contrary to the recommendations of the Cork Report. It is to be observed that, in Ireland, an action for reckless trading may be commenced where a company is in liquidation, or where an execution of a judgment in favour of a creditor has been returned unsatisfied, or where it is proved to the satisfaction of the court that a company is unable to pay its debts, taking into account its prospective and contingent liabilities. In addition to an action for reckless trading being commenced by a liquidator, the action may be also be brought by a receiver, liquidator, or any creditor or contributory.

[23] In accordance with IA 1986, s.214(2)(c), the court cannot make a declaration under s.214 in any case where the "relevant time before the commencement of the winding up", was before 28th April 1986. It should be noted that under the Cork Report's proposals, there would have been no such restriction.

[24] Section 214 is without prejudice to IA 1986, s.213 (see IA 1986, s.214(8)).

[25] IA 1986, s.214(6). In relation to the winding up of a company, a debt will include prospective, future and contingent liabilities, see the Insolvency Rules 1986, r.13.12. Note that, contrary to the recommendations of the Cork Report, insolvency is not defined to include instances of cash flow insolvency.

the drafting of section 214 may, as a matter of principle, be criticised on the premise that it is ambiguous in its failure to identify the type of corporate malpractice which it seeks to regulate.[26] This ambiguity may be contrasted with the proposed type of conduct which would have given rise to the implementation of the provision under both the terms of the Cork Report and White Paper, namely, the ambit of the proposed provision had been identified as being confined to a situation whereby a company continued to trade and incur debts at a time when the company's directors knew or ought to have known that there was no reasonable prospect of the company being able to meet those debts.

In the absence of any specific guidance of the type of conduct which will give rise to the implementation of the provision, the scope of section 214 would appear very wide and applicable to any situation in which a director is responsible for misconducting the affairs of a company at a time when he knew or ought to have concluded that there was no reasonable prospect that the company would avoid going into insolvent liquidation. Yet, the scope of the provision is impliedly limited by reference to the nature of a director's potential liability. As the nature of that liability is one, whereby, following a company's insolvent liquidation, a director may be held personally liable to contribute to the company's assets, it is logical to assume that the type of misconduct which the provision was intended to govern was conduct which a director knew or ought to have known would, at a time prior to the commencement of the winding up of the company, deplete the available assets against which creditors could lay claim. Obviously, the nature of the prejudicial conduct so envisaged by the terms of the provision will include the type of wrongful trading which both the Cork Report and the White Paper had intended the provision to cover. However, in addition, the width of the provision is such that it will be applicable to any type of conduct which had the effect of depleting a company's distributable assets. Examples of such conduct would, during a period in which a company was insolvent, include over generous dividend payments, the sale of corporate assets at an undervalue, and excessive payments of directors remuneration.

4.4 Establishing liability — the reasonable diligent person test

To establish that a director is *prima facie* liable under section 214, the liquidator must show that at a specified time prior to the liquidation of the company, the director, in conducting the affairs of the company, was aware

---

[26] See, L Doyle "Anomalies in the Wrongful Trading Provisions" (1992) 13 Co Law 96.

or ought to have been aware that there was no reasonable prospect of the company avoiding liquidation. In determining whether a director ought to have been aware that there was no reasonable prospect of the company avoiding liquidation, section 214(4) provides that:

"... the facts which a director of a company ought to know or ascertain, the conclusions which he ought to reach and the steps which he ought to take are those which would be known or ascertained, or reached or taken, by a reasonably diligent person having both —

(a) the general knowledge, skill and experience that may reasonably be expected of a person carrying out the same functions as those which were carried out by that director in relation to the company,[27] and
(b) the general knowledge, skill and experience of the director".

Inevitably, the assessment of the viability of an action under section 214 will be determined by a retrospective consideration of the financial state of the company at the moment in time relied upon by the liquidator to establish that the director was aware or ought to have been aware that there was no reasonable prospect of the company avoiding liquidation. For the court to avoid reaching the conclusion that a director ought to have been aware that there was no reasonable prospect of the company avoiding liquidation, the liquidator must establish that the director's expectation of the company's ability to halt its decline into liquidation was unreasonable. Accordingly, a director's expectation of the company's future survival, based solely upon business instinct and which is speculative in its nature, will be viewed with much caution, whereas an expectation based upon factual evidence, indicative of a possible reversal in the company's fortunes, will be more apt in convincing the court that the company had a reasonable prospect of avoiding liquidation.[28] The determination of the state of a company's financial health will be gauged by, for example, examining the company's profit and loss accounts, its purchase and sales figures, its order books and its banking accounts. In respect of ascertaining whether, at a specified date, a director ought to have concluded that there was no reasonable prospect of the company avoiding liquidation, the court will also be mindful of evidence which may be supportive of a finding that the company was unable to escape from its insolvent state. Examples of this type of evidence could include:

---

[27] This includes functions with which the director was entrusted, notwithstanding that these functions had not been carried out by the director, see IA 1986, s.214(4).
[28] See, Oditah, "Wrongful Trading" [1990] LMCLQ 205, at pp.207-212.

(a) corporate creditors pressing for judgment orders in respect of outstanding debts;

(b) the withdrawal, suspension or reduction of financial support from the company's bankers;

(c) the withdrawal of support from the company's holding company;

(d) the resignation of directors, in an attempt to divorce themselves from any potential liability following the collapse of the company;

(e) the loss of contracts, or the inability to attain new contracts;

(f) the non payment of Crown debts;

(g) an unrealistic forecast of expected profits; and

(h) an inadequate or non existent business plan.

In the first reported case in which section 214 was considered, namely *Re Produce Marketing Consortium Ltd*,[29] Knox J construed section 214(4) in the following manner.

"The facts which the [directors] ought to have known or ascertained and the conclusions that they ought to have reached are not limited to those which they themselves, showing reasonable diligence and having the general knowledge, skill and experience which they respectfully had, would have known, ascertained or reached, but also those that a person with the general knowledge skill and experience of someone carrying out their functions would have known, ascertained or reached".[30]

---

[29] [1989] 5 BCC 569. This case concerned the activities of a company (PMC) which had been incorporated in 1964 to carry on a wholesale fruit importing business. Between 1980 and 1984, PMC's fortunes declined, to the extent that, by 1984, the company was trading in an insolvent state. The two directors of PMC had been aware of the company's insolvent state but had believed, up until the beginning of 1987, that the company could trade itself out of its difficulties. From 1984, until its liquidation in October 1987, the company constantly abused its overdraft facility. Although in 1986/7 the company managed to reduce the amount of its overdraft, the reduction was financed out of an increased indebtedness to the company's largest creditor; at the date of the company's liquidation the company owed this particular creditor £175,062. PMC was put into liquidation with an estimated deficiency of £317,694. The liquidator claimed, and Knox J agreed, that by the end of July 1986 the directors ought to have been aware that the turnover of the business was well down on the previous year, a loss which compounded the company's already precarious position. Accordingly, as of July 1986, the directors should have concluded that there was no reasonable prospect of the company avoiding liquidation. In reality, the company's directors had allowed the company to continue trading at a time when there was no reasonable justification for the company's continued existence. The directors' forlorn hope that the company's fortunes would improve was totally unjustifiable.

[30] *Ibid.*, at p.593.

This interpretation confirmed the importance of considering both the subjective and objective elements of the section, albeit that its emphasis and tone was more prescriptive of a finding that the subjective part of the test should be viewed to be subsidiary to the objective standard prescribed by section 214(4)(a). Indeed, although section 214(4)(b) creates a flexible standard against which a director's awareness of a company's pending liquidation should be measured, it does not permit a purely subjective consideration of whether an individual director (at whatever level of skill or experience) was himself justified in believing (albeit mistakenly) that the company would have a reasonable prospect of avoiding liquidation. The particular level of skill, knowledge and experience attributable to any given director must be viewed through the eyes of and in accordance with the expectations of the reasonably diligent person. Further, although section 214(4)(b) fails to stipulate any minimum standard of competence to be expected of a director in respect of his level of skill, knowledge or experience, the fact that the competence of a director is measured in the context of a standard ascribed to a reasonably diligent person is such, that a level of skill, experience or general knowledge which falls below that objective standard will be ignored in relation to the subjective part of the assessment. For example, the reasonable diligent person, in acting as a company director, will be expected to be familiar with those parts of the companies legislation which prescribe the duties of a company director. Accordingly, a director will not be able to rely on his ignorance of such matters.

Although the objectivity of the reasonably diligent person test dominates the construction of section 214(4), it would be very wrong to discard the potential importance of section 214(4)(b). In some circumstances, the subjective nature of section 214(4)(b) is permissive of different levels of competency against which the standards of company directors may be gauged. Knox J, commenting on the effect of section 214(4)(b), stated that,

> "... the general knowledge, skill and experience postulated will be much less extensive in a small company in a modest way of business, with simple accounting procedures and equipment, than it will be in a large company with sophisticated procedures".[31]

Further, it is probable that the potential scope of section 214(4)(b) will be extended beyond distinguishing between modest and well established business ventures. For example, in accordance with section 214(4)(b), it may be assumed that in the normal course of events, an executive director will be expected to exhibit more awareness of the inevitability of a company's

---

[31] *Ibid.*, at p.594-5.

pending liquidation than a non-executive director;[32] a director with considerable business experience more awareness of the inevitability of a company's pending liquidation than an inexperienced director; and a director with a relevant professional qualification, in a field related to say accountancy or corporate law, more awareness of the inevitability of a company's pending liquidation than a director who is absent of such qualifications.

It is also to be observed that, according to Knox J, the knowledge to be imputed in determining whether a director knew or ought to have concluded that there was no reasonable prospect of the company avoiding liquidation should not be limited to the documentary material which would have been available to the director at the date (as specified by the liquidator) when he should have realised that there was no reasonable prospect of the company avoiding liquidation. Knox J justified this contention on the premise that section 214(4) employs the term "ought to ascertain". As such, the factual information which is deemed to be available to a director will not only include ascertained information but also, given the reasonable diligence and the appropriate level of general knowledge, skill and experience of the director in question, information which the director could have ascertained. For example, in *Re Produce Marketing Consortium Ltd*, the respondent directors of the company argued that they could not have realised, at the date specified by the liquidator, that there was no reasonable prospect of the company avoiding liquidation, in so far as at the specified date they had not been in possession of the accounting figures which subsequently revealed the company's perilous position. The said argument was rejected because, regardless of the absence of the accounts, the directors ought to have been aware, from their active positions in the management of the company, that the company's dire financial position had become irreversible.

Whilst, prior to its liquidation a company may, to the knowledge of its directors, have been trading in an insolvent state, it must be stressed that it does not necessarily follow that knowledge of the company's insolvent state will automatically deem that the directors should have presumed that there was no reasonable prospect of the company avoiding liquidation. In determining a director's potential liability under section 214, the courts must be mindful that their assessment of the alleged wrongful trading will be made with the benefit of hindsight. Accordingly, a director's judgment in allowing a company to continue to trade in an insolvent state must be assessed in relation to the circumstances prevailing at the time that the decision was made.

---

[32] But see Chapter 1, at p.4, for a discussion on the standards expected of non executive directors.

In *Re Sherborne Associates Ltd*,[33] his Honour Jack QC, sitting as a High Court judge, dismissed an action under section 214 because the evidence of the case was inconclusive of a finding that during the period in which the company was specified by the liquidator to have been party to wrongful trading, the directors ought to have been aware that there was no reasonable prospect of the company avoiding liquidation. The case involved a company (an advertising agency), the creation of which had been the brainchild of S, a well respected and successful businessman. S acted as the company's chairman and was one of the three non executive directors against which the section 214 action had been commenced. The three non executive directors were the company's major shareholders but had no specialist knowledge of the world of advertising. Accordingly, three executive directors were appointed to the company; the three appointees had an expertise in advertising matters and were expected to attract business. It should be noted that during the short life span of the company, six different persons were to occupy the three executive posts.

The company was incorporated in January 1987, in the first five months of trading, its trading loss was £27,638, and by the close of 1987, the company's audited accounts showed the loss at £78,904. Indeed, by the end of 1987, the company's liabilities exceeded its assets and the company was insolvent. Further, in January 1988, the company suffered a further setback to its future prospects, in so far as the company's most productive fee earner resigned from his position as an executive director. In February 1988, at a company board meeting, S warned his fellow directors that unless the company's fortunes radically improved the company would be placed into liquidation. However, notwithstanding its insolvent state, the company continued to trade throughout 1988, drawing finance from an overdraft facility and its general creditors. Although the company's financial plight was aided by an injection of share capital, to the sum of £36,000, the company's fortunes continued to decline and during the period between January and June 1988, three further persons resigned from their positions as executive directors of the company. In December 1988, as a consequence of the company's failure to secure further accounts, S resigned as a non executive director of the company. The company was put into liquidation in February 1989, with debts amounting to £178,788 and a deficiency of assets over liabilities of £109,237.

In effect, the liquidator's ability to establish that the three non executive directors were liable under section 214, depended, in the first instance, on establishing S's liability. If the action against S could not be substantiated, the court recognised that the proceedings against the other two non executive

---

[33] [1995] BCC 40.

directors would also fail. An unfortunate complication in this matter was that S had died prior to the commencement of the proceedings. Although his Honour Jack QC held that the statutory right and obligation under section 214 survived the death of a respondent in a situation where the respondent's estate was sufficient to meet any contribution which might be ordered against him,[34] it is to be noted that, as a consequence of S's death, the learned judge was mindful that any evidence which implicated S should be viewed with caution. The authorities dictated[35] that the court had to be aware of the possibility that, had S lived, he may have been able to advance explanations which could have rebutted or had a tendency to rebut the liquidator's case. Accordingly, the court could not reject the effect of any probable explanation, which may have been advanced by S, unless it was satisfied, after rigorous examination, that such an explanation would have had no effect on the outcome of the proceedings.

In contending that S and his fellow non executive directors were liable under section 214, the liquidator alleged, that, by the end of January 1988, the directors ought to have concluded that there was no reasonable prospect of the company avoiding liquidation. At this specified date, the company had been trading for ten months and had incurred losses in the region of £80,000; in the three months prior to the specified date, the company's losses amounted to £30,000. On an examination of the company's board minutes for January 1988, it was evident that S had clearly appreciated the financial plight of the company. His Honour Jack QC concluded that, by the specified date, S should have been aware that the likelihood of the company's liquidation was a strong possibility. However, notwithstanding the company's dire financial position, the learned judge refused to accept that S ought to have been aware that there was no reasonable prospect of the company avoiding liquidation at

---

[34] The IA 1986, s.214 refers to a person who is or has been a director of a company, although it fails to specifically refer to that person's estate or personal representatives. However, as the learned judge pointed out, it is not usual for an Act of Parliament to indicate whether a right or obligation will pass on death by reference to a person's estate or personal representative. His Honour Jack QC considered that s.214 created a cause of action which was capable of surviving the death of the respondent in accordance with the Law Reform (Miscellaneous Provisions) Act 1934, s.1(1). However, even if that interpretation of a s.214 action was incorrect, the learned judge held that, to determine whether a right or obligation will pass, one must look at the intention of the legislation in question. Where that intention of the legislation serves a commercial purpose, as in the case of s.214, then the presumption would be that the purpose of the provision would not be defeated by the death of the respondent.

[35] See, for example, the *dictum* of Brett MR in *Re Garnett* (1866) 31 Ch D 1, at p.9.

the date specified by the liquidator.[36] This decision was justified on the basis that, whilst in January 1988, the resignation of the company's most effective fee earner from his post as an executive director of the company was harmful to the company's interests,[37] it was not crucial to the future survival of the company. Further, although it was unclear why S had continued to allow the company to trade beyond January 1988, that decision had been made on the basis of detailed sales projections (although the projections were, with the benefit of hindsight, clearly over optimistic) and with the reasonable expectation of securing the services of a further executive director, who it had been hoped, would bring to the company, a much needed injection of business. The learned judge described S as a "hard headed man" who he considered to be sincere in his belief that the company's fortunes could be turned around. His Honour Jack QC, opined that,

"In the absence of contrary evidence and in the light of the discretion I have set out concerning the case against him, I should be slow to reject what he stated".[38]

But for S's death and its effect on the manner in which the evidence of the case was dealt with, it is perhaps more than a speculative assumption to suggest that S and possibly the two other non executive directors of the company would, ordinarily, have been found liable under section 214. Although S and his co-respondents were inexperienced in the advertising business, it is to be noted that the three respondents were all experienced businessmen. It should also be noted that S was a cost accountant and therefore should have been expected to portray a level of skill and

---

[36] A conclusive factor in the outcome of this case was the liquidator's decision to specify the January 1988 date as the time at which the directors ought to have concluded that the company's liquidation was inevitable. Given the fact of S's death and with the benefit of hindsight, the liquidator's choice of date was perhaps over optimistic in its presumption of the date at which the company's directors ought to have realised that there was no reasonable prospect of the company avoiding liquidation. Indeed, his Honour Jack QC intimated, in the course of his judgment, that it was not until approximately three months after the date chosen by the liquidator that a reasonable assumption could have been made, as to the near certainty of the company's liquidation. The liquidator was refused the opportunity to substitute new dates for the ones pleaded, on the premise that to do so would have prejudiced the preparation of the respondent's defence.

[37] The executive director in question generated 15.7% of the company's annual income.

[38] *Supra*, n.33, at p.55.

understanding of the financial affairs of the company at a standard which went beyond the capacity of the average company director.[39]

In seeking to substantiate a director's conclusion that there was a reasonable prospect of the company avoiding liquidation, the court will be mindful of evidence which portrays a creditable and realistic attempt to reverse the fortunes of the company.[40] Examples of evidence which may be supportive of the company's attempted regeneration, may include the following:

(a) an injection of share capital which significantly reduces the level of the company's indebtedness;

(b) a review of directors and employees remuneration and in appropriate circumstances a reduction in the said levels;

(c) the employment of cost cutting measures to reduce corporate expenditure;

(d) support from the company's creditors in respect of the company's continued trading;

(e) holding regular board meetings and the constant review and monitoring of corporate policy;

(f) the production of up to date accounts and a detailed and realistic business plan;

(g) a re-organisation or re-structuring of the day to day management of the company;

(h) a reasonable expectation of securing a new and lucrative contract, the effect of which would seek to reverse the company's dire financial position; and

(i) professional advice which was supportive of the company's continued trading.

In relation to example (i), it is submitted that it may be unjust for a director to be made liable under section 214 in circumstances where he relied upon

---

[39] Although the evidence of the case against S and the other respondents was largely dependent upon documentary evidence, namely the company's accounts and the minutes of the company's board meetings, it must be observed that, as a consequence of S's death, the standard of proof required to establish S's liability was impliedly shifted from the civil standard based on a balance of probabilities to a standard approaching that of reasonable doubt. As such, it should be stressed that the eventual outcome of this case, namely a finding that S and the other respondents were not liable under s.214, should, as a matter of precedent, be restricted to the particular facts of the case.

[40] It is to be noted that an authoritative form of guidance would have been introduced if the Cork Report's proposal for an anticipatory declaration had not been rejected by the legislature.

independent professional advice,[41] the nature of which was later established to have been inaccurate or misleading in its portrayal of the company's capacity to rescue itself from its insolvent position. In this type of situation, the court would most probably be reluctant to conclude that the director's judgment and knowledge of the company's affairs would have been sufficient to override the recommendations of a professional advisor.[42] By analogy, a court would be unlikely to ignore the impact of the recommendations of a professional advisor in a situation where a director allowed the company to continue trading contrary to the recommendations of that advisor. Indeed, following the lead taken by Vinelott J in *Re Purpoint*,[43] the court would be apt to conclude that where a professional advisor recommended that a company's continued existence was futile, the director ought, on receiving that advice, to have been heavily persuaded that there was no reasonable prospect of the company avoiding liquidation. However, in assessing the impact and importance which a director should have attached to professional advice, it must be observed that the court should also be mindful of the

---

[41] A bank's decision to extend or renew a company's overdraft facility, whilst possibly portraying an optimistic view of the company's potential to trade itself out of its difficulties, would be very unlikely to be considered as a factor negating a director's ability to reach the conclusion that there was no reasonable prospect of the company avoiding liquidation.

[42] By analogy, see *Re Bonus Breaks Ltd* [1991] BCC 546, discussed in Chapter 5, at p.108 *et seq.*

[43] [1991] BCLC 491, at pp.494-495. This case involved a company (Purpoint Ltd), which had but a short existence. The company, which officially started trading in May 1985, was put into liquidation in May 1988; it ceased trading in November 1987. The company had two directors, a husband and wife team, who were also the only shareholders of the company. The husband dominated the running of the company's business and it was against him that the s.214 action was commenced. The first and only general meeting of the company was held in June 1986 and although the company appointed a firm of accountants, no audited accounts were ever prepared; this was as a consequence of the directors' failure to keep accounting records. The company ran up large Crown debts and other debts to trade creditors. By the date of its liquidation, the company's deficiency was £63,685. The trade debts, incurred after the date which the liquidator relied upon as being the date when the director ought to have concluded that there was no reasonable prospect of the company avoiding liquidation (May 1987), amounted to £13,500. In May 1987 (confirmed by a letter in June 1987), the director had been advised by the company's accountants of the likelihood of a wrongful trading action being brought against him. The accountants advised the director that he should stop drawing a salary from the company and that he should also exclude himself from the day to day management of its affairs. In addition, the director was advised that the company should prepare detailed cash flow forecasts. Unfortunately, the director did not heed the advice and took no steps with a view to minimising the potential loss to the company's creditors. The director was found liable under s.214. Vinelott J held that the latest date the director should have realised that the company's liquidation was inevitable was in May 1987, although the judge believed that such a conclusion should have been obvious to the director by January 1987. The director was also held liable under IA 1986, s.212 (discussed further in Chapter 2).

director's own level of skill, knowledge and experience and the type and size of company in which he held office.

4.5 The every step defence (section 214(3))

Liability under section 214 may be avoided in circumstances where the section 214(3) defence is satisfied. The defence will be established where the court is convinced that the director, after first becoming aware that there was no reasonable prospect of the company avoiding liquidation, took every step, with a view to minimising the potential loss to the company's creditors.

In appraising whether the steps taken by a director comply with the terms of the section 214(3) defence, the director will be assessed by applying the reasonable diligent person test, provided by section 214(4). Therefore, to satisfy the section 214(3) defence, the court must be persuaded that a reasonable diligent person, imputed with the director's own skill, experience and knowledge would, in seeking to minimise the loss to corporate creditors, have been unable to take any further steps than those that had actually been taken by the respondent director, following his realisation that there was no reasonable prospect of the company avoiding liquidation. The defence, in requiring that "every step" must be taken with a view to minimising the potential loss to the company's creditors, sets a daunting standard which, if construed literally, may, save in the most exceptional cases, render its application to be most improbable.

In the absence of any detailed judicial pronouncements on the scope and the requirements for establishing the section 214(3) defence,[44] the potential application of this defence remains uncertain. However, for a director to convince the court that he took every step to safeguard the interests of creditors, it is patently obvious that he will ordinarily be required to establish that his participation in the company's affairs was, as from the date upon which he realised that there was no reasonable prospect of the company

---

[44] The s.214(3) defence was briefly considered by Knox J in *Re Produce Marketing Consortium Ltd* (1989) 5 BCC 569, at p.596. Here the learned judge came to the obvious conclusion that the defence would not be applicable in a situation where a director's belief in his ability to deflect the company's dire financial position was not substantiated by any positive action on the part of the director to achieve that objective. In this case, Knox J found that, as the company had continued to trade in an insolvent state for a year after the date on which the directors ought to have realised that there was no reasonable prospect of the company avoiding liquidation, it was obvious that they had given very little thought to the plight of the company's creditors. Further, the learned judge held that the directors could not contend that, in seeking to improve the position of the company's principal creditor, they had taken the necessary steps to bring themselves within the s.214(3) defence. The defence required the directors to have taken every step to minimise potential losses in respect of the interests of the creditors as a whole.

avoiding liquidation, both active and geared to the protection of the interests of corporate creditors. Accordingly, in seeking to establish the defence, a director would be advised to attend all board meetings, ensuring that his opinions were recorded in the board minutes. In addition, a director should seek to ensure that the company's accounts are kept up to date and where necessary he should be an active player in instigating meetings with the company's creditors. It is important that the company's creditors are aware of, and support the company's proposed methods for minimising losses, because clearly, the status of corporate creditors, following the company's decline into an insolvent state will be transformed. Essentially, the creditors will become the beneficial owners of the company's assets and as such the company's directors will have a duty to safeguard their interests.[45]

It is suggested that the first step a respondent director would be expected to take to bring himself within the ambit of the section 214(3) defence would be to be present at the board meeting at which the company's dire financial position was confirmed and discussed. The respondent director would be expected to support any proposal which recommended that the board should seek professional guidance with a view to obtaining an assessment of the viability of the company's capacity to continue its trading activities.

In a situation where a company's position was such that it was evident that there was no reasonable prospect of its debts and liabilities being reduced by its continued trading, then the obvious and logical step for a director to take would be to support a motion which would have the effect of ending the company's trading activities. However, even in circumstances where a company was unable to escape its insolvent state, it must be noted that the cessation of business activity, followed by the company's liquidation, may not always be the most appropriate option available. Although an expeditious liquidation would be likely to minimise any further depletion of the company's existing assets, it may not be the most effective way of maximising the value of existing or potential assets. For example, the interests of creditors may, in the short term, be more effectively safeguarded if the company continued its existence for the purpose of, for example, completing existing contracts, collecting outstanding debts, or disposing of assets with less haste and at a better return than might otherwise be the case had the assets been disposed of in the course of the liquidation process.[46]

As an alternative to supporting the continued existence of the company's management team, a more appropriate step for a director to take in respect of the section 214(3) defence may be to recommend or support the appointment

---

[45] See, for example, *West Mercia Safetywear Ltd v. Dodd* [1988] BCLC 250.

[46] In determining the appropriate course of action, it would, in most cases, be imperative to consult with the company's creditors.

of an administrator. Although an administration order triggers a moratorium period,[47] which in effect prolongs the settlement of corporate debts, administration may, in relation to the interests of corporate creditors, be a welcomed alternative to allowing the company to operate under the control of what may be perceived to be a failed management team. An administrator must be a qualified insolvency practitioner and as such his experience in dealing with insolvent companies may provide the means by which a more efficient and effective realisation of the company's assets may be achieved.

Another option open to a director would be to recommend that the company be put into receivership; a receiver must also be a qualified insolvency practitioner. However, the appointment of a receiver may only be made by a creditor of the company with an interest secured by way of a floating charge. In addition, it is probable, although by no means certain, that the appointment of a receiver would, if it was to take place, occur prior to the point in time at which there was no reasonable prospect of the company avoiding liquidation. As the holder of a floating charge will wish to maximise the value of the charged assets, a delay in the appointment of a receiver, to a point in time where the company's liquidation had become virtually inevitable, would be likely to result in a less favourable return on the charged assets than would otherwise have been the case had the receiver been appointed at an earlier date.

A final and controversial aspect of the every step defence concerns the significance to be attached to a director's resignation from office, following his realisation that there was no reasonable prospect of the company avoiding liquidation. Where a director's proposals to alleviate the potential prejudice to the company's creditors have been rejected by the company's board, (proposals which, had they been implemented may have successfully improved the creditors' position) is it, in such circumstances, advisable for the director to resign his office or should the director continue in office as an active and opposing voice to the majority view?

In exceptional cases, a director's resignation from office may be viewed as the final and possibly the only step available to the director, for example, in circumstances where the resignation followed a prolonged but unsuccessful attempt on the part of the director to convince the board of its folly in pursuing a course of action. However, in the majority of cases, resignation will probably be viewed as indicative of the fact that the director failed to take every step to minimise the potential loss to creditors. Clearly, evidence which supports a director's claim to have taken every step to safeguard creditors interests will be more readily found from the director's continued and active participation in the affairs of the company. Indeed, resignation may be viewed

---

[47] See IA 1986, s.11.

as a step which was designed to protect the interests and integrity of the individual director, rather than seeking to confer any benefit on the company in respect of minimising the potential loss of its creditors.

4.5.1 *The applicability of the section 727 defence?*

A director may be excused from liability arising out of his negligence, breach of duty or breach of trust where, in accordance with section 727 of the Companies Act 1985, the court is of the opinion that the director acted honestly and reasonably and, as a consequence of his actions, ought fairly to be excused from liability. At first sight, it would appear that section 727 could be invoked as a defence to a section 214 action, because in cases commenced under section 214, a director's conduct will rarely be of a dishonest nature (if it were otherwise, an action under section 213 of the Insolvency Act 1986 would seem more appropriate), and, in addition, at a time when the company is trading in an insolvent state, the conduct giving rise to a section 214 action will inevitably involve a breach of duty to the company as a whole, that is, the conduct may be viewed as a breach of duty in so far as it adversely affects the interests of corporate creditors.

However, in respect of a section 214 action, the section 727 defence must surely fail in so far as the defence will only apply in cases where a director's conduct is viewed to be both honest and reasonable. Accordingly, where in the context of a section 214 action, a director's conduct fell below the standard of a reasonably diligent person, it would be improbable to contend that regardless of that fact, the conduct could still be viewed to have been of a reasonable standard in the context of the section 727 defence.[48]

In *Re Produce Marketing Consortium Ltd*,[49] it is to be noted that Knox J concluded that the section 727 defence was incompatible with the objective nature of the test to determine liability under section 214. The learned judge opined that it was very difficult to marry the two distinct tests applicable to section 214 and section 727 in so far as section 727 invited an essentially subjective approach, whereas liability under section 214 was primarily determined by an objective test. Although the nature of the distinction drawn by Knox J in relation to the two tests may be viewed with some caution (section 727 cannot, in its use of the term "reasonably", be properly viewed as

---

[48] However, note that in *Re D'Jan of London Ltd* [1993] BCC 646, Hoffmann LJ found that it was possible for conduct to be viewed as reasonable for the purposes of the s.727 defence notwithstanding that the very same conduct was, in respect of the s.214(4) test, found to have been of an unreasonable nature. This case was concerned with the availability of the s.727 defence in relation to proceedings under IA 1986, s.212. The case is discussed further in Chapter 2, at p.32.

[49] [1989] BCLC 513.

supporting a test which is absent of any objective element, and the section 214 test, whilst primarily objective in nature, does contain a subjective element), the learned judge's assertion that the two tests cannot be applied on a concurrent basis, is clearly representative of the correct approach.[50]

4.6 Applications under section 214

A company's liquidator is the only person who is permitted to make an application under section 214.[51] In so restricting the availability of the provision, section 214 is drafted in a manner which is quite contrary to the recommendations advocated by the Cork Report. Indeed, given that the White Paper approved the Cork Report's objective of wishing to create a stricter regime for the regulation and control of directors involved in the wrongful trading activities of insolvent companies, it is disappointing that the White Paper should have in fact recommended that the potential scope of section 214 should be restricted in the manner represented by section 214. However, in following the recommendations of the White Paper, it is suggested that the legislature was influenced by a desire to protect the potential survival of a company in receivership or a company which was subject to an administration order. For example, had a receiver, administrator or an individual creditor of a company been permitted to make an application under section 214, (in accordance with the recommendations of the Cork Report) the resulting action, although targeted against a director(s) of the company, may have had the effect of undermining the confidence and stability in an already vulnerable enterprise.

Although restricting the availability of the provision to a situation where a company is in insolvent liquidation may enhance the stability of a corporate enterprise which is, for example, in receivership or administration, the said restriction may well be contrary to the immediate interests of unsecured creditors; the very class of person which the provision was designed to protect. For example, a creditor who is a victim of an act of wrongful trading may be placed in such a financial position whereby the recovery of sums owed to him by the company becomes imperative to his own survival. The creditor's financial position may be perilous, to the extent that any suspension of proceedings under section 214, until such a time as the company is put into liquidation, may cause the creditor's own business to be put in serious jeopardy. Further, when a company is in receivership, a company's assets may, during the receivership process, be completely dissipated, with the result

---

[50] See also, *Re DKG Contractors Ltd* [1990] BCC 903.
[51] This follows the recommendations of the White Paper.

that the company may never be placed into insolvent liquidation, thereby negating the possibility of an action under section 214.[52]

Although it is doubtful whether it is justifiable to restrict the commencement of proceedings under section 214 to a situation where a company is in liquidation, it is even more difficult to understand the plausibility of the provision in its failure to allow an individual creditor to make an application under section 214, following the company's insolvent liquidation. While this restriction may be defended on the premise that individual applications would interfere with the liquidator's task of attempting to safeguard the interests of all unsecured creditors, the restriction is especially unfair in a situation where a debt, which is owed to a creditor by the insolvent company, represents a large proportion of the total amount of an expected contribution order. In such circumstances, it would appear unjust that an individual creditor should, on having to rely on the liquidator to make an application, be expected to take an equal share with other creditors in the sum of the contribution order,[53] especially where the claims of the company's other creditors may have arisen in circumstances quite distinct from those which would have resulted in an action under section 214.[54] Further, it must be remembered that a creditor will, irrespective of the amount of his claim against the insolvent company's assets, be devoid of any right to compel the liquidator to proceed with an application under section 214.[55]

4.7 Persons who may incur liability under section 214

Unlike section 213 of the Insolvency Act 1986, liability under section 214 may only be imposed against company directors. Had the proposals of the Cork Report been followed, liability would have been applicable to any person who had played a substantive role in the wrongful trading of a company.[56] The legislature's decision to restrict liability under section 214 to company directors may, in part, be explained by its decision to retain (contrary to the recommendations of the Cork Report) the civil offence of fraudulent trading;

---

[52] See, Williams & McGhee "Curbing Unfit Directors — Is Personal Liability an Empty Threat" [1993] *Insolvency Lawyer* 2.

[53] In respect of the distribution rules, see, the Insolvency Rules 1986, r.4.181.

[54] *Supra*, n.52.

[55] For example, a liquidator may decline to commence an action under s.214 because of the expected cost of the proceedings.

[56] It is to be observed that, in Ireland, an action for reckless trading may be commenced against any officer of the company. An officer is defined to include a company director (including a shadow director), the company secretary, the company's auditor, liquidator or receiver.

which is, of course, permissive of actions against persons other than company directors.[57] The decision may also be explained on the premise that had "any person" been able to incur liability under section 214, creditors may have been less willing to offer financial support to ailing companies, because the procurement of assistance may have been construed to have taken place at a time when the creditor ought to have realised that there was no reasonable prospect of the company avoiding liquidation, thus bringing the creditor's assistance within the terms of section 214.

Although liability under section 214 is restricted to company directors, the definition of a director is not confined to a person who was appointed to the company's board of directors (a *de jure* director) but will also include a *de facto* director,[58] that is, a person who, notwithstanding an absence of a formal appointment to the company's board was in the habit of performing managerial tasks of a type ordinarily associated with a *de jure* director. Further, section 214(7) specifically provides that liability under section 214 will arise where a person acts in the capacity of a shadow director. A shadow director is defined as a person in accordance with whose directions or instructions the directors of the company are accustomed to act. Accordingly, although a creditor of a company cannot, as of right, incur liability under section 214, it may be possible for a creditor to be held liable as a shadow director of the company. Indeed, it is to be noted that in *Re a Company (No. 005009 of 1987), ex parte Copp*,[59] Knox J refused to strike out a claim in which it was alleged by the liquidator that the company's bank should, on the premise that the bank had acted as the company's shadow director, be made liable as a party to the company's wrongful trading. In this case, the bank had actively involved itself in the company's affairs, for example, the bank had appointed inspectors to report on the company's financial state and as a consequence of the inspectors' report the company had been obliged, in order to retain the bank's support, to implement the bank's recommendations. Although Knox J was not called upon to adjudicate on the success or otherwise of the liquidator's claim, the fact that the claim was allowed to proceed is, itself, sufficient to justify the contention that a bank (or other creditor) may, in the future, be exposed to a potential liability under section 214.

A more probable finding of the existence of a person having acted as a shadow director may be advanced in respect of a corporate group relationship, that is, where a holding company controls the corporate

---

[57] See Chapter 3 at p.44.
[58] See the comments of Millet J in *Re Hydrodam (Corby) Ltd* [1994] 2 BCLC 180, at pp.182–183.
[59] [1989] BCLC 13.

policy of its subsidiary. However, from the decision of Millet J in *Re Hydrodam (Corby) Ltd*,[60] although a holding company may, under the terms of section 214, be found to be a shadow director of its subsidiary company, it is unlikely that the directors of the holding company will be deemed to have acted as shadow directors of the subsidiary company, notwithstanding that the said directors shared a collective responsibility in conducting the affairs of the holding company in its relationship with the subsidiary. Millet J opined,

> "The liquidator submitted that where a body corporate is a director of a company, whether it be a *de jure*, *de facto* or shadow director, its own directors must *ipso facto* be shadow directors of the company. In my judgment that simply does not follow. Attendance of board meetings and voting, with others, may in certain limited circumstances expose a director to personal liability to the company of which he is a director or its creditors. But it does not, without more, constitute him a director of any company of which his company is a director".[61]

Therefore, in attempting to establish that a director of a holding company acted as a shadow director of the holding company's subsidiary, it will be necessary to produce evidence which is indicative of a finding that the director dominated and controlled the affairs of the holding company in its relationship with the subsidiary, to the extent that the subsidiary company acted, not on the instructions of the company's board, but rather, on the instructions of the individual director.

4.8 The beneficiaries of a contribution order

In circumstances where a court finds a director to be liable under the terms of section 214, the contribution order (if any) must be paid into the general assets of the company. The potential beneficiaries of the contribution order are the company's unsecured creditors. However, as section 214 fails to provide otherwise, *prima facie*, it would appear feasible to suggest that a creditor with a floating charge over the company's undertaking should, following the crystallisation of the charge, be entitled to a first claim on the amount of any contribution. As the contribution payment becomes a part of the general assets of the company in liquidation, it would appear to be caught by the terms of such a charge. Indeed, in *Re Produce Marketing Consortium Ltd*,[62] a secured creditor's entitlement to the proceeds of a contribution order

---

[60] *Supra*, n.58.
[61] *Ibid.*, at p.184.
[62] [1989] 5 BCC 569.

was impliedly confirmed by the terms of the order.[63] The contribution order provided that the company's bank, which held a floating charge over the company's undertaking,

> "will have a charge over anything which the [respondent directors] contribute pursuant to my order".[64]

However, following the Court of Appeal's decision in *Re Oasis Merchandising Services Ltd*,[65] the presumption of a priority being afforded to a holder of a floating charge can no longer be sustained.[66] In *Re Oasis Merchandising Services Ltd*, the Court of Appeal held that the fruits of a section 214 action (the sum of a contribution order) could not be regarded as a property right of a company. Therefore, the sum of any contribution order was incapable of being made the subject of a charge. Accordingly, and following the spirit of the Cork Report,[67] the fruits of a section 214 action are free from the prior claims of any floating charge.[68]

Although, potentially, all the unsecured creditors of a company will benefit from the terms of a contribution order, it is to be observed that in accordance with section 215(4) of the Insolvency Act 1986, the court may direct that the whole or part of any debt owed by the company to a creditor and any interest thereon shall rank in priority after all other debts owed by the company and after any interest on those debts. Primarily, the purpose of this provision is to preclude a company director, in his capacity as a creditor of the company, from contending that regardless of his participation in the wrongful trading activities of the company, he should still, in accordance with section 214(1), be entitled, as an unsecured creditor of the company, to an equal participation in a share of the contribution order.[69]

---

[63] For a comprehensive discussion of whether a secured creditor should be entitled to participate in assets which are comprised of the proceeds of a contribution order, see, Oditah "Wrongful Trading" (1990) LMCLQ 205, Prentice "Creditor's Interests and Director's Duties" (1990) 10 OJLS 265, Hicks "Advising on Wrongful Trading" (1993) 14 Co Law 16, 55, & Wheeler "Swelling the Assets for Distribution in Corporate Insolvency" [1993] JBL 256.

[64] *Supra*, n.49, at p.598.

[65] [1997] 1 WLR 764. This case is discussed in detail at p.86 *et seq*.

[66] This position will also be true of a contribution order made under IA 1986, s.213.

[67] See, paras 1797, 1806.

[68] The fruits of the s.214 action will be preserved for the benefit of the company's unsecured creditors. However, it must be noted that, where corporate assets are insufficient to discharge the debts of a secured creditor, the chargeholder will also be able to participate in the distribution of the fruits of the action.

[69] See, *Re Purpoint Ltd* [1991] BCC 121.

4.9 The extent of a director's liability under section 214

Under section 214, the extent of a director's liability is determined at the discretion of the court. The court may declare that the director make such contributions (if any) to the company's assets as it thinks proper. Although section 214 provides no method or guidance for calculating the amount of a director's contribution, existing case law[70] confirms that the maximum amount of any contribution will ordinarily be discerned in proportion to the effect which the period of wrongful trading had on the depletion of the company's assets.[71] The period runs from the date on which the director should have first realised that the company had no reasonable prospect of avoiding liquidation. While section 214 incorporates a potential penal or public element, in so far as the court may, where a director is liable under section 214, impose a disqualification order against him under section 10 of the Company Directors Disqualification Act 1986,[72] it is to be observed that the ability to establish a director's liability under section 214 is absent of any requirement to prove fraudulent intent. Consequently, and in contrast to the calculation of the extent of a director's liability under section 213 of the Insolvency Act 1986,[73] the sum of a contribution order under section 214, will primarily be of a compensatory nature.

However, as the court is given a wide discretion in determining the amount of any contribution order, the court may, in exercising its discretion, consider the extent of the director's participation in, and his culpability for, the company's wrongful trading. Therefore, whereas the court may view the conduct of the honest, albeit, naive director with some leniency,[74] a director who exhibits a reckless and blatant disregard for the interests of corporate

---

[70] See, for example, *Re Produce Marketing Consortium Ltd* [1989] 5 BCC 569, *Re Purpoint Ltd* [1990] BCC 121.

[71] However, in *Re DKG Contractors Ltd* [1990] BCC 903, his Honour John Weeks QC, sitting as a High Court judge, prescribed a variant method for calculating the amount of the contribution. The learned judge held that the director's contribution to the company's assets should be equated to the amount of the trade debts on or after the date on which the director ought to have realised that there was no prospect of the company avoiding liquidation. This method of calculation may have some merit because a director's contribution to the company's assets is made exclusively for the purpose of relieving the debts of unsecured creditors, which are incurred as a consequence of the company's wrongful trading.

[72] The disqualification order may be imposed for a period up to a maximum of fifteen years. The CDDA 1986, s.10 is discussed further in Chapter 7, at p.145.

[73] Discussed in Chapter 3, at p.54.

[74] See, *Re Produce Marketing Consortium Ltd* [1989] 5 BCC 569.

creditors may be expected, in relation to the calculation of the contribution order, to be treated with much less sympathy.[75]

Finally, it must be noted that, in accordance with section 215(2) of the Insolvency Act 1986, the court may, in relation to the terms of a contribution order, place a charge over the director's obligation to discharge his liability. The charge will be secured against any debt or obligation due from the company to the director, or on any mortgage or charge, or any interest in a mortgage or charge on assets of the company held by, or vested in the director or any person on his behalf, or any person claiming to be his assignee. Under the terms of section 215(2), the court is given the power to make further orders which may be deemed necessary for the enforcement of the charge.

4.10 Financing an application under section 214

Following a company's insolvent liquidation, a liquidator's application under section 214, will ordinarily be financed from assets which have been realised during the liquidation process. Further, section 115 of the Insolvency Act 1986, provides that all the expenses incurred in the winding up of a company are payable out of the company's assets in priority to all other claims, the expenses in question relate, to the realising or getting in of any of the assets of the company.[76] However, in respect of proceedings under section 214, can such an action be regarded as an attempt to realise or get in an asset of the company? Although a section 214 action may result in a contribution being made to the company's assets, the said contribution (assets) would have had no existence at the time when the action was commenced.

If, as is to be implied from the decision of Millet J in *Re M C Bacon Ltd (No. 2)*,[77] an asset of a company will not, for the purposes of section 115 of the Insolvency Act 1986, include a contribution which did not form part of the company's property at the commencement of its winding up, then in many instances the funds available to finance section 214 proceedings may be minimal, because the liquidator will be unable to claim liquidation expenses in relation to the section 214 action (the conclusion reached by Millet J was approved in *obiter* comments made by the Court of Appeal in *Re Oasis Merchandising Services Ltd*).[78] In so far as the liquidator must, in distributing assets, apply them in accordance with priority rules, then accordingly, after the debts of the company's secured and preferential creditors have been

---

[75] See, *Re DKG Contractors Ltd* [1990] BCC 903.
[76] See, the Insolvency Rules 1986, r.4.218(1).
[77] [1990] BCC 430.
[78] [1997] BCC 282, at p.290.

discharged, the company's assets may be severely depleted or indeed non existent.

However, following the decision of the Court of Appeal in *Katz v. McNally*,[79] the standing of *Re M C Bacon Ltd (No. 2)* may now be doubted in relation to its conclusion that contributions which do not form a part of the company's property at the commencement of its winding up cannot be properly regarded as assets of the company. In *Katz v. McNally*, the Court of Appeal considered (albeit without the benefit of in depth argument in relation to the issue) that the statutory scheme for determining the identification of liquidation expenses was permissive of a liquidator's ability to claim expenses in respect of financing an action to recover assets of the company, irrespective of whether or not those assets were derived from part of the company's property.[80] Phillips LJ, in delivering the leading judgment of the court, considered that Rule 12.2 of the Insolvency Rules 1986 put the matter beyond any doubt. Rule 12.2 provides:

"All fees, costs, charges and other expenses incurred in the course of winding up or bankruptcy proceedings are to be regarded as expenses of the winding up, or, as the case may be, of the bankruptcy".

While the Court of Appeal's common-sense approach to the determination of liquidation expenses is to be applauded, it is nevertheless questionable, without a more detailed and thorough judicial examination of the matter, whether the *obiter* comments in *Katz*, can be relied upon as providing a definite and conclusive alternative to the decision reached in *Re M C Bacon Ltd*. Indeed, a literal interpretation of section 115 of the Insolvency Act 1986, when read in conjunction with rule 4.218 of the Insolvency Rules 1986 would seem to infer that the "realising or getting in of any of the assets of the company" is indicative of the fact that the term "assets" refers to those assets which form a part of the company's property at the commencement of its winding up. Accordingly, one may argue that rule 12.2 should not be construed in isolation to, but rather in conjunction with section 115 and rule 4.218.

Although a liquidator may be unwilling or unable to commit corporate assets for the purpose of funding an application under section 214, the liquidator may nevertheless proceed with the application where a creditor(s) of the company decides to fund the action. Obviously, a creditor(s) in considering whether to fund an application must carefully determine whether

---

[79] [1997] BCC 784.
[80] For example, actions under IA 1986, ss.213, 214, 238 and 239.

the pursuit of the section 214 action would be financially sustainable in relation to the probable cost of the proceedings.[81]

4.10.1 *The ability of a third party to fund a section 214 action*

Where a liquidator of a company is of the opinion that an action under section 214 is sustainable but the company's financial position would not warrant the funding of the application, it would appear, other than where an unsecured creditor(s) is willing to fund the action (or legally assign the debt to a third party who is willing to fund the action)[82] that the application will be lost. In such circumstances, the only method by which the application could proceed would be if the liquidator had an authority to assign the section 214 action, or the fruits of the future section 214 action, to a third party.[83] Although an outright legal assignment of a section 214 action is not possible, in so far as section 214 proceedings may only be commenced and conducted by a liquidator, the plausibility of an equitable assignment would, providing it was supported by consideration, appear to be a more logical possibility. The equitable assignment would take the form of an agreement between the liquidator and a third party, whereby the third party would agree to fund the section 214 action in return for a share in the fruits of the action.

The competence of a liquidator to enter into an agreement to cause an equitable assignment of a section 214 action was recently considered by the Court of Appeal in *Re Oasis Merchandising Services Ltd*.[84] In this case, the liquidator of Oasis Mechandising Services Ltd entered into an agreement with London Wall Litigation Claims Ltd (LWL) (a company which provided a specialist litigation support service for liquidators) under which LWL agreed to finance a section 214 action in return for the assignment of the fruits of the action. The objective of the agreement was that LWL would be reimbursed for the expenditure arising from the litigation and that any excess obtained on

---

[81] See, for example, *Katz v. McNally*, *supra*, n.79.

[82] An absolute transfer of the debt, as a transfer of property, will normally carry with it the right to prosecute any cause of action to recover the debt, see *Camdex International Ltd v. Bank of Zambia* [1996] 3 WLR 759. Although a transfer of a debt will not give the transferee a right to commence an action under s.214, the transferee will have the right to finance the action, albeit that any contribution recovered as a result of the action will be directed towards the company's assets and will therefore benefit all of the company's unsecured creditors and not solely the creditor (transferee) who financed the litigation.

[83] The authorities confirm that a liquidator or trustee in bankruptcy has a right to exercise a power of sale to assign a cause of action for valuable consideration, see, e.g. *Re Park Waggon Works Co* (1881) 17 Ch D 234 (this case concerned an assignment of a cause of action in relation to a misfeasance claim).

[84] [1997] 1WLR 764, [1997] 1 BCLC 689.

judgment would, depending on the amount of the excess, be divided between LWL and the liquidator, in varying percentages. The liquidator's percentage was to increase from 10% to a maximum of 50% on any excess of £500,000. The agreement was expressed to be by way of an equitable assignment of the fruits of the action. Although the claim was to be pursued by the liquidator, it was, however, of a champertous nature,[85] in so far as LWL exerted influence over the liquidator in respect of the manner in which the action could be pursued (a fact which was not disputed by the parties to the action).[86] Obviously, had the assignee not been accorded a right to interfere in the proceedings, no question of champerty would have arisen.[87]

Notwithstanding that the agreement was of a champertous nature, the liquidator contended that paragraph 6 of Schedule 4 of the Insolvency Act 1986 permitted the equitable assignment of the fruits of the action, because the statutory provision gave a liquidator the power to "sell any of the company's property". Accordingly, the liquidator submitted that he was afforded a statutory authority to sell the fruits of a section 214 action as a property right; an authority which validated what would otherwise have been a champertous agreement.

The liquidator sought the approval of the companies court prior to entering the agreement with LWL. Although approval was initially given, it was to be subsequently set aside by Robert Walker J,[88] who, in staying proceedings, declared the agreement to have been champertous and contrary to public policy. In a detailed judgment, Robert Walker J held the agreement to be invalid on two distinct counts. First, the learned judge refuted the liquidator's contention that the definition of a company's property, within section 436 of

---

[85] A champertous agreement is one whereby encouragement or assistance is given to a litigant by a person with no direct interest in the litigation in consideration of a share in the fruits of the action. Such an agreement is contrary to public policy or otherwise illegal, see Criminal Law Act 1967, s.14(2).

[86] By the terms of the agreement, the liquidator was to institute, carry on and prosecute the s.214 action and to do all such lawful acts and things as LWL might require for the purpose of instituting, carrying on and prosecuting the s.214 action. LWL had the right to appoint solicitors in respect of the action and to direct and instruct LWL in relation to the conduct of the proceedings.

[87] See, for example, *Glegg v. Bromley* [1912] 3 KB 474. Also see *Katz v. McNally* [1997] BCC 784 where the Court of Appeal found that there had not been a champertous agreement in respect of proceedings under IA 1986, s.239 (proceedings to recover preference payments) in so far as the proceedings had been financed by a creditor with an interest in the litigation. Further, the liquidators had not surrendered their right to pursue the litigation in a manner which they considered appropriate.

[88] [1995] 2 BCLC 493.

the Insolvency Act 1986,[89] was wide enough to cover the equitable assignment of the fruits of a section 214 action. Although Robert Walker J accepted that the section 436 definition of property included a right of action which, on the company's liquidation, could be pursued by a liquidator,[90] the learned judge viewed the right of action to be subject to the condition that it had been vested in the company at a time up until the commencement of the company's winding up.[91]

Although the "property issue" was, of itself, a sufficient ground to defeat the validity of the agreement, Robert Walker J also sought to refute the efficacy of the agreement on an alternative ground. The learned judge opined that as section 214 incorporated a potential penal or public element, namely, the court in the course of section 214 proceedings had a power, under section 10 of the Company Directors Disqualification Act 1986, to impose a disqualification order,[92] it followed that even a partial loss of the liquidator's control over the proceedings should be viewed as objectionable to the public interest.

The case proceeded to the Court of Appeal, where the decision of Robert Walker J, was unanimously affirmed.[93] In giving the judgment of the court, Peter Gibson LJ confirmed that the fruits of a section 214 action should not be regarded as the property of a company for the purposes of paragraph 6 of Schedule 4 of the Insolvency Act 1986. In addition to the explanations advanced by Robert Walker J, Peter Gibson LJ justified the correctness of differentiating between a right of action acquired prior to a company's winding up and a right of action arising after a liquidator's appointment on other grounds.[94] His lordship pointed out that unlike the personal

---

[89] Section 436 specifies that property includes "money, goods, things in action, land and every description of property wherever situated and also obligations and every description of interest, whether present or future or vested or contingent, arising out of or incidental to property ...".

[90] It should be noted that according to Lightman J in *Grovewood Holdings plc v. James Capel & Co Ltd* [1994] 2 BCLC 782, at 788, the IA 1986, para. 6, Sch. 4 conferred no exception from the law of champerty on a sale of the fruits of an action when the sale included provision for the purchaser to finance the litigation. Robert Walker J and subsequently Peter Gibson LJ, in giving the judgment of the Court of Appeal, had much difficulty with the view expressed by Lightman J. Whether, a liquidator's sale of a cause of action was exempted from being a champertous agreement by the statutory power of sale was a matter to be determined by reference to the nature of the cause of action in conjunction with a construction of the statutory power of sale.

[91] Robert Walker J found support for his interpretation of "property of the company" in the decisions of Knox J in *Re Ayala Holdings (No. 2)* [1996] 1 BCLC 467 and Millet J in *Re M C Bacon (No. 2)* [1990] BCLC 607.

[92] Discussed further in Chapter 7, at p.145.

[93] The appeal was instigated on behalf of LWL. The liquidator was not a party to the appeal.

[94] See also, *Re M C Bacon Ltd* [1990] BCLC 607.

bankruptcy provisions of the Insolvency Act 1986,[95] the Act, in its treatment of corporate insolvency, failed to specify whether an asset acquired after a company's liquidation could be regarded as the property of a company so as to substantiate a company's ability to assign that property in accordance with paragraph 6 of Schedule 4. Further, Peter Gibson LJ also noted that if the fruits of a section 214 action constituted a property right, it would have been difficult to contend that such a right was incapable of being made subject to a charge expressed to have been taken over the company's present and future assets. In such a case, the holder of the charge would have been accorded a prior claim to the fruits of a section 214 action, a scenario which would have defeated the provision's very purpose of protecting the interests of the company's unsecured creditors.

In addition to dismissing LWL's contention that the fruits of a section 214 action could be regarded as falling within the ambit of paragraph 6 of Schedule 4 of the Insolvency Act 1986, the Court of Appeal also refused to accept an alternative argument, to the effect that the agreement could, regardless of whether or not the assignment of the fruits of the section 214 action constituted an assignment of a property right, still be validated in accordance with paragraph 13 of Schedule 4 of the Insolvency Act 1986. Paragraph 13 of Schedule 4 provides the liquidator with a power to do all such things as may be necessary for the winding up of the company's affairs and the distribution of the company's assets. LWL contended that the liquidator had, under the terms of paragraph 13, the power to override what would otherwise have been a champertous agreement. Despite the apparent width of paragraph 13, the Court of Appeal considered that its interpretation should be restricted to a legitimate exercise of a liquidator's power. Therefore, it could not, as in the present case, be employed for the purpose of allowing a liquidator to enter into an agreement which was contrary to public policy or otherwise illegal.

Although the Court of Appeal held the agreement in *Re Oasis Merchandising Ltd* to be invalid, it is to be noted that the court recognised that, as a matter of policy, a liquidator should be able to enter into an agreement with a third party, the purpose of which was to fund a section 214 action in return for a share in the fruits of the action. The validity of such an agreement would be dependent upon a liquidator's ability to commence the

---

[95] By IA 1986, s.307, the trustee in bankruptcy may by notice claim for the bankrupt's estate any property which has been acquired by or has devolved upon the bankrupt since the commencement of the bankruptcy, and by s.351, references to property comprised in the bankrupt's estate include any property which would be such property if a notice in respect of it were given under s.307. By para. 9 of Sch. 5, the trustee has a power to sell any part of the property for the time being comprised in the bankrupt's estate.

section 214 proceedings without any form of interference from a third party. Peter Gibson LJ stated that,

> "As a matter of policy we think that there is much to be said for allowing a liquidator to sell the fruits of an action ... provided that it does not give the purchaser the right to influence the course of, or to interfere with the liquidator's conduct of the proceedings. The liquidator as an officer of the court exercising a statutory power in pursuing the proceedings must be free to behave accordingly".[96]

The above statement is to be welcomed. Although an agreement, irrespective of whether or not it is touched by champerty, cannot be validated in accordance with the liquidator's statutory power of sale under paragraph 6 of Schedule 4 of the Insolvency Act 1986,[97] the Court of Appeal recognised that the scope of the liquidator's statutory power, contained in paragraph 13 of Schedule 4 of the Insolvency Act 1986, is permissive of a liquidator's ability to assign the fruits of a section 214 action in cases where no champerty is involved. However, although the recognition of a liquidator's ability to assign the fruits of a section 214 action is to be welcomed, it is to be observed that in many cases a third party may be most reluctant to enter into an agreement where he is unable to direct or otherwise influence the manner in which proceedings are to be conducted.

By comparison, it is interesting to note that under the Australian jurisdiction, sections 588M and 588W of the Corporations Law 1991, a liquidator is permitted, under his statutory power of sale, to assign the fruits of an insolvent trading action (this is similar to wrongful trading action). Unlike the UK legislation, the Australian legislation is framed in a manner whereby the loss or damage caused by a company's insolvent trading and which is attributable to a director (or holding company), is deemed to be a debt recoverable by the company. The debt arises once the conditions of liability have been fulfilled. Therefore, the debt can properly be regarded as part of the company's property which the liquidator is empowered to sell.[98] To prevent the fruits of the insolvent trading action from being made the subject matter of a charge which would otherwise take priority over the

---

[96] [1997] 1 WLR at p.777.

[97] This observation is the very product of the judicial reasoning which underpinned the decision in *Re Oasis Merchandising Services Ltd*, where it was made clear that an assignment of the fruits of a s.214 action cannot be regarded as an assignment of the company's property.

[98] See, *R E Movitor Pty Ltd* (1995) 19 ACSR 440, a case which was referred to by the Court of Appeal in *Re Oasis Merchandising Services Ltd*.

interests of unsecured creditors, the Australian legislation specifically provides that moneys recovered under the insolvent trading provision cannot be used to discharge a secured debt unless all the company's unsecured debts have been paid in full.[99]

4.11 A concurrent action under section 212 and section 214 of the Insolvency Act 1986

Where a director is a party to the unwarranted depletion of corporate assets, at a time when he ought to have been aware that there was no reasonable prospect of the company avoiding liquidation, the director, in addition to incurring liability under section 214, may also be made the subject of a misfeasance claim under section 212 of the Insolvency Act 1986.[100] Conduct giving rise to an action under section 214 may substantiate proceedings under section 212 in so far as a director's participation in the wrongful trading of a company will inevitably result in a breach of the director's duty to the company, namely, the wrongful trading will prejudice the interests of corporate creditors, who, following the company's insolvency, may be properly regarded as a constituent part of the company, to whom duties are owed.

Where a liquidator makes successful applications under both sections 214 and 212, the extent of a director's liability will, in accordance with the decision of his Honour John Weeks QC in *Re DKG Contractors Ltd*,[101] be calculated on a concurrent basis. This decision would appear particularly just in circumstances where the liquidator relied upon the same misconduct to substantiate both applications. In such circumstances, the total sum of a director's liability under section 214 may be satisfied in circumstances where his liability under section 212 was equal to, or in excess of the amount of a contribution order under section 214.[102]

Nevertheless, although it may be just for a section 214 contribution order to be satisfied by a concurrent liability under section 212, a difficulty may arise in

---

[99] The Corporations Law 1991, s.588Y.

[100] The IA 1986, s.212 is discussed in Chapter 2.

[101] *Supra*, at n.75.

[102] It is to be noted that in *Re Purpoint Ltd* [1991] BCC 121, Vinelott J ordered the respondent's liability under s.214 and s.212 should be cumulative. However, in this case, the contribution payable under s.212 was in respect of a breach of duty which had occurred prior to the date on which the director ought to have realised that there was no reasonable prospect of the company avoiding liquidation. In other words, the course of conduct which was penalised under s.214 was distinct from the course of conduct that gave rise to the contribution order under s.212.

relation to priority issues. Although a sum contributed to a company's assets, pursuant to an order under section 212, may be regarded as the property of the company and therefore be caught by the terms of a floating charge,[103] the decision of the Court of Appeal in *Re Oasis Merchandising Services Ltd*,[104] establishes that a contribution order under section 214 will not be caught by the terms of a floating charge. Accordingly, where liability under section 214 is satisfied by the terms of a contribution order under section 212, a problematical conflict arises in relation to priority issues, namely, in such a case would the floating charge attach to the sum of the concurrent liability or should the sum of the liability, in so far as it incorporates a contribution order under section 214, be reserved for the company's unsecured creditors? This question highlights a present state of affairs which is quite ludicrous, especially when it may be presumed that conduct giving rise to a section 214 action would, also, substantiate a claim for a breach of duty under section 212.[105] Indeed it seems bizarre that the law should be willing to differentiate between a section 214 and section 212 action on the premise that the proceeds of the former action, unlike the proceeds of the latter, are not regarded as assets of the company.

4.12 Evidential problems in commencing an action under section 214

4.12.1 *Establishing the date on which the alleged wrongful trading first took place*

In seeking to commence an action under section 214, the liquidator is required to elect a relevant date which he deems to be conclusive of a finding that the respondent director should have been aware or ought to have been aware that the company had no reasonable prospect of avoiding liquidation. The selection of a specified date will be determined by a retrospective consideration of the company's financial state prior to its liquidation. The evaluation of the date will often be problematic, especially where the company's financial records are incomplete, or, in some cases, non-existent. In selecting a specified date, the liquidator will be mindful that the court, in ordering any contribution payable by a director, will normally calculate the extent of that contribution on the basis of losses incurred by creditors from the period commencing from the specified date. Accordingly, in seeking to maximise the amount of the director's potential contribution, the liquidator

---

[103] *Re Anglo-Printing & Publishing Union* [1895] 2 Ch 891.
[104] *Supra*, at n.78.
[105] Discussed further in Chapter 2, at p.37.

will seek to select a time period which accentuates the possibility of the highest attainable contribution. However, whilst seeking to maximise the amount of the contribution, the liquidator must ensure that the specified date is conclusive of a finding that, as of that date, there was no reasonable prospect of the company avoiding liquidation.

The selection of the specified date is crucial and will, if it does not accurately prescribe the period of wrongful trading, be fatal to the liquidator's case. For example, in *Re Sherborne Associates Ltd*,[106] his Honour Jack QC, sitting as a High Court judge, dismissed an action under section 214 on the premise that, although it was probable that the date chosen by the liquidator was indicative of a period in which the company had been operating in an insolvent state, the date was not however, conclusive of a finding that there was no reasonable prospect of the company avoiding liquidation. Indeed, on the contrary, the judge concluded that on the date specified by the liquidator, there had been a reasonable prospect to which the directors had addressed their minds, that the company could avoid liquidation. The learned judge refused to allow the liquidator to substitute a new date for the one which had been pleaded, on the premise that this would have prejudiced the preparation of the respondents' defence.

4.12.2 *Limitation periods*

In seeking to prosecute an action under section 214, the liquidator should ensure that it is prosecuted within the limitation period prescribed by section 9(1) of the Limitation Act 1980. Section 9(1) provides that,

> "An action to recover any sum recoverable by virtue of any enactment shall not be brought after the expiration of six years from the date on which the cause of action accrued".

The failure to prosecute within the requisite period may result in the action being stayed in circumstances where the court is satisfied that, as a consequence of an inordinate and inexcusable delay on the part of the liquidator, there was a substantial risk to the fairness of the trial, or that the effect of the delay was likely to cause or had caused serious prejudice to the respondents.

The applicability of section 9(1) of the Limitation Act 1980 to a section 214 action was confirmed by the Court of Appeal in *Re Farmizer (Products)*

---

[106] [1995] BCC 40.

Ltd.[107] In this case, the liquidator contended that a section 214 action was either, inconclusive of any prescribed limitation period under the Limitation Act 1980,[108] or alternatively, that if the Limitation Act 1980 did prescribe a limitation period for a section 214 action, the said period should be set in accordance with section 8(1) of that Act, namely, for a period of twelve years.

The liquidator's first contention, namely that the Limitation Act 1980 was inapplicable to a section 214 action, was based on the argument that the wording of section 214 was permissive of an action being commenced at any time during the winding up process, that is, the prosecution of an action was not restricted to any period specified by the Limitation Act 1980. The liquidator relied upon section 39 of the Limitation Act 1980, which provides,

"... the Limitation Act shall not apply to any action ... for which a period of limitation is prescribed by or under any other enactment (whether passed before or after this Act)".

The validity of this argument was dismissed by the Court of Appeal on the basis that section 39 of the Limitation Act 1980 would only be applicable where a statutory provision made it expressly clear that a specified limitation period, other than the one identified by the 1980 Act, was to apply. The Court of Appeal concluded that the wording of section 214 was far too inconclusive of such an intention.

The liquidator's alternative contention, namely that section 8(1) and not section 9(1) of the 1980 Act should apply to a section 214 action, was advanced on the premise that liability under section 214 was derived from the exercise of the court's discretionary jurisdiction, and not, as required by section 9(1) of the 1980 Act, the terms of the enactment. Section 8(1) of the Limitation Act 1980 provides that,

"An action upon a specialty shall not be brought after the expiration of twelve years from the date on which the cause of action accrued".

Further, the liquidator contended that under the terms of the court's discretionary judgment the nature of the director's liability was not restricted to a "sum recoverable" but rather a contribution (if any) to the company's assets; a contribution which would not necessarily take the form of a sum of money. Although the Court of Appeal conceded that section 214 provided

---

[107] [1997]1 BCLC 589; affirming the judgment of Blackburne J, [1995] 2 BCLC 462.

[108] Section 39 of the Limitation Act 1980 provides that "... the Limitation Act shall not apply to any action ... for which a period of limitation is prescribed by or under any other enactment (whether passed before or after this Act)".

the court with a discretion, in respect of the nature and extent (if any) of a contribution order, the court found that the discretion was a power derived from the terms of the enactment. In respect of the term "contribution" the court held that its inclusion within the context of section 214 should be afforded the same meaning as that which was ascribed to it by related provisions of the Insolvency Act 1986, namely sections 212 and 213 of the Insolvency Act 1986. Accordingly, the construction of the term "contribution" was indicative of a liability by way of the payment of a sum of money, albeit that a liquidator was not necessarily precluded from accepting property other than moneys to satisfy that liability.

4.12.3 *Striking out an action for want of prosecution*

Where, as in *Re Farmizer (Products) Ltd*,[109] the court concludes that a delay in the prosecution of a section 214 action exceeded the specified limitation period, the court may, in circumstances where the delay occasioned additional prejudice to the prejudice already caused by the late commencement of the proceedings,[110] strike out the action for want of prosecution. The additional prejudice in question need be no more than minimal.[111] In *Re Farmizer (Products) Ltd*, the additional prejudice existed in so far as the delay in the prosecution resulted in a diminishing of the ability of the witnesses to recall events relevant to the action. On this point, the Court of Appeal refused to accept the liquidator's contention that the events pertinent to this particular action were almost exclusively represented in the form of accessible documentary evidence. Peter Gibson LJ, giving the judgment of the court stated that,

> "The liquidators will no doubt rely on the documents to prove their case, but it will be for Mr Gadd [the director] to explain the documents and his thinking at various times, and that is where the fading of memory becomes relevant".[112]

4.13 Section 214 — a failure or a success?

Section 214 was introduced with the expectation of producing a regime under which a director of an insolvent company would be more readily susceptible to

---

[109] *Supra*, at n.107.

[110] By analogy, see, striking out actions for want of prosecution in relation to disqualification orders, discussed in Chapter 9 at p.214.

[111] See, e.g. *Birkett v. James* [1978] AC 297, *Roebuck v. Mungovin* [1994] 2 AC 224.

[112] *Supra*, n.107, at p.602.

the imposition of personal liability in circumstances where the company's assets had been depleted at a time when the director was aware, or ought to have been aware, that there was no reasonable prospect of the company avoiding liquidation. The section 214 provision was generally heralded as a major breakthrough, an innovation which sought to penetrate the protective shield of a company's limited liability status. Together with the emergence of case law establishing that directors of insolvent companies owed a duty to consider the interests of corporate creditors, section 214 appeared indicative of a new era in corporate law. As one learned commentator observed,

"The above two developments, particularly section 214, have greatly altered the topography of company law. The threat to directors that they will be made personally liable for the debts of a company which has continued to trade at the expense of its creditors has significantly eroded the principle of limited liability. This, in many ways, is unquestionably one of the most important developments in company law this century".[113]

However, despite the provision's potential to significantly displace the director's protective shield of limited liability, section 214 has, in reality, failed to fulfil its objective of achieving an efficient means by which the wrongful trading activities of directors can be successfully penalised. Evidence which is indicative of the provision's ineptitude may be found from the diminutive number of reported cases concerning actions under section 214. While a lack of reported cases[114] may not, in itself, be conclusive of the provision's failure to achieve a more efficient regulation of the wrongful trading activities of directors,[115] it is clearly a strong indicator of the inadequacy of the provision. Indeed, given that since 1986, there have been on average, some 18,000 insolvent liquidations per annum, it is surely a

---

[113] Prentice "Creditor's Interests and Director's Duties" (1990) 10 OJLS 265, at p.277.

[114] Of course, unreported cases may exist. An example of one such unreported case is *Re Fairmont Tours (Yorkshire) Ltd* (15 February 1989). This case was heard in the Huddersfield County Court. For a detailed account of this case see, L. Doyle "Ten Years of Wrongful Trading" [1996] *Insolvency Lawyer* 10.

[115] It has been argued that s.214 may be having some positive effect on curbing wrongful trading in the sense that directors, who may have been liable under the terms of the provision, have sought to settle their liability out of court, see Hicks "Wrongful Trading — Has it been a Failure" (1993) 8 *Insolvency Law and Practice* 134. However, save where the evidence of a case is without reproach, it is unlikely that such settlements will become commonplace, given that the liquidator's ability to establish liability under section 214 may be both an arduous and expensive task, see Williams & McGhee "Curbing Unfit Directors — Is Personal Liability an Empty Threat" [1993] *Insolvency Lawyer* 2.

hallmark of the provision's ineffectiveness that more actions have not been brought.[116]

The problems associated with section 214 have been well documented in this chapter, but further consideration may be given to what is undoubtedly the provision's principal aberration, namely, the problem of financing a section 214 action. Given that a section 214 action may prove to be expensive venture, especially when the evidence to sustain the action cannot readily be obtained from company records, the cost of the proceedings may be such as to prohibit the liquidator's ability to finance even the most worthy case. The financial restraints placed upon a liquidator are expounded in that it is doubtful whether the costs of a section 214 action can be recovered as liquidation expenses.[117] Further, even where the liquidator pursues a successful action, there can be no guarantee that a director will be able to meet the costs of the action, let alone the terms of any contribution order made against him.[118]

To redress the financial constraints of pursuing an action under section 214, and to attain a more efficient means of penalising the wrongful trading activities of directors, careful consideration must be given to the plausibility of maintaining the liquidator as the only party who is permitted to commence proceedings under section 214. However, if the position of the liquidator, as the only permissible applicant, is to be maintained, then clearly a reform of the method of financing the proceedings must be found. One method of reform would be to treat the fruits of a section 214 action as a property right, thus enabling a liquidator to claim the costs of an action as a liquidation expense. However, if the fruits of a section 214 action were deemed to be the property of the company, an additional reform to the provision would be essential, so as to ensure that the sum of any contribution order would not be made subject to the prior claims of a holder of a floating charge.

Finally, it is suggested that a more radical solution to the problem of financing section 214 proceedings would be to create a central fund from which selected actions could be financed. Although initially, such a fund

---

[116] By comparison, provisional statistics published by the Department of Trade and Industry on 7 February 1997 showed that in 1996 there had been 946 disqualification orders made under the Company Directors Disqualification Act 1986. This represents an increase of 49% over the 1995 figure.

[117] However, see *Katz v. McNally* [1997] BCC 784, discussed further at p.85.

[118] A company may, by virtue of CA 1985, s.310(3)(a), take out insurance, on behalf of a director, to protect the director against the imposition of personal liability in circumstances where he breached his duty to the company. Clearly a director will be in breach of his duty in circumstances where he is found liable under s.214, i.e. the director will have acted contrary to the interests of corporate creditors.

would require to be paid for from the public purse, the scheme would, it is suggested, eventually become self financing. Under such a scheme, the ability of a liquidator to apply for central funds to aid an action under section 214 would be determined by a vetting procedure to establish the viability of the proposed litigation. In cases where central funding was provided, the central fund would be reimbursed where a director was found liable under section 214. The fund would be reimbursed from the costs which were awarded against the director. In addition, a percentage of any contribution order would also be paid over to the central fund, thereby enabling it to sustain any losses incurred as a result of funding actions which were unsuccessful, or in cases where a director defaulted on the payment of costs.

Chapter 5

THE PHOENIX SYNDROME (SECTIONS 216 AND 217 OF THE INSOLVENCY ACT 1986)

5.1 Introduction

The "phoenix syndrome" describes a situation in which the controllers of a company place that company into liquidation or receivership with the objective of seeking to continue its business activities under the banner of a newly constituted company (the successor company). The effect of this conduct may be prejudicial to the public interest in the sense that the successor company will be devoid of any responsibility or accountability in respect of the corporate debts of the first company. Further, the creditors of both the first company and the successor company may be mistakenly induced into advancing credit facilities to the successor company in the belief that it is but an extension of the first company, when in reality, the two enterprises are distinct and separate legal entities. The extent and degree of prejudice which the effect of the phoenix syndrome may cause, will vary, but it is likely to be more prejudicial in circumstances where, for example, the controllers of the first company are able to purchase the assets of that company at a significant undervalue, or where, in order to benefit from any goodwill which remains from the business activities of the first company, the successor company adopts a name which is the same as, or closely associated with the name of the first company.

5.2 Reform

The prejudicial effect of the phoenix syndrome was severely criticised in the Report of the Review Committee into Insolvency Law and Practice (The Cork Report).[1] The mischief with which the report was concerned was identified as,

> "...the ease with which a person trading through the medium of one or more companies with limited liability can allow such a company to become insolvent, form a new company, and then carry on trading as

---

[1] Cmnd. 8558, see Chapter 44, paras 1813, 1826-1837.

much before, leaving behind him a trail of unpaid creditors, and often repeating the process several times".[2]

The Cork Report dealt with this mischief in a series of comprehensive proposals,[3] the sum of which resulted in a recommendation for statutory intervention. The effect of that recommendation would have been to impose personal liability on any person who had been involved or concerned in the management of two or more companies, in circumstances where:

(1) that person had been a participant in, or had been concerned (whether directly or indirectly) in the management of a company[4] in liquidation (the first company), at any time during the period of two years prior to the commencement of the insolvency of that company;[5]

(2) that person had also been a participant in or been concerned in the management of a successor company (whether directly or indirectly)[6] which had a paid up share capital of less than £50,000;[7]

(3) The successor company, after commencing or continuing trading within 12 months after the commencement of the insolvent winding up of the first company, had, itself, within a period of three years from the winding up of the first company, been placed into insolvent liquidation.

Where the above points (1-3) were satisfied, a person would have been deemed personally liable (unless the court otherwise directed)[8] for the unpaid liabilities of the successor company (and any other company falling within points 2 and 3) in circumstances where those liabilities were created or

---

[2] *Ibid.*, at para. 1813.

[3] *Ibid.*, at paras 1826-1837.

[4] *Ibid.*, at para. 1828. The terms of the recommendation also encompassed the managerial activities of any person who had acted as a *de facto* or shadow director of the company.

[5] The Cork Report (*ibid.*, at paras 1836-1837) considered that there was a problem arising from cases where the first company would not be put into liquidation, but would nevertheless cease to trade. In such circumstances, the Cork Report recommended that consumer creditors (but not commercial creditors) should be eligible for legal aid so as to obtain a winding up order against the company. The Report suggested that this proposal would cover a householder with a limited income and no capital resources other than his home, who had, for example, paid a deposit to a company for roof repairs that had never been properly carried out, or had paid in advance for goods which had never been delivered.

[6] *Supra*, n.5.

[7] *Supra*, n.2, at para. 1834. However, liability would not attach in a situation where the company was a wholly owned subsidiary of a company which had a paid up share capital of not less than £50,000.

[8] Cmnd. 8558 at para. 1831. The Cork Report suggested that the court should have wide powers to defer the imposition of liability in circumstances where the failure of either the first or successor company was unrelated to a person's conduct of those companies.

incurred within two years after the commencement of the winding up of the first company.

5.3 Sections 216 and 217 of the Insolvency Act 1986

Legislation to combat essential characteristics of the phoenix syndrome was introduced by sections 216 and 217 of the Insolvency Act 1986.[9] This legislation represents a radical departure from the proposals advanced by the Cork Report, a departure which is, in part, exemplified by the fact that a contravention of section 216 will give rise to criminal liability. However, in accordance with section 217, a person who acts in contravention of section 216, or a person who knowingly assists a person who acted in contravention of section 216, may also be made personally liable for the debts and liabilities of the successor company. Section 217 defines the extent and nature of a person's potential personal liability.

Although sections 216 and 217 are undoubtedly connected with the regulation of the phoenix syndrome, the marginal note to section 216 introduces the provision as one which is concerned with "The Restriction on the re-use of company names". Although the marginal note is instructive of an essential characteristic of the mischief which the provision seeks to regulate, it may nevertheless be described as misleading in the sense that it fails to identify the principal objective of the provision, which is to restrict the ability of a director to be involved in a company which adopts a prohibited name.[10] The following subsections of section 216 provide that:

(1) This section applies to a person where a company[11] ("the liquidating company") has gone into insolvent liquidation[12] on or after the appointed day[13] and he was a director or shadow director of the company at any time in the period of 12 months ending with the day before it went into liquidation.

---

[9] First introduced in the guise of s.17 of the Insolvency Act 1985.
[10] See the comments of Peter Gibson LJ, in *Thorne v. Silverleaf* [1994] BCC 109, at p.111.
[11] The term "company" includes a company which may be wound up under Part V of the Insolvency Act 1986 (IA 1986, s.216(8)).
[12] A company goes into insolvent liquidation if it goes into liquidation at a time when its assets are insufficient for the payment of its debts and other liabilities and the expenses of the winding up (IA 1986, s.216(7)).
[13] The relevant day is the day on which the Insolvency Act 1986 came into force, namely 29 December 1986.

(2) For the purposes of this section, a name[14] is a prohibited name in relation to such a person if—

(a) it is a name by which the liquidating company was known at any time in that period of 12 months, or

(b) it is a name which is so similar to a name falling within paragraph (a) as to suggest an association with that company.

(3) Except with leave of the court[15] or in such circumstances as may be prescribed, a person to whom this section applies shall not at any time in the period of 5 years beginning with the day on which the liquidating company went into liquidation—

(a) be a director of any other company that is known by a prohibited name, or

(b) in any way, whether directly or indirectly, be concerned or take part in the promotion, formation or management of any such company, or

(c) in any way, whether directly or indirectly, be concerned or take part in the carrying on of a business carried on (otherwise than by a company) under a prohibited name.

(4) If a person acts in contravention of this section, he is liable to imprisonment or a fine, or both.[16]

5.3.1 *The prohibited mischief*

Although section 216 does not completely eradicate the full force of the phoenix syndrome, the provision does have a potential to seriously disturb the ability of a person to continue the business activities of a liquidated company, in the guise of another company. The effect of section 216 is, however, limited, to a situation where the successor company adopts a name

---

[14] References to a name by which a company is known are references to the name of the company at that time or to any name under which the company carries on business at that time. The company's "name" is not restricted to the company's registered name, but also applies to any business name which it goes or went under (IA 1986, s. 216(6)).

[15] "The court" means any court having jurisdiction to wind up companies, i.e. in England and Wales the High Court or a county court, or in Scotland the Court of Session or a sheriff court. The reference to "any" court confirms that it need not be the same court as that which had been involved in the winding up of the liquidating company.

[16] A director or shadow director is liable on conviction on indictment to up to two years' imprisonment and/or a fine or, on summary conviction, to up to six months' imprisonment and/or a fine of up to the statutory maximum (IA 1986, Sch. 10). Following the decision of the Court of Appeal (Criminal Division) in *R v. Cole, Lees & Birch* [1998] BCC 87, a sentence imposing community service may be appropriate in respect of a contravention of s.216.

which is the same as or similar to that of the liquidated company. The justification for the prohibition is to protect the public interest, albeit that the protective nature of the provision is geared towards safeguarding the interests of corporate creditors. The mischief which section 216 seeks to curb is therefore of a type which clearly falls short of the corporate malpractice which was identified by the terms of the Cork Report. Accordingly, the provision may be criticised on the premise that it fails to completely eradicate the malpractice represented by the phoenix syndrome. Indeed, in accordance with the terms of section 216, other than where the name of the successor company is the same as, or similar to the name of the first company, a person may still allow a company to be placed into insolvent liquidation, form another company, and then carry on trading as much before.[17]

Nevertheless, although section 216 identifies the ambit of the mischief in terms which are far narrower than those advocated by the Cork Report, the provision does, in one sense, achieve a more efficient and stringent method of regulation than had been advocated by the Cork Report, because, under section 216, the imposition of liability is not dependent on the successor company having been placed into liquidation within a defined period.[18] Indeed, a person may be liable under section 216, even in circumstances where the new company is a solvent and a successful enterprise.[19] Further, unlike the proposals advanced by the Cork Report, a person's liability under section 216 (although not under section 217) may be established in circumstances where the successor business is not a registered company.

Although the ambit of section 216 is of a restrictive nature, it is to be observed that in an attempt to curb the prejudice suffered by corporate creditors as a consequence of the phoenix syndrome, specific provisions of the Insolvency Act 1986,[20] have sought to restrict the ease in which controllers of a company are permitted, during the company's liquidation, to purchase the assets of the first company at an undervalue, a practice which became known as "centrebinding", so called after the case of *Re Centrebind Ltd*.[21] The

---

[17] The scope of the provision is additionally limited by the fact that liability will only be invoked against a relevant person, where that person's participation in the first company was during a period of up to 12 months prior to the first company's liquidation; this time period may be contrasted with the two year period specified in the Cork Report.

[18] The period prescribed by the Cork Report was that, after 12 months from the commencement of the insolvent winding up of the first company, the successor company had, itself, within a period of three years from the winding up of the first company, been placed into liquidation.

[19] However, it is to be observed that IA 1986, s.216(3) does provide that a person's liability under the provision will only be maintained for a period of five years after the date on which the first company went into liquidation.

[20] See, IA 1986, ss.98, 99, 114, 166 and 388.

[21] [1967] 1 WLR 377.

aforementioned provisions are designed to make directors and liquidators more accountable for their actions in respect of the disposal of corporate assets.[22]

5.4 Establishing a person's liability under section 216

As a prerequisite to establishing a person's criminal liability under section 216,[23] it will be necessary to show that the defendant acted as a director[24] or shadow director[25] of the liquidated company, within the twelve months prior to its liquidation. Having established that fact, it must then be proved that the defendant took part or was concerned, whether directly or indirectly,[26] in the promotion, formation or management of a successor company or business, the name of which was the same as that of the first company, or so similar to the name of the first company as to indicate an association with that company. Section 216 may be retrospectively enforced against a person in circumstances where the successor company adopts a prohibited name in a period of twelve months prior to the day before the liquidating company goes into liquidation. In relation to the name of a company, it must be noted that the prohibition is not confined to the first company's registered name, it will also apply where the first company's business was carried on under some other trade name. The defendant's involvement in the successor company, which may be a newly incorporated company, or a company which has

---

[22] Albeit, that the legislation does not prevent the controllers of the first company from seeking to enforce prior ranking security interests over the company's assets.

[23] In so far as s.216 imposes a criminal sanction, a defendant's liability must be established beyond a reasonable doubt.

[24] A director includes any person occupying the position of a director, by whatever name called, see IA 1986, s.251. Accordingly, the provision will apply to a *de facto* director. The characteristics which define a *de facto* director are discussed in Chapter 1 at p.4 and in Chapter 8 at p.154.

[25] A shadow director is defined by IA 1986, s.251 as "... a person in accordance with whose directions or instructions the directors of the company are accustomed to act (but so that a person is not deemed a shadow director by reason only that the directors act on advice given by him in a professional capacity)". The characteristics associated with a person who acts as a shadow director are discussed in Chapter 1 at p.4 and in Chapter 8 at p.156.

[26] The use of the term "indirectly" would appear to suggest that a person may be exposed to liability under s.216 in circumstances where he is able to exert influence over the management functions of the successor company. Accordingly, it is not inconceivable that a majority shareholder of the company could *qua* shareholder, be made subject to the terms of the provision; especially in a situation where he has a capacity to determine the outcome of a motion placed before the general meeting.

altered its name to the prohibited name, must have occurred within a period of five years from the date of the first company's liquidation.

5.4.1 *Corporate name*

A potential difficulty in establishing a person's liability under section 216 may arise in circumstances where the name of the successor company is similar, but not identical to the name of the first company. In such a case, the provision will only take effect where the name of the successor company was so similar to the name of the first company as to indicate an association with the first company. Therefore, if the first company's name was, for example, Fred Bowers (Construction) Ltd and the successor company's name was Frederick or Freddy Bowers (Construction) Ltd, or, Fred, Frederick or Freddy Bowers Ltd, or alternatively, Fred, Frederick, or Freddy Bowers (Builders) Ltd, it is probable that in such a case an association would be made. However, if the successor company's name was, for example, F Bowers Ltd, then notwithstanding that the company shared the name "Bowers" with the first company, it would be unlikely that the relevant association would be made. Clearly the letter "F" in the successor company's name would not necessarily be representative of an association with the name "Fred", so used in the first company's name, that is, the letter "F" could be indicative of a number of very different names, for example, Frans, Frank, Francis, etc.[27] If, however, the successor company's name was F Bowers (Construction) Ltd or Bowers (Construction) Ltd, it is probable that the requisite association would be made on the basis that both the first and second companies shared the name Bowers and that both were, from the names used, implied to be companies associated with the construction business. The matter would be more difficult to resolve where the successor company employed the name F Bowers (Builders) Ltd or Bowers (Builders Ltd). In such a case, although the first and successor companies may have been associated by a common business purpose, it is likely that such an association would, of itself, be insufficient to justify the attention of the provision in so far as the provision is specific in its requirement that the association be one made by name and not business activity.[28]

---

[27] By anology, see *Durham Fancy Goods v. Michael Jackson (Fancy Goods) Ltd* [1968] 2 QB 839, discussed in Chapter 6.

[28] Obviously, much will depend upon the vigilance of the Registrar of Companies, see CA 1985, s.28.

5.5 Dispensations from the incursion of liability under section 216

Although section 216 seeks to exclude a person from becoming involved in the management of a company (the successor company) which adopts the name of, or a similar name to a liquidated company in which that person acted as a director, the prohibitive effect of the provision may be excluded where, in accordance with section 216(3), one of the exceptions prescribed by rules 4.228, 4.229 and 4.230 of the Insolvency Rules 1986, is applicable. Further, a person may, under section 216(3), apply to the court for leave to be associated with the management of a successor company.[29] The circumstances which may give rise to a successful leave application are not alluded to by the provision or by the Insolvency Rules 1986 and accordingly, the method by which leave will be determined will be left to the discretion of the court.

5.6 The exceptions to section 216 as prescribed by rules 4.228, 4.229 and 4.230 of the Insolvency Rules 1986

5.6.1 *Rule 4.228 of the Insolvency Rules 1986*

This exception will operate in a situation where a person to whom section 216 would otherwise apply, seeks to be associated with the management of a successor company which acquires the whole or substantially the whole of the business of the insolvent company, under arrangements made by an insolvency practitioner acting as its liquidator, administrator or administrative receiver, or as a supervisor of a voluntary arrangement under Part 1 of the Insolvency Act 1986. The successor company is required to give twenty-eight days' notice from the completion of the arrangements to all the creditors of the insolvent company of whose addresses the successor company is aware. The notice must specify:

(i) the name and registered number of the insolvent company and the circumstances by which its business was acquired by the successor company;

(ii) the name which the successor company has assumed, or proposes to assume for the purpose of carrying on its business, if the name is, or will be, a prohibited name under section 216;

---

[29] Other than where a case falls under one of the exceptions provided by the Insolvency Rules or, alternatively, where leave is obtained under IA 1986, s.216(3), the effect of s.216 is to create a strict liability offence, see, for example, *R v. Cole, Lees & Birch* [1998] BCC 87.

THE PHOENIX SYNDROME

(iii) any change of name which it has made or proposes to make for that purpose under section 28 of the Companies Act 1985;[30] and

(iv) the name of the person to whom section 216 may apply and the nature and duration of that person's directorship in respect of the insolvent company.

Where the notice requirements are met, the person to whom section 216 would otherwise have applied, may be associated with the successor company without the need to apply to the court for leave to so act.

5.6.2 *Rule 4.229 of the Insolvency Rules 1986*

Unlike rules 4.228 and 4.230, the effect of the exception represented by rule 4.229[31] is of a temporary nature. The purpose of this exception is to provide a transient period during which a person will be allowed to continue to be associated with a successor company. The exception operates where, in accordance with section 216(3), an application for leave is made not later than seven days from the date on which the company went into liquidation. The transient period commences from the beginning of the day on which the company went into liquidation and ends either, on the day falling six weeks after that date, or on the day on which the court disposes of the application for leave, whichever of those days occurs first.

5.6.3 *Rule 4.230 of the Insolvency Rules 1986*

In accordance with rule 4.230, a person who is associated with the management of a successor company which has traded under a name by which it has been known for the whole of the period of twelve months ending with the day before the liquidating company went into liquidation, may, providing that the successor company has not, at any time in the said period, been dormant within the meaning of section 250(3) of the Companies Act 1985,[32] be exempted from the prohibitive effect of section 216. As in a majority of cases the period of time between a company's insolvency and its liquidation will frequently exceed a period of twelve months, it is worth noting the relative ease with which a director of a company may, by complying with rule 4.230, avoid the effect of section 216.

---

[30] The CA 1985, s.28 provides that a company may change its name by special resolution.

[31] Introduced, with effect from 11 January 1988, by the Insolvency (Amendment) Rules 1987 (SI 1987/1919).

[32] The CA 1985, s.250(3) provides that a company is dormant during a period in which no significant accounting transaction occurs, i.e. no transaction which is required by CA 1985, s.221 to be entered in the company's accounting records; and a company ceases to be dormant on the occurrence of such a transaction.

5.7 The court's discretionary power to grant leave

In accordance with section 216(3) and rule 4.226 of the Insolvency Rules 1986, the court may exercise a discretionary power to grant leave to enable a person to be associated with the management of a company (or business) which has adopted a prohibited name.[33] Where the court exercises this discretionary power the applicant will be exempted from the prohibitive effect of section 216. In respect of an application for leave, section 216(5) provides that the Secretary of State or the Official Receiver may appear and call the court's attention to any matters which may have a bearing on the application. The court may call on the liquidator (or former liquidator) of the liquidating company for a report into the circumstances surrounding the liquidated company's insolvency and the extent by which the applicant's conduct may have contributed to the company's demise.[34]

In *Re Bonus Breaks Ltd*,[35] the first reported case in which an application for leave under section 216(3) was considered, an applicant sought leave to be involved as a director of a company named Bonus Break Promotions Ltd; the applicant having previously been a director of the liquidated company, Bonus Breaks Ltd. The liquidated company's insolvency was described by Morritt J as having been substantial, the liquidator's report confirming a total deficiency of £343,917 in relation to the claims of the company's unsecured creditors. Although the liquidator's report concluded that there was no evidence to suggest that the applicant had ever conducted the affairs of the liquidated company in a dishonest manner, the report did indicate that the company had been allowed to continue to trade for almost two years after it had fallen into a state of insolvency. The liquidator's report noted that in such circumstances the company's continued trading may ordinarily have given rise to a presumption of wrongful trading under section 214 of the Insolvency Act 1986.[36] However, no proceedings under section 214 had been commenced because the applicant, in allowing the company to continue to trade, had relied upon the advice of two professional advisors, namely, the company's auditor and the company's bank manager.

In respect of the successor company (Bouns Break Promotions Ltd), the arrangements were such that it was to have a paid up share capital of £50,000, divided into 1,000 £1 ordinary shares and 49,000 £1 redeemable shares. The applicant was to be one of the company's two directors, the other director

---

[33] See, Wilson "Delinquent Directors" (1996) 47 NILQ 344.
[34] See, Insolvency Rules 1986, r.4.227.
[35] [1991] BCC 546.
[36] See, Chapter 4.

being a man of considerable commercial and financial experience; the fact that the second director had expertise in financial matters was relevant in so far as the applicant had not been well versed in financial matters in relation to the management of the liquidated company. In seeking leave under section 216(3), it is to be noted that the applicant had the support of two of the liquidated company's major creditors.

In determining the leave application, Morritt J considered that it was necessary for the court to consider the successor company's ability to avoid the pitfalls which had resulted in the liquidated company's demise. Whilst Morritt J welcomed the appointment of the second director, he was particularly anxious about the manner in which the successor company's share capital had been structured, in so far as it was comprised of 98% redeemable shares. Morritt J feared that if such shares were redeemed within a short period, then the company would be left under capitalised and heavily dependent upon bank borrowings. The concern expressed by Morritt J was undoubtedly driven by the learned judge's desire to protect creditor interests in respect of the successor company, an anxiety which was justifiable given the seriousness of the liquidated company's insolvency. However, in so far as the applicant was willing to give an undertaking to the court, the effect of which was to alleviate a threat of an immediate reduction of the company's capital base, Morritt J approved the leave application. The undertaking provided that, except in a situation where the company appointed a third and independent director and that director approved a reduction in the company's capital, the company would not redeem shares for a period of two years, or, alternatively, purchase its own shares out of distributable profits during the said two year period.

However, following the subsequent cases of *Penrose v. Official Receiver*[37] and *Re Lightning Electrical Contractors Ltd*,[38] the manner by which Morritt J sought to determine the leave application in *Re Bonus Breaks Ltd* may now be viewed as the source of some contention. In *Penrose v. Official Receiver*, the applicants, who had been directors of a liquidated company (Hudson Coffee Houses Ltd) sought the court's leave to be involved as directors of a successor company, a company named, Hudson Coffee Houses (Holdings) Ltd. The Official Receiver's report concluded that the failure of the liquidated company had been attributable to factors which included the withdrawal of a bank overdraft facility, the company's rapid but poorly managed expansion, and the company's general lack of capital.

At first instance, District Judge, Sankley considered that the application for leave should be determined by examining the way in which the successor

---

[37] [1996] 1 WLR 482.
[38] [1996] BCC 950.

company was structured and its potential to avoid the commercial difficulties which had befallen the liquidated company. This approach was similar, if not identical to the approach adopted by Morritt J, in *Re Bonus Breaks Ltd*. The examination undertaken by the district judge revealed that the successor company was, in a like manner to the liquidated company, undercapitalised, and trading exclusively on bank borrowings. Further, the district judge found that the applicants, albeit persons of an honest and enthusiastic disposition, were unequivocally inexperienced in the affairs of a limited company. District Judge Sankley concluded that the leave application should be refused.

On appeal, Chadwick J disapproved of the manner by which District Judge Sankley had sought to determine leave under section 216(3). Chadwick J considered that the district judge's method of investigating both the applicants' competence to conduct the affairs of a limited company and the business merits of the successor company, was unnecessary, given that the applicants' participation in the management of the liquidated company had never been called into question on the ground that they had been unfit to be concerned in the management of a company. Although the learned judge pointed out that there were similarities between section 216(3) and the leave procedure under section 17 of the Company Directors Disqualification Act 1986 (CDDA 1986), Chadwick J observed that the leave procedure under section 216(3) was quite distinct from an application under section 17 CDDA 1986, in so far as under section 17 CDDA 1986 the court would naturally be compelled to instigate a thorough investigation of the applicant and the affairs of the company in which he sought leave to act, because the applicant in seeking leave would be doing so in a situation where his previous conduct of the affairs of a company had already been adjudged to have been of an unfit standard. Accordingly, Chadwick J concluded that the court should only refuse an application for leave under section 216(3) in circumstances where the applicant's conduct in the affairs of the liquidated company warranted the attention of the CDDA 1986. Chadwick J observed that it was patently wrong for the court to refuse an application for leave under section 216(3) on the basis that the applicants' involvement in a subsequent corporate venture would carry a degree of commercial risk. The learned judge pointed out, that the creation of any corporate enterprise always entailed an element of risk. Accordingly, as the legislators had not, in respect of a leave application under section 216(3), sought to prohibit the incorporation of undercapitalised companies nor sought to prohibit inexperienced persons from becoming involved in the management of a company, Chadwick J held that the circumstances of the case did not justify a refusal of the leave application.

The reasoning adopted by Chadwick J, to resolve the leave application in *Penrose v. Official Receiver*, was subsequently affirmed by the decision of E W Hamilton QC, (sitting as a deputy judge of the Chancery Division) in *Re*

Lightning Electrical Contractors Ltd.[39] In this case, the applicant sought leave to be involved as a director of Lightning Electrical Construction Ltd and five other dormant companies, having previously been a co-director, with his brother, of a company which, prior to its liquidation, had traded under the name Lightning Electrical Contractors Ltd. The liquidated company, which had been incorporated in 1977, prospered for a period of approximately ten years, but following a deterioration in the relationship between the two directors, the company's financial position plummeted. The crisis in the breakdown of the relationship culminated in 1994, when the applicant pursued an action under section 459 of the Companies Act 1985, to prevent his brother from making unjustified drawings from the company's bank account. In November 1995, the company went into receivership and shortly thereafter was made subject to a compulsory winding up order.

In February 1996, the applicant sought leave to continue to act as a director of Lightning Electrical Construction Ltd and the five other dormant companies. The application was supported by the company's administrative receivers and the applicant's bankers. Although the report of this case fails to allude to the liquidated company's deficiency in relation to its creditors, it may, given the favourable response of the administrative receivers, be presumed that such a deficiency was not of a substantial nature; to some extent this presumption is confirmed by the fact that in prosecuting the case, the Secretary of State did not request a report from the company's liquidator in relation to the affairs of the liquidated company.[40]

In approving the leave application, E W Hamilton QC fully endorsed the approach to the determination of leave as advocated by Chadwick J in *Penrose v. Official Receiver*, although interestingly, the learned judge sought to deny the existence of any substantive distinction between that approach and the one adopted by Morritt J in *Re Bonus Breaks Ltd*. E W Hamilton QC opined that, in *Re Bonus Breaks Ltd*, Morritt J had never sought to suggest that the court should approach applications under section 216(3) in a similar fashion to applications made under section 17 of the CDDA 1996 (indeed, Morritt J never expressly mentioned the CDDA 1996). E W Hamilton QC further contended that Morritt J had been justified in investigating the future trading prospects of the successor company in so far as there had been an inference from the facts of the case that the applicant may have been a party

---

[39] [1996] BCC 950.

[40] Indeed, the circumstances of this case came close to fulfilling the requirements of the statutory exception to s.216, as provided by r.4.228 of the Insolvency Rules 1986. Overall, the applicant had a most cogent case in respect of his leave application, a case which was undoubtedly strengthened by the support he received from the administrative receivers and also his bankers.

to the wrongful trading of the liquidated company, a fact which, if substantiated, may have led to the conclusion that the applicant's conduct had been of an unfit nature thereby justifying his disqualification under either section 6 or section 10 of the CDDA 1986.[41]

Although, E W Hamilton QC, sought to reconcile the methods adopted by Morritt J and Chadwick J in respect of the determination of leave, the attempted reconciliation must be viewed with caution given the fact that in *Re Bonus Breaks Ltd*, Morritt J did not seek to challenge the liquidator's finding that a wrongful trading action could not have been sustained as a consequence of the applicant having relied upon professional advice in allowing the company to continue to trade. Accordingly, it is difficult to contend that Morritt J was cautious in his approach to granting leave on the basis of an unsubstantiated allegation of wrongful trading. Indeed, the principal concern of Morritt J, in respect of determining the leave application in *Re Bonus Breaks Ltd*, was clearly directed at ensuring that the capital structure of the successor company was secure, Morritt J was anxious to prevent the successor company from falling into the trap which had already snared the liquidated company. Indeed, notwithstanding the contrary intimations of E W Hamilton QC,[42] it is contended that had it not been for the applicant's undertaking, Morritt J would not have allowed the leave application in *Re Bonus Breaks Ltd*.

5.7.1 *An examination of the judicial methods to determine a leave application*

In applying its discretion to grant leave under section 216(3), the court will naturally seek to protect the interests of corporate creditors in circumstances where there is a danger that the public interest may be exploited by permitting an applicant to participate in the business activities of the successor company. In analysing the respective methods by which leave under section 216(3) has hitherto been determined, it may be said that the stricter approach adopted by Morritt J in *Re Bonus Breaks Ltd* may, in one sense, be commended, in that it is a more efficient means of safeguarding the public interest from the effects of the mischief represented by the phoenix syndrome.[43] However, this approach is subject to one major flaw, namely, the mischief against which section 216 is aimed is only concerned with prohibiting the exploitation of a successor

---

[41] The CDDA 1986, s.10 is discussed in Chapter 7, at p.145, the CDDA 1986, s.6 is discussed in Chapter 8.

[42] In *Penrose v. Official Receiver*, Chadwick J also suggested that Morritt J may have granted leave irrespective of whether an undertaking had been given.

[43] See Milman "Curbing the Phoenix Syndrome" [1997] JBL 224.

company which adopts a prohibited name; the provision does not, contrary to the approach prescribed by Morritt J, seek to prohibit the phoenix syndrome in a manner which was, for example, prescribed by the terms of the Cork Report.

In respect of the method to determine leave as advocated by Chadwick J in *Penrose v. Official Receiver*, this approach may also be criticised. The approach may be criticised on the premise that it places too much emphasis on the nature of the applicant's misconduct in respect of his management of the affairs of the liquidated company. While the approach advocated by Chadwick J is undoubtedly correct in its assumption that leave should not be granted in circumstances where an applicant's conduct of the affairs of a liquidated company is deemed to be unfit, because otherwise, if leave was granted under section 216(3), the applicant could still be subject to a disqualification order under the terms of the CDDA 1986, the approach assumes that the prohibitive nature of section 216 will have no effect other than where the applicant's conduct is adjudged to have merited the imposition of a disqualification order. The problem with this assumption is that it fails to recognise that there may be circumstances where the public interest is, given the potential danger of the successor company's adoption of a prohibited name, prejudiced in a situation where an applicant's conduct fell below the appropriate standard to justify the attention of the CDDA 1986, especially in so far as the ability to substantiate an allegation of unfit conduct, is, for the purposes of the CDDA 1986, set at an arduous standard.[44]

5.8 Establishing a person's liability under section 217

In accordance with section 217(1)(a), a person will be deemed to be personally responsible for all the relevant debts of a successor company[45] where, in being involved in the management[46] of that company, he acts in contravention of the terms of section 216. Liability is not dependent upon a conviction under section 216. Further, section 217(1)(b) extends the imposition of personal

---

[44] The ability to substantiate an allegation of a director's unfit conduct is discussed in Chapter 8, at p.160 *et seq.*

[45] The term "company" refers to a company which exists in contravention of s. 216 and which is capable of being wound up under IA 1986, Part VI. In accordance with IA 1986, s.217(3)(a), the relevant debts of the company are such debts and other liabilities of the company as are incurred at any time when that person was involved in the management of the company.

[46] The IA 1986, s.217(4) provides that a person is involved in the management of a company if he is a director of the company or if he is concerned with, whether directly or indirectly, or takes part in, the management of the company.

liability for the relevant debts[47] of the successor company to any person who, being involved in the management of the successor company, acted or was willing to act on the instructions (without the leave of the court) of his principal, being aware that the principal was, in relation to his involvement in the successor company, acting in contravention of section 216. To establish a person's willingness to act on instructions, section 217(2) provides that, a name is prohibited in relation to such a person if—

    (a) it is a name by which the liquidating company was known at any time in that period of 12 months, or

    (b) it is a name which is so similar to a name falling within paragraph (a) as to suggest an association with that company.

A person who is deemed to be personally responsible for the relevant debts of a company, will be jointly and severally liable in respect of those debts with the company and any other person who, is deemed to have been liable under section 217, or otherwise.[48] Further, it must be noted that in addition to the imposition of personal liability, a contravention of section 216 may also be regarded as cogent evidence of a director's unfit conduct for the purposes of disqualification under section 6 of the Company Directors Disqualification Act 1986.[49]

5.8.1 *The beneficiaries of a section 217 order*

Following a contravention of section 216, any creditor of the successor company may seek to recover a debt or other outstanding liability from any person who, in accordance with section 217, is deemed to be personally responsible for the relevant debts of the company. Indeed, in accordance with the decision of the Court of Appeal in *Thorne v. Silverleaf*,[50] a creditor of a successor company will not be precluded from pursuing an action under section 217, even in circumstances where the creditor's involvement in the affairs of the successor company was such as to give rise to a finding that he aided and abetted the commission of the section 216 offence.

In *Thorne v. Silverleaf*, the principal creditor (S) of a company named Mike Spence Classic Cars Ltd (the successor company), sought, under section 217, to

---

[47] In this case, the relevant debts are such debts and liabilities of the company as are incurred at a time when that person was acting or willing to act on instructions given by a person whom he knew to be in contravention of s.216. (IA 1986, s.217(3)(b)).

[48] IA 1986, s.217(2).

[49] See, for example, the comments of Browne Wilkinson V-C in *Re Travel Mondial (UK) Ltd* [1991] BCLC 120, at p.123. See also, *Re Keypak Home Care Ltd (No. 2)* [1990] BCLC 440.

[50] [1994] BCC 109.

recover a debt of £134,600 from T, the director of the successor company. The successor company had been incorporated in January 1990, but had been placed into liquidation in November 1992. T had also been previously involved as a director of two other companies, namely Mike Spence Reading Ltd, which had been put into liquidation in February 1990, and Mike Spence (Motorsport) Ltd, which had been put into liquidation in October 1989. In its adoption of the name "Mike Spence" the successor company was known by a prohibited name and, as such, T was in contravention of the terms of section 216.

In defending the action under section 217, T alleged that S had been actively involved in the day to day administration of the affairs of the successor company and that as S had been aware that T had previously been a director of two companies with names which were very similar to the name adopted by the successor company. In effect S had aided and abetted the commission of the criminal offence specified in section 216. Accordingly, T claimed that S should not be permitted to benefit from that crime. Alternatively, T contended that S's involvement in the affairs of the company was such that he should either be estopped from asserting his right to recover the sum claimed or be treated as having waived that right.

In determining the issue, the Court of Appeal dispensed with the argument based upon estoppel and waiver on the basis that S had never made a representation or promise to refrain from seeking to recover the sums claimed and, further, that T had never sought to rely on such a representation or promise. In respect of the allegation that S had aided and abetted the commission of the section 216 offence, the court asserted that public policy demanded that the enforcement of a right would be precluded in circumstances where its existence had evolved as a direct result of the commission of a crime. However, the court was of the opinion that S should not be precluded from seeking to rely on section 217, in so far as the enforcement of that right was totally unrelated to his alleged involvement in commission of the section 216 offence.[51] The right to pursue the action under section 217 had arisen as a result of S's legitimate right to enforce a debt against the company. Peter Gibson LJ considered that the determination of the public policy issue was comparable with the manner in which the applicability of the maxim *ex turpi causa non oritur actio* had been

---

[51] Indeed, the Court of Appeal considered that S had not aided and abetted the s.216 offence in so far as S had never had any influence in relation to T's appointment as a director of the successor company nor had he any responsibility for determining the name of the successor company.

determined by Lord Browne Wilkinson in *Tinsley v. Milligan.*[52] Lord Browne Wilkinson determined the issue in the following manner,

"In my judgment the time has come to decide clearly that the rule is the same whether a plaintiff founds himself on a legal or equitable title: he is entitled to recover if he is not forced to plead or rely on the illegality, even if it emerges that the title on which he relied was acquired in the course of carrying through an illegal transaction".[53]

---

[52] [1993] 3 WLR 126.
[53] *Ibid.*, at p.153.

Chapter 6

SECTION 349(4) OF THE COMPANIES ACT 1985

6.1 Introduction

Section 349(4) is derived from established historical roots, its wording remains virtually unaltered from section 31 of the Joint Stock Companies Act 1856,[1] a provision which may be heralded as one of the first statutory attempts to protect corporate creditors from the liberalism which emanated from the creation of the limited company. Nevertheless, while the last decade has witnessed an increase in the number of actions commenced under section 349(4), the provision has generally been the subject matter of but a handful of reported cases. Nevertheless, despite its infrequent appearance in the law reports, the potential consequences of a breach of section 349(4) cannot be underestimated.

6.2 Section 349(4) of the Companies Act 1985

Section 349(4) of the Companies Act 1985 provides that,

> "If an officer of a company or a person on its behalf signs or authorises to be signed on behalf of the company any bill of exchange, promissory note, endorsement, cheque or order for money or goods in which the company's name is not mentioned as required by subsection (1),[2] he is liable to a fine; and he is further personally liable to the holder of the bill of exchange, promissory note, cheque or order for money or goods for the amount of it (unless it is duly paid by the company)".

---

[1] Hereafter, referred to as JSCA 1856. The wording of s.349(4) is identical to the wording of its statutory predecessor, namely CA 1948, s.108, save that in relation to s.349(4) there is no maximum sum attributed to the fine payable for non compliance with its terms. The wording of the provision, as contained within the 1948 Act, was marginally altered from the original wording of the 1856 provision, in so far as it was expanded to apply to all registered companies. Prior to the 1948 Act, the provision was only applicable to companies which had been registered with a limited liability status.

[2] In accordance with the CA 1985, s.349(1), every company must, where necessary, have its name mentioned in legible characters.

The protection afforded by section 349(4) is therefore one of an assurance to the recipient of a relevant instrument in which the form of the corporate name had been misdescribed, whereby, if the liability evidenced by the instrument is not met by the debtor company, then the person(s) responsible for the instrument's endorsement will be deemed personally liable to discharge that liability. While personal liability may be incurred at a time when a company is solvent, in practice, section 349(4) is more likely to be invoked where a company is itself unable to meet the terms of the relevant instrument,[3] that is where the company is insolvent. In addition, personal liability may be attached to any officer of a company who knowingly authorised the endorsement of an instrument containing a misdescribed form of the company's name,[4] although following the case of *Wilkes Ltd v. Lee (Footwear) Ltd*,[5] an officer of a company, having authorised the endorsement of an instrument, will not incur liability under section 349(4) where, in applying a "reasonable man" test, that officer was unaware that the instrument in question contained a misdescription of the company's name. A breach of the provision is also punishable as an offence under the criminal law, the penalty being the imposition of a fine.

As previously noted, the present wording of section 349(4) is derived from section 31 of the JSCA 1856, a provision which was introduced in an attempt to suppress the fears of a commercial community, justifiably suspicious of the then radical ability to incorporate a business medium in the guise of a limited liability company.[6] Prior to 1855, the majority of business structures had been unincorporated associations of an unlimited liability status.[7] In *Penrose v. Martyr*,[8] the first reported case in which section 31 of the JSCA 1856 was subjected to judicial scrutiny, Crompton J opined that the intention of the provision was to,

---

[3] Where a company retains its trading existence, an individual in breach of s.349(4) would ordinarily be indemnified by the company providing that, in endorsing the instrument, the individual acted on behalf of the company with valid authority and in accordance with his duties.

[4] See, e.g. *Civil Service Co-Operative Society v. Chapman* [1914] WN 369.

[5] [1985] BCLC 444.

[6] The availability of incorporating a company with a limited liability status was first introduced by the Limited Liability Act 1855.

[7] Indeed, in respect of small domestic companies, a mistaken presumption that the members would remain personally accountable for the debts of the company prevailed throughout the nineteenth century. The recognition of the limited liability status of such companies was finally confirmed by the decision of the House of Lords in *Salomon v. A Salomon & Co Ltd* [1897] AC 22.

[8] (1858) EB & E 499. Here, a director of a company was made personally liable on a bill of exchange as a result of omitting to include the company's limited liability status.

"... prevent persons from being deceived into the belief that they had a security with the unlimited liability of common law, when they had but the security of a company limited".[9]

However, if the intended purpose of the provision had been originally conceived as one which sought to curb the potential abuses associated with the creation of the limited liability company, the provision's purpose was to be subsequently expanded by the judicial construction of its wording. The ambit of the provision was, in the adoption of a strict adherence to the literal rule of construction broadened, to encompass the forbiddance of any mistake in the linguistical characteristics of the representation of a company's name. For example, in *Atkin & Co v. Wardle*,[10] directors of a company registered as the "South Shields Salt Water Baths Co Ltd", accepted a bill of exchange drawn in favour of one of the company's shareholders. The bill of exchange incorrectly represented the company's name as the "South Shields Salt Water Baths Co". Although the directors of the company, in accepting the bill, failed to make mention of the company's limited liability status, the plaintiff, in addressing the bill to the company, had included the word "limited" in the title of the company's name. However, the plaintiff mistakenly placed the words "limited" and "South Shields" in the wrong order, thereby addressing the bill to the "Salt Water Baths Co, Limited, South Shields". Denman J remarked that,

"... the intention of the Act was to insure extreme strictness in all transactions on behalf of limited companies as regards the use of the registered name of the company not only in enforcing the use of the word limited but in all other respects. Cases may easily be conceived in which a very slight variation from the registered name might lead a person to believe that he was taking a bill off a totally different kind of company from that to which the directors signing the bill really belonged.... On the whole, though not without considerable doubt, I am of the opinion that the two variations from the proper designation of the company are sufficient to bring the defendants within the provision of section 42 of the Act [Companies Act 1862]".

Almost 150 years after its original introduction as section 31 of the JSCA 1856, the judicial interpretation of the provision now represented by section 349(4), has remained consistent with a historically binding attachment to a strict and arbitrary construction of its terms. As a consequence of its rigid

---

[9] *Ibid.*, at p.503.
[10] (1889) 61 LT 23, aff'd (1889) 5 TLR 734.

interpretation, even a minor spelling mistake or error in the order in which a company's name is properly represented may invoke the implementation of the provision. For example, in *Hendon v. Adelman*,[11] Mackenna J held that a cheque endorsed in the name "L R Agencies Ltd" was, in so far as the correct name of the company should have been represented as "L & R Agencies Ltd", contrary to the terms of the provision. Therefore, the simple omission of an ampersand between the letters "L" and "R" was sufficient to supplicate the implementation of the provision. Similarly, in *Barber & Nicholls Ltd v. R & G Associates (London) Ltd*,[12] the omission of the parenthesised word "London" from the name of the company was sufficient to justify the utilisation of the provision.

The austere construction of section 349(4) is such that a person authorised to endorse an instrument on behalf of a company may not rely, in an attempt to avoid personal liability, on the fact that the misdescription of a corporate name had no adverse effect on the decision of the recipient of the instrument, to enter into the transaction to which the instrument related.[13] Therefore, the method of determining liability under section 349(4) is solely concerned with an objective and technical examination of the accuracy of the name of the company as identified in the instrument. As such, a defendant's potential liability is not determined by a subjective or even objective consideration of motive or intent in relation to the nature of the misdescription. Accordingly, a negligent misdescription of a company's name, albeit born of an honest misunderstanding of the requirements of the provision, will be penalised in the same manner as if the representation had been of a fraudulent nature. For example, in *Maxform v. Mariani & Goodville Ltd*,[14] the defendant, the sole director and shareholder of a company registered under the name of "Goodville Ltd", purported to endorse bills of exchange on behalf of the said company. However, instead of the bills being signed on behalf of "Goodville Ltd", the bills were signed on behalf of "Italdesign", a trading name of Goodville Ltd. Mocatta J held that the provision, in its requirement for the "name" of a company to be properly mentioned on an instrument, would, as a matter of logic, be construed as an obvious reference to the company's registered corporate name as opposed to a registered trade name. The defendant was liable irrespective of the fact that the holder of the bills had been fully aware that the trading name "Intaldesign" was a name used by and registered to Goodville Ltd.

---

[11] (1973) 117 SJ 631. (Applying the Companies Act 1948, s.58.)

[12] (1981) 132 NLJ 1076.

[13] See, for example, the comments of Donaldson J in *Durham Fancy Goods Ltd v. Michael Jackson (Fancy Goods) Ltd* [1968] 2 QB 839, at p.846.

[14] [1979] 2 Lloyd's Rep 385; aff'd [1981] 2 Lloyd's Rep 54.

6.3 Exceptions to the application of section 349(4)

Although the inclusion of certain words within the title of a corporate name may be legitimately represented by abbreviations, for example, the word "limited" may be abbreviated to "Ltd",[15] the word "company" may be replaced by the abbreviation "Co",[16] also the word "and" by the ampersand "&",[17] such abbreviations of corporate identity are the only accepted exceptions to the otherwise rigid statutory construction of section 349(4). The aforementioned abbreviations are permitted in so far as they represent commercially acceptable shorthand versions of words commonly used in the description of corporate names.[18] Nevertheless, while such exceptions provide the only acceptable anomalies to the otherwise stringent interpretation of section 349(4), examples of other diversions from the severe construction of the provision do exist to dilute the absolute rigidity of the provision in its imposition of a standard of strict liability.

The first of the said diversions is to be found in *The Dermatine Company Ltd v. Ashworth*.[19] This case involved a bill of exchange which was drawn up by The Motor and General Tyre Company (Limited), in favour of the plaintiff company. Although the bill was addressed with the complete and accurate name of the drawee company, the acceptance part of the bill omitted to mention the fact that the drawee was a limited liability company. The omission was caused by a failure to ensure that a rubber stamp, impressed with the complete and accurate name of the company, had been properly placed on the acceptance part of the bill. The misplacement of the rubber stamp resulted in the omission of the word "limited" in the representation of the company's name. Notwithstanding the said omission, Channell J found that the provision[20] had not been contravened. The learned judge reached this conclusion on the premise that the drawee and acceptor of a bill of exchange had to be, and in the instant case were, the same person.[21] Therefore,

---

[15] See, for example, *F Stacey & Co v. Wallis* (1912) 106 LT 376. Likewise, it is perfectly acceptable to shorten the term "public limited company" to the abbreviation "plc", see the Companies Act 1985, s.27.

[16] See, for example, *Banque de L' Indochine of de Suez SA v. Euroseas Group Finance Co Ltd & Others* [1981] 3 All ER 198.

[17] See, for example, *Hendon v. Aldelman* (1973) 117 SJ 631.

[18] In relation to the general availability of being permitted to abbreviate part of a corporate name, see the comments of Scrutton J in *F Stacey & Co Ltd v. Wallis* (1912) 28 TLR 209, at p.211.

[19] (1905) 21 TLR 510.

[20] Companies Act 1862, s.42.

[21] In compliance with the Bills of Exchange Act 1882, s.17.

providing the drawee's complete and accurate name was properly included on some part of the bill it was immaterial that the name had not been properly mentioned in the acceptance part of the bill. Indeed, Channell J believed that providing an obvious and accurate reference to the company's name had been included in some part of the bill, the acceptance of the instrument could, for example, have taken the form of "on and behalf of the said company".[22]

Yet, despite the trifling nature of the mistake which resulted in the mis-description of corporate identity in *The Dermatine Company Limited v. Ashworth*, it is respectfully submitted that in accordance with a strict interpretation of the provision, the decision to dismiss the action was incorrect. Although the bill had been addressed with the complete and accurate name of the company, the acceptance part of the instrument was crucial to the formation of a binding contractual relationship between the parties; it was the acceptance part of the bill which would be "signed" so as to bind the company. Accordingly, the inclusion of the accurate representation of the company's name, other than in the acceptance part of the instrument, should have been quite irrelevant in determining whether or not the instrument had been "signed on behalf of the contracting company" so as to bind it to the terms of the instrument.

Indeed, the case of *Nassau Steam Press v. Tyler*[23] lends support to the above contention. Here, it was held that the directors of a company properly named the "Bastille Syndicate Ltd" had infringed the terms of the provision by accepting bills of exchange in a form whereby the company's name was represented as the "Old Paris Bastille Syndicate Ltd", notwithstanding that the bills had been correctly addressed to "Bastille Syndicate Ltd". In this case, the manner in which the bills were accepted was considered crucial to the determination of whether the directors were to be held personally liable under the terms of the provision.[24]

The second diversion from the accepted construction of section 349(4) occurred in *Durham Fancy Goods Ltd v. Michael Jackson (Fancy Goods) Ltd*.[25] This case concerned a bill of exchange which had been accepted on behalf of a company named "Michael Jackson (Fancy Goods) Ltd". The plaintiff, the drawer of the bill, incorrectly addressed the bill by identifying

---

[22] *Supra*, n.19, at p.511.

[23] (1894) 70 LTR 376.

[24] See also, *Durham Fancy Goods Ltd v. Michael Jackson (Fancy Goods) Ltd* [1968] 2 QB 839 and *Lindholst & Co A/S v. Fowler* [1988] BCLC 166. In both the aforementioned cases, the acceptance part of the relevant bills of exchange was considered the crucial part of the instrument for determining whether a company's name had been correctly mentioned therein, for the purpose of determining whether liability under the provision could be evaded.

[25] [1968] 2QB 839.

the company's name as "M Jackson (Fancy Goods) Ltd". Further, and definitive to the outcome of the case, was the fact that the plaintiff stipulated that the bill should be signed by a director of the company in the form "for and behalf of M Jackson (Fancy Goods) Ltd". The bill was subsequently signed and accepted by a director of Michael Jackson (Fancy Goods) Ltd, in accordance with the plaintiff's instructions, namely the director's signature was placed above the wording "for and on behalf of M Jackson (Fancy Goods) Ltd".

In accepting that the first part of the company's name, "Michael", should not have been abbreviated by the letter "M" and that the endorsement of the abbreviated name would have ordinarily resulted in the defendant being made liable under the terms of the provision,[26] Donaldson J nevertheless found that the circumstances of the case were such to preclude the provision's application. The justification for this finding was based upon an imaginative employment of the equitable doctrine of estoppel, a device ordinarily used to defend the validity of a promise to suspend the enforcement of a contractual obligation, in circumstances where the promise to suspend is unsupported by consideration.[27] In attempting to apply the components of the equitable doctrine of estoppel to the facts found in *Durham Fancy Goods Ltd v. Michael Jackson (Fancy Goods) Ltd*, it is to be observed that the defendant sought to enforce the suspension of a statutory obligation, as opposed to the suspension of a contractual obligation. Secondly, the plaintiff failed to make any representation to the effect that it agreed to suspend the enforcement of the statutory obligation; indeed the parties to the action were, at the time of the transaction, quite ignorant as to the existence of the statutory obligation. Thirdly, if it was possible to imply from the parties' conduct that the representation to suspend the statutory obligation had been made, then given the fact that Michael Jackson (Fancy Goods) Ltd was, shortly after the transaction, placed in liquidation, could it be justifiably argued that the promisee had obtained the representation in equitable circumstances? Finally, the application of the doctrine of equitable estoppel in *Durham Fancy Goods Ltd v. Michael Jackson (Fancy Goods) Ltd* had the effect of totally extinguishing the operative "legal obligation" despite the fact that the plaintiff was denied an opportunity to furnish reasonable notice of its intention to terminate the "implied" promise.[28]

---

[26] Companies Act 1948, s.108.

[27] The roots of the doctrine of equitable estoppel may be traced to *Hughes v. Metropolitan Railway Co* (1877) 2 App Cas 439; see, especially, the judgment of Lord Cairns at p.448.

[28] In seeking to enforce the provision, it is arguable that the plaintiff was giving notice to the effect that the suspension of the statutory obligation was at an end. By analogy see, *Tool Metal Manufacturing Co Ltd v. Tungsten Electric Fire Co Ltd* [1955] 1 WLR 761.

Indeed, it is to be observed that subsequent attempts to apply the equitable doctrine of estoppel to deny the enforcement of the provision have all failed. For example, in *Lindholst & Co A/S v. Fowler*,[29] the plaintiff addressed bills of exchange to a company incorporated as the "Corby Chicken Co Ltd", but in doing so omitted its limited liability status from the representation of the company's name. The defendant, the managing director of Corby Chicken Co Ltd, accepted the bills on behalf of the company but failed to correct the error of identity, the consequence of which was that the bills were erroneously accepted on behalf of the "Corby Chicken Co". The defendant contended that following the application of the doctrine of equitable estoppel in *Durham Fancy Goods Ltd v. Michael Jackson (Fancy Goods) Ltd*, the plaintiff, in so far as it had introduced the error of identity into the instrument, should be estopped from relying on the provision.

Donaldson LJ, in delivering the judgment of the Court of Appeal, denied the validity of the defendant's argument and thereby distinguished his own earlier decision in *Durham Fancy Goods Ltd v. Michael Jackson (Fancy Goods) Ltd*. The basis for distinguishing the decision was that in *Lindholst*, the introduction of the error of corporate identity into the acceptance part of the bills had not, unlike the circumstances found in *Durham Fancy Goods Ltd v. Michael Jackson (Fancy Goods) Ltd*, resulted from the plaintiff's insistence upon a form of acceptance which incorporated the use of an incorrect representation of the company's name. Therefore, in the absence of the plaintiff's insistence upon a specific form of acceptance, the defendant had a responsibility, which had been ignored, to ensure that the company's name had been correctly mentioned as the acceptor of the bills.

The third diversion from the accepted construction of section 349(4) is also derived from the case of *Durham Fancy Goods Ltd v. Michael Jackson (Fancy Goods) Ltd*. It may be implied from observations made by Donaldson J in respect of comments intimating that it would have been inequitable for the plaintiff to have enforced the statutory liability imposed by the provision

---

[29] [1988] BCLC 166. See also, *Rafsanjan Pistachio Producers Co-operative v. Reiss* [1990] BCLC 352, in which Potter J opined that the application of the doctrine of equitable estoppel in *Durham Fancy Goods Ltd v. Michael Jackson (Fancy Goods) Ltd* should be confined to the peculiar facts of that case. In *Rafsanjan*, the defendant contended that the plaintiff should be estopped from relying on the s.349(4) provision because two out of five cheques signed by the defendant in favour of the plaintiff, but bearing a misdescription of the company's name, had been cashed by the plaintiff. The defendant argued that by accepting the cheques and by the presentation and payment of two of the cheques, the plaintiff had represented that the cheques, albeit in a form which contained a misdescription of the company's name, were acceptable. The defendant's argument failed in that the plaintiff had never made any promise to refrain from enforcing the terms of provision should the cheques not be met.

without having first given the defendant the option to correct the error contained within the bill.[30] In effect, such a suggestion amounted to the acceptance of the availability of a defence based upon the equitable remedy of rectification, irrespective of the fact that rectification is normally only available as a defence where a person intending to sign a document in one capacity, mistakenly does so in another;[31] in *Durham Fancy Goods Ltd v. Michael Jackson (Fancy Goods) Ltd*, the defendant had always been of a mind to sign the bill with the intention of binding the company. In reality, the defendant's mistake was one related to the technical identity of the company's formal name as opposed to a mistake affecting the substance of the director's intended objective of binding the company to the terms of the instrument. With respect to the learned judge, it seems quite improbable to suggest that rectification could ever be advanced as a means to evade the provision. Indeed, in subsequent cases the courts have constantly denied the possibility of the equitable remedy being used as a device to evade the liability arising from a breach of the provision. For example, in *Blum v. OCP Repartition SA*,[32] the Court of Appeal unanimously declared that the employment of the equitable remedy would have distorted the will of Parliament, if it could have been used as a mechanism to escape the liability exacted by the statutory provision.[33]

The final and most recent judicial diversion from the strict and arbitrary interpretation of section 349(4) is to be found in *Jenice Ltd v. Dan*.[34] This case

---

[30] *Supra*, n.25 at p.848.

[31] *Druiff v. Parker* (1868) LR 5 Eq 131.

[32] [1988] BCLC 170.

[33] It is interesting to note that in *Blum v. OCP Repartition SA*, the error of corporate identity had been caused by a mistake on the part of the company's bank; the company's cheques failed to mention its limited liability status. The director of the company who was responsible for endorsing the cheques initiated a counterclaim against the bank for negligence and asked the court for a stay of execution (RSC Ord. 47, r.1(1)) in relation to his liability to meet the terms of the cheques in accordance with the provision (Companies Act 1948, s.108). The Court of Appeal refused to grant the stay of execution on the basis that the bank had an independent cross claim against the director which if substantiated would have negated any financial benefit derived from any claim the director may have had based on the bank's negligence. Nevertheless, this case highlights the possibility of an action for negligence in a situation where a third party, for example, a bank, was responsible for the introduction of the error of corporate identity into the relevant instrument. While such a negligence claim would not affect the liability of a person incurred as a consequence of a breach of s.349(4), it would no doubt ease that person's financial burden to meet the liability. In such a case, it is inevitable that the party responsible for introducing the error of corporate identity would seek to establish contributory negligence in that the person responsible for endorsing the instrument would have been under the statutory obligation (s.349(4)) to ensure that the instrument contained the correct representation of a corporate name.

[34] [1993] BCLC 1349.

concerned an action in respect of the endorsement of five cheques by a director of the payee company, "Primekeen Ltd". As a result of a bank error, the cheques contained an incorrect representation of the company's name; the middle letter "E" having been omitted from the company's correct title. As such, the company's name was described as "Primkeen Ltd" instead of Primekeen Ltd (emphasis added).

Despite the misstatement of the company's name, Titheridge QC, sitting as a deputy High Court judge, held that the spelling error would not justify the application of section 349(4). The learned Judge took the view that as the spelling error was incapable of causing any confusion in relation to the identity of the company, then commonsense dictated that the company's name had been identified in accordance with the terms of the provision. Although Titheridge QC considered that a commonsense approach to the construction of section 349(4) would not be inconsistent or overshadowed by any binding precedent of a contrary disposition,[35] it is respectfully submitted that, in reality, the so called "commonsense" approach portrayed a total contradiction to the accepted judicial norm, in so far as judicial pronouncements in relation to the construction of the provision have clearly been dominated by the view that it is extraneous to consider the issue of whether a recipient of a relevant instrument was confused by a misrepresentation of corporate name.

Therefore, it may be stated that in common with other strict liability provisions, section 349(4) is drafted in a manner which provides the ultimate means of encouraging compliance with its legislative objective. The nature of the conduct necessary to substantiate the implementation of the provision is devoid of any subjective or objective consideration appertaining to the extent of an individual's culpability[36] and is also unrelated to the determination of whether or not the recipient of a relevant instrument was misled or confused by an erroneous representation of corporate identity.[37]

As the objective of the provision endeavours to protect the commercial community from misleading misstatements relating to a company's legal identity, it is perhaps surprising that the wording of section 349(4) is absent of any requirement associated with the investigation of matters pertinent to the

---

[35] *Ibid.*, at p.1356.

[36] The court will have a discretion in relation to the criminal sanction, i.e. in deciding upon the level of the fine which is to be imposed against the defendant. Prior to the passing of the Companies Act 1985, the provision had always contained an express stipulation that the criminal sanction would amount to a fine not exceeding fifty pounds, see, e.g. CA 1948, s.108. The provision now represented by s.349(4) does not specify a maximum penalty to be incurred as a result of the transgression of s.349(4), albeit that the maximum fine to be imposed will be that incurred as of a summary trial.

[37] Although the liability attached to a breach of s.349(4) CA 1985 is of a strict standard, a contravention of the provision will inevitably involve negligent conduct.

determination of whether a misstatement of corporate identity had or could reasonably be perceived to have had a misleading effect on the recipient of an instrument. Certainly, it would appear that the provision's failure to consider the actual or potential effect of a misdescription of identity is indicative of a vastly overprotective stance which is deficient of any resemblance to the law's general treatment of contractual misrepresentations, or indeed with the development and treatment of contractual misrepresentations specifically governed by the companies legislation.[38]

In reality, the scope of the provision, coupled with the severity of the penalty imposed for its breach, must now be regarded as an outmoded and unnecessary blemish on the character and status of modern company law.[39] Although officers of a company may, on occasions, be perceived to be advantageously treated by the corporate legal structure it would be inequitable to suggest that such a position is, for example, justly counter-balanced by a provision such as section 349(4). While statutory provisions which are designed to counter the exploitation of the corporate form are essential to the pursuit of the just treatment of creditor interests, an over protective approach of such interests must surely be discouraged as counter productive to the maintenance of a balanced and just regulation of corporate law.

---

[38] For example, statutory provisions relating to the regulation of an issue of shares, made to the public for the first time, seek to prevent the contents of an advertisement for such shares, as contained within a company's prospectus or listing particulars, from being of an untrue or misleading nature. A subscriber to a public share issue having suffered loss as a result of an untrue or misleading statement contained within a prospectus or listing particulars may rescind the contract for the purchase of such shares or/and claim damages. See the Financial Services Act 1986, s.150 in respect of misrepresentations contained within listing particulars and s.154A (inserted by the Public Offers of Securities Regulations 1995) in relation to misrepresentations included in a prospectus offering securities for which a listing is sought. See the Public Offers of Securities Regulations 1995, reg. 14 in respect of a prospectus relating to an unlisted company. The aforementioned statutory provisions do not require any form of reliance upon an untrue or misleading statement although it should be noted that it is a defence for the issuer of the shares to show that the person suffering loss as a result of the acquisition of the shares to which the prospectus related was aware that the statement was false or misleading at the time the shares were acquired, see the Public Offers of Securities Regulations 1995, reg. 15(5).

[39] For a detailed discussion of the possible ways in which s.349(4) could be reformed, see Griffin "Section 394(4) of the Companies Act 1985 — An Outdated Victorian Legacy" [1997] JBL 438.

Part II

DISQUALIFICATION OF COMPANY DIRECTORS

General introduction

Part II of this book is concerned with an analysis of the disqualification of company directors. The disqualification process comprises the imposition of what may tentatively be described as a *quasi* penal provision. During a period of disqualification, the liberty attached to a director's capacity to participate in the activities of a limited company is temporarily removed, in a manner which is, in an abstract sense, comparable with a convicted person's removal from society.[1] A convicted criminal and a disqualified director are, for the duration of their respective exclusion periods, removed from their own social domains. The justification for the imposition of a disqualification order and a term of imprisonment are also comparable in the sense that both are exacted to protect the public interest. A further similarity between the two sanctions is that both carry the stigma of social disgrace.

However, despite the fact that the disqualification process seeks to protect the public interest, a disqualification order is, in essence, a civil and not a penal sanction. Although a person who is made subject to a disqualification order will suffer a form of constraining punishment, that is, he will temporarily be precluded from involving himself in the management of a company's affairs, he will not, as a result of being disqualified (other than where he breaches the terms of a disqualification order) be liable to pay a debt to society in the form of a fine or a term of imprisonment.

Part II of this book has been split into three distinct chapters. The first of the said chapters, Chapter 7, is concerned with the historical background pertinent to the current system of disqualification orders. This chapter also seeks to provide a general overview of the Company Directors Disqualification Act 1986.[2] Chapter 8 deals specifically with disqualification orders made under section 6 of the CDDA 1986. Section 6 orders are by far, the most common type of order under the CDDA 1986 and unlike other operative provisions of the CDDA 1986, section 6 provides a mandatory form of disqualification order. In addition, while the majority of the provisions of the CDDA 1986 may be invoked against a director of a solvent or insolvent company, section 6 specifically provides for the disqualification of directors involved in the management of insolvent companies. Finally, Chapter 9 is concerned with the procedural and evidential requirements of the CDDA 1986. These matters are far ranging and have generated an abundance of case law.

---

[1] See, Dine "The Disqualification of Company Directors" (1988) 9 Co Law 213.
[2] Hereafter, referred to as the CDDA 1986.

Chapter 7

THE COMPANY DIRECTORS DISQUALIFICATION ACT 1986: THE HISTORICAL BACKGROUND AND A GENERAL OVERVIEW OF THE ACT

7.1 The historical background

The roots of the modern day disqualification procedure originate from the Companies Act of 1929; this Act was passed following the recommendations of the Greene Committee.[1] However, at its conception the disqualification process was severely limited. The 1929 legislation was restricted to the introduction of two types of disqualification. First, it prohibited undischarged bankrupts from taking part in the management of a company without the leave of the court[2] and secondly, it empowered the courts to disqualify company directors in circumstances where a director had been found to be in breach of the fraudulent trading provisions.[3]

Section 188 of the Companies Act 1948, sought to expand the type of conduct which could give rise to disqualification proceedings. The section enabled the court to impose disqualification orders in circumstances where a director had been found guilty of an offence(s) connected with the fraudulent promotion, formation, or management of a company.[4]

The scope of activities regulated by the disqualification procedure was further extended by section 28(1) of the Companies Act 1976. This provision allowed the courts to disqualify a director for up to five years in circumstances

---

[1] The Committee was set up in 1925 to investigate the effect of corporate failure on economic activity within the business community. The principal recommendation of the Committee was a procedure for creditors' voluntary liquidation, a recommendation which was first introduced into the legislation by the Companies Act 1929.

[2] Now incorporated into the CDDA 1986, s.11.

[3] The fraudulent trading provisions were also introduced by the 1929 legislation. Fraudulent trading is discussed in detail in Chapter 3.

[4] This would now be regulated under the CDDA 1986, ss.2 or 4.

where the director had been persistently in default of any provision of the companies legislation which required any return, account or other document to be filed with or sent to the registrar of companies.[5]

Following the introduction of section 9 of the Insolvency Act 1976 (this provision was subsequently incorporated into the Companies Act 1985, as section 300) a mechanism was introduced to give effect to a disqualification procedure which allowed a director of an insolvent company to be disqualified where he was considered unfit to be concerned in the management of a company. Although, in theory, the section created a deeper net into which incompetent directors might fall subject to a disqualification order, the efficiency of section 9 was marred in three material respects. First, the courts' power to grant a disqualification order was a discretionary one. Secondly, a court's ability to impose a disqualification order was limited by the requirement that the order could only be made against a director who had been involved in the management of two or more companies which had faltered into insolvent liquidation; the second liquidation having occurred within five years of the first. Thirdly, following a contravention of section 9 the maximum disqualification period which a court could impose was for five years.

In 1982, the Cork Committee Report was published.[6] The Report devoted a chapter of its findings to disqualification proceedings.[7] The Report, in analysing the shortcomings of section 9 of the Insolvency Act 1976, proposed substantive reforms to that provision. Whilst the Report retained the concept of unfitness as the main criterion for determining the disqualification of directors of insolvent companies, it addressed a principal criticism of section 9, by recommending that the court's power to disqualify should no longer be subject to a discretionary power, but should be replaced by a mandatory disqualification period of at least two years, up to a maximum of fifteen years. The Report also recommended that in the context of section 9, a disqualification order should be applicable where a director's corporate misconduct related to a single company.[8]

Following the publication of the Cork Committee Report, in February 1984 the government, in the form of a White Paper, published its own proposals for the reform of insolvency law.[9] The Insolvency Bill, which followed the

---

[5] This is now regulated by the CDDA 1986, s.3.

[6] Cmnd. 8558.

[7] *Ibid.*, Chp. 45 paras 1807-1826.

[8] It should be noted that the Cork Report suggested that the power to instigate disqualification proceedings under IA 1976, s.9 should be made available to liquidators; a proposal which has never been enacted in respect of disqualification based upon establishing a director's unfit conduct in the affairs of an insolvent company (now governed by the CDDA 1986, s.6).

[9] "A revised Framework for Insolvency Law", Cmnd. 9175.

White Paper, was introduced into the House of Lords in December 1984. Following many amendments to its original form (the Bill had been introduced into Parliament after only a minimum consultation period following the publication of the White Paper) the Bill reached the statute book as the Insolvency Act 1985. Shortly after its introduction, the 1985 Act was superseded by new insolvency legislation in the guise of the Insolvency Act 1986; the 1986 Act received its Royal Assent on 29 December 1986. The Insolvency Act 1986 was introduced for the purpose of consolidating the majority of insolvency laws into one statute, something which the 1985 Act had failed to achieve. However, in relation to disqualification proceedings, Parliament decided that new legislation should be introduced for the specific purpose of consolidating the law's treatment and regulation of this area of the law. The consolidating legislation became the Company Directors Disqualification Act 1986.

7.2 An overview of the CDDA 1986

7.2.1 Disqualification following the collapse of a corporate enterprise

It is to be expected, and indeed it is confirmed by the reported cases, that examples of corporate mismanagement giving rise to the imposition of a disqualification order will be most evident following the collapse of a corporate enterprise. Accordingly, while many of the provisions of the CDDA 1986 may be implemented against a person involved in the management of a solvent company, the majority of disqualification proceedings will inevitably be commenced against persons who were involved in the management of insolvent companies. In the majority of cases, the person against whom a disqualification order is instigated will have acted as a company director, although other than for sections 6 and 8 of the Act, a disqualification order may be imposed against a person whose management activities are not necessarily defined as those of a company director.

7.2.2 The power to impose a disqualification order

The CDDA 1986 aims to protect the general public from the activities of delinquent persons who are, or who have been, involved in the management of a company.[10] Section 1(1) of the CDDA 1986 provides that in accordance with the circumstances specified in the Act, a court may, and under section 6

---

[10] A disqualification order may be made against a person as opposed to an individual. Therefore, an order may be made against a corporate body, see CDDA 1986, s.14.

shall, make a disqualification order against a person with the effect that the person shall not, without the leave of the court—

(a) be a director of a company; or
(b) be a liquidator or administrator of a company; or
(c) be a receiver or manager of a company's property; or
(d) in any way, whether directly or indirectly, be concerned or take part in the promotion, formation or management of a company.

A disqualification period takes effect from the date of the order, and while the period of disqualification is operative, section 1(1) will, following the judgment of the Court of Appeal in *Re Cannonquest. Official Receiver v. Hannan*,[11] have the effect of disqualifying a person from acting in all the capacities indicated by section 1(1) (a)–(d). Accordingly, the court is not permitted to restrict the operation of the order to preclude any of the categories listed in section 1 (a)–(d).

Although section 1 stipulates that a disqualification order is to take effect from the date of the order, it is interesting to note that, under rule 9 of the Insolvent Companies (Disqualification of Unfit Directors) Proceedings Rules 1987,[12] it is provided that, unless the court otherwise directs, a disqualification order is to take effect at the beginning of the 21st day after the day on which the order was made. Accordingly, there would appear to be some doubt as to the date on which an order will commence. However, in accordance with the decision of Evans-Lombe J in *Secretary of State for Trade and Industry v. Edwards*,[13] there would appear to be no apparent inconsistency between section 1(1) and rule 9, in so far as the learned judge considered that rule 9 merely suspended the effect of the order by banning the respondent from acting as a director for a period of 21 days after the order was made. However, notwithstanding this judgment, there remains an inconstancy between the wording of section 1(1) and rule 9. The solution to this inconsistency is unclear,[14] although the procedural advantage of giving

---

[11] [1997] BCC 644. The fact that the court should not restrict the operation of the order was recognised by Robert Reid QC, sitting as a deputy High Court judge in *Re Gower Enterprises Ltd (No. 2)* [1995] 2 BCLC and by Lindsay J in *Re Polly Peck International plc* [1994] 1 BCLC 574, at pp.581-582. However, in some earlier cases the courts took a contrary position, for example, in *Re Rolus Properties Ltd* [1988] 4 BCC 446, Harman J held that the court could limit the effect of the order to encompass but s.1(1)(a) and s.1(1)(d).
[12] SI 1987/2023.
[13] [1997] BCC 222.
[14] This inconsistency was identified by the Court of Appeal in *Secretary of State v. Bannister* [1995] 2 BCLC 271, but unfortunately the court felt that on the facts of the case it was unnecessary to decide the matter; albeit that Morritt LJ did consider that it was a problem which the rule making authorities might direct their attention, *ibid.*, at p.276.

effect to the wording of rule 9 is obvious in the sense that the 21 day period would enable a respondent to apply for a disqualification order to be stayed or suspended at a time prior to the actual date from which the order was supposed to take effect.[15]

7.2.3 *The courts' discretionary power to impose a disqualification order*

In respect of section 6 of the CDDA 1986, the imposition of a disqualification order is mandatory where a director's conduct was unfit in relation to the management of a company. However, in relation to the other provisions of the CDDA 1986, under which a disqualification order may be imposed, namely sections 2, 3, 4, 5, 8 and 10, the court's power to make a disqualification order is a discretionary one. The court's primary concern in exercising its discretion will be the protection of the public interest, that is, where a person's managerial practices have prejudiced the interests of innocent third parties it will, *prima facie*, be beneficial to the public interest to remove that person's capacity to participate in the future management of a company. However, in some cases, the imposition of a disqualification order may be harmful to the public interest. For example, although a person may have conducted the management of a company in a delinquent manner, that person may also be actively involved in the management of a further company which is both solvent and successful. In such a case, the imposition of a disqualification order could seriously disturb the successful company's business activities (especially where the person to be disqualified is a dominant and essential character in the running and organisation of the company's affairs) and as such, may seriously harm the interests of the company's creditors, shareholders and employees.

The courts, in exercising their discretion to impose a disqualification order, will also consider the interests of the person who is the subject matter of the disqualification proceedings. The decision of the Court of Appeal in *R v. Holmes*[16] provides a good example of the courts' consideration of such matters. In this case, the Court of Appeal quashed a disqualification order made under section 2 of the CDDA 1986, in circumstances where, in addition to a disqualification order, the director had been ordered to pay a compensation order in the sum of £25,000. The Court of Appeal quashed the disqualification

---

[15] In *Re Continental Assurance Co plc* [1997] BCLC 48, Chadwick J preferred to follow rule 9 of the Disqualification Rules in so far as the convenience of the 21-day period prescribed by rule 9 would save the court from formally having to adjudicate upon whether there was a need to stay proceedings pending a possible appeal or application under CDDA 1986, s.17.
[16] [1991] BCC 394.

order on the ground that it had been wrong for the trial judge to disqualify a director following the making of the compensation order in circumstances where, once disqualified, the director would have had no obvious means by which he could discharge its terms. The Court of Appeal emphasised that in making a compensation order (which in this case the Court of Appeal also quashed), care must be taken not to reduce or inhibit a director's means to pay off the order.[17]

7.2.4 *The consequences attached to a breach of a disqualification order*

In accordance with section 13 of the CDDA 1986, a person in breach of a disqualification order or a person acting in contravention of section 12(2)[18] or section 11[19] of the CDDA 1986, is liable, on conviction on indictment, to a maximum penalty of two years' imprisonment and/or the imposition of a fine, and on summary conviction, to imprisonment for not more than six months, or a fine not exceeding the statutory maximum, or both. In addition, under section 15(1)(a) of the CDDA 1986, a person in breach of any disqualification order, or a person who acts in contravention of section 11 of the CDDA 1986, will be made jointly and severally liable with the company and any other person who is liable for any debts of the company which were incurred at a time when that person acted in a manner which was contrary to the terms of the order. Section 15(b) of the CDDA 1986 further provides that where a person is involved in the management of a company he will be liable for the debts and other liabilities of the company during a period of time in which he acted on instructions (without the leave of the court) given by a person who he knew to be an undischarged bankrupt, or a person who he knew was at that time subject to a disqualification order.

In a situation where a company is in breach of a disqualification order, section 14 of the CDDA 1986 states that the company will be subject to a

---

[17] However, it should be noted that in quashing the disqualification order, it is probable that the Court of Appeal was influenced by the director's subsequent formation of another company, a company which had proved itself to be successful, and a company which had a significant number of employees.

[18] The CDDA 1986, s.12 precludes a person from acting as a director or liquidator or from directly or indirectly taking part in the promotion, formation or management of a company in circumstances where, other than with the leave of the court, the person has been made the subject of an order under s.429 of the Insolvency Act 1986. Section 429 is concerned with the revocation of an administration order under Part VI of the County Courts Act 1984.

[19] The CDDA 1986, s.11 provides that, except with the leave of the court, it is an offence for an undischarged bankrupt to act as a director or directly or indirectly to take part in or be concerned in the promotion, formation or management of a company.

penal sanction in the form of a fine, and that any of its officers, or persons acting in such a capacity, who were aware of the company's contravention of the order, or who were negligent in not acting to prevent the company from contravening the order, will themselves be subjected to a criminal sanction.

7.2.5 *The register of disqualification orders*

Under section 18(2) of the CDDA 1986, the Secretary of State is obliged to maintain a register of disqualification orders which is open to public inspection on the payment of a small fee. The register contains the names of persons subject to a disqualification order. The Secretary of State maintains the register with information obtained from officers of the court. The Secretary of State must, by section 18(1) of the CDDA 1986, be kept informed of matters specified under the Companies (Disqualification Orders) Regulations 1986.[20] The regulations provide that an officer of the court must notify the Secretary of State when a disqualification order is made, where any action is taken by a court to vary or terminate an order, and where leave is granted by the court under section 17 of the CDDA 1986. Where the duration of a disqualification order has expired, the Secretary of State must, in accordance with section 18(3) of the CDDA 1986, remove the entry from the register and all particulars relating to the order.

7.3 Disqualification for general misconduct under sections 2–5 of the CDDA 1986

7.3.1 *Introduction*

Under sections 2-5 of the CDDA 1986, an application for a disqualification order may be made by the Secretary of State or the Official Receiver, the liquidator, or any past or present member or creditor of a company, against any person who committed an offence or other default governed by sections 2-5.[21] Other than for an application under sections 2 and 5 of the CDDA 1986, (discussed below), an application for a disqualification order must always be made to a court which has a jurisdiction to wind up the company in question.[22] In accordance with sections 2-5, a person who intends to make an

---

[20] SI 1986/2067.

[21] The list of applicants is in line with the recommendations of the Cork Report. However, it must be noted that only the Secretary of State may make an application under CDDA 1986, s.8. Contrary to the recommendations of the Cork Report, applications made under CDDA 1986, s.6, may only be made by the Secretary of State or the Official Receiver.

[22] Where a company's paid up share capital is in excess of £120,000, the relevant court will be the High Court, where it is less, the relevant court will be the County Court.

application must give the person against whom the order is sought, at least ten days' notice of his intention. The attitude of the courts to the making of disqualification orders under sections 2-5 is, as in all cases involving disqualification, dominated by a consideration of whether the order would benefit and protect the public interest.

7.3.2 *Disqualification following the conviction of an indictable offence (section 2 CDDA 1986)*

Under section 2 of the CDDA 1986, the court may, at its discretion, make a disqualification order against any person convicted of an indictable offence in connection with the promotion, formation, management or liquidation of a company, or with the receivership or management of a company's property. Although the relevant conviction must be for an indictable offence, it is not a pre-requisite for a person to have been convicted on indictment. For the purposes of this section, a conditional discharge is not to be interpreted as a conviction.[23]

Although the commission of an indictable offence may be related to a person's involvement in the affairs of a company, it is necessary for a court to determine whether the offence can properly be equated to a person's involvement in the management functions of a company. The determination of such matters will vary depending upon, for example, the size and type of company in which the person is involved. Following the judgment of the Court of Appeal in *R v. Goodman*,[24] it is unnecessary to establish that the offence was connected with the internal management of the company, such as an offence related to the keeping of accounts or the filing of returns. In giving the judgment of the Court of Appeal, Staughton LJ considered that it was unnecessary to establish that the offence was committed in the course of the day to day management of the affairs of a company.[25] Indeed, according to his lordship, the only pre-requisite for disqualification under section 2 is that

---

[23] See, for example, *R v. Young* [1990] BCC 549.

[24] [1994] BCLC 349 (Court of Appeal — criminal division).

[25] Many of the case examples concerning CDDA 1986, s.2 have been related to matters of internal or external management. For example, in *R v. Georgiou* (1988) 87 Cr App R 207, the defendant carried on an insurance business through the company without the authorisation of the Secretary of State and, accordingly, transgressed provisions of the Insurance Companies Act 1982. It was held that the offence was connected with the management of the company. See also, *R v. Corbin* (1984) 6 Cr App R 17 — obtaining corporate assets by deception; *R v. Austen* (1985) 7 Cr App R 214 — carrying out fraudulent hire purchase transactions through a number of limited companies. In this latter case, the Court of Appeal defined the management of a company as involving the company's internal or external affairs in relation to any activity covering the company's birth, life, or death.

the offence must have had some factual connection with the management of the company. Although Staughton LJ failed to define the exact meaning of the term "factual situation" it may be implied from his judgment that an offence connected to the management of a company extends beyond one which is associated with an improper exercise or abuse of the administration of a company's affairs. In *R v. Goodman*, the relevant offence was insider dealing, an offence which is not connected to the administration of a company's affairs but one which nevertheless demands a factual connection with the management of a company, that is, the offence is committed as a consequence of the defendant's knowledge of the company's affairs. In *R v. Goodman*, the defendant acquired the requisite inside knowledge in his capacity as the company's chairman, an office which is undoubtedly associated with the management of the company's affairs.[26]

For the purposes of section 2, any court with a jurisdiction to wind up the company may impose a disqualification order. Alternatively, section 2(2) provides that the disqualification order may be imposed by the court in which the person was convicted of the indictable offence. Where an order under section 2 is made by a court of summary jurisdiction, (magistrates' court) the maximum period of disqualification is five years. Where the disqualification order is imposed on indictment, the maximum period of disqualification is 15 years.

7.3.3 *Persistent breach of the companies legislation (section 3 CDDA 1986)*

In accordance with section 3 of the CDDA 1986, a disqualification order may be made against a person who persistently breached provisions of the companies legislation which required any return, account or other document to be filed with, delivered or sent, or notice of any matter to be given to the Registrar of Companies.[27] Section 27(7) of the CDDA 1986 defines the expression "the companies legislation" as comprising the Companies Acts, Parts I to VII of the Insolvency Act 1986 and, sections 411, 413, 414, 416 and 417 of Part XV of that same Act. Section 3(2) of the CDDA 1986 provides that without prejudice to its proof in any other manner, a person will be conclusively established to have been in persistent default of a relevant

---

[26] The Court of Appeal in dismissing the defendant's appeal confirmed that he was to be disqualified for a period of ten years. The defendant was also sentenced to 18 months' imprisonment (nine months suspended) in respect of a guilty plea to s.1 of the Company Securities (Insider Dealing) Act 1985.

[27] See, for example, *Re Civica Investments Ltd & Ors* [1983] BCLC 456.

provision of the companies legislation, where it is shown that in the five years ending with the date of the application, the person was found guilty of three or more defaults of the relevant provisions of the companies legislation. Section 3(3) then specifies that a person is adjudged to be guilty of a default of the companies legislation if;

(a) he is convicted (whether on indictment or summarily) of an offence consisting in a contravention of, or failure to comply with a provision of the companies legislation (whether on his own part or on the part of a company); or

(b) a default order is made against him under (whether on his own part or on the part of a company) any of the following provisions —
    (i) CA 1985, s.244 (the delivery of company accounts);
    (ii) CA 1985, s.245B (the preparation of revised accounts);
    (iii) CA 1985, s.713 (the delivery or notice to the registrar of a document or other specified matter);
    (iv) IA 1986, s.41 IA (a receiver or manager's legal obligation to file, deliver or make returns);
    (v) IA 1986, s.170 (a liquidator's legal obligation to file, deliver or make returns).

In determining whether a person has been in persistent breach of a relevant provision of the companies legislation, the court may not take into account any offence which was committed, or a default order made, before 1 June 1977 (CDDA 1986, Sch. 2, para. 5). In accordance with section 3(2), the convictions which may substantiate a finding of persistent default may have taken place on different occasions, or may have taken place on the same occasion.

In respect of the manner by which "default" is defined in section 3(3), the said provision does not specify in relation to disqualification proceedings whether the court should consider the culpability attached to a particular default.[28] However, where a person's culpability is established, it would appear logical to assume that the length of a disqualification period would naturally reflect the degree and nature of that culpability. In disqualifying a person under section 3, the relevant court may make an order for a maximum period of five years.

---

[28] However, it should be noted that the term "in default" as defined by CA 1985, s.730(5) does specify that a person is in default where he "knowingly and wilfully authorises or permits the default...".

7.3.4 *Disqualification for fraudulent conduct (section 4 CDDA 1986)*

The imposition of a disqualification order under section 4 of the CDDA 1986 will occur where, during the winding up of a company, evidence is placed before the court which establishes that a person involved in the management activities of the company, acted in a fraudulent manner in the conduct of the company's affairs. For the purposes of a section 4 order, a person will be adjudged to have acted in a fraudulent manner where he appears to have been guilty of:

(a) fraudulent trading, under section 458 of the Companies Act 1985,[29] irrespective of whether that person has been convicted; or
(b) where he has otherwise been guilty, while an officer,[30] liquidator, receiver of the company, or manager of the company's property, of any fraud connected with the management of the company or any breach of duty to the company.

Under section 4, a person may be disqualified up to a maximum period of fifteen years. In defining the term "officer of a company", it is to be noted that section 4(2) makes no specific reference to an administrator or a supervisor of a voluntary arrangement. However, it is submitted that both positions carry extensive powers of management and as such it would be most unlikely that persons holding office in these said positions would be construed as falling outside the activities of a person who, in accordance with section 4, "acts as a manager of a company's property".

7.3.5 *Persistent breaches of the companies legislation (summary jurisdiction under section 5 CDDA 1986)*

The circumstances giving rise to a court's ability to impose a disqualification order under section 5 of the CDDA 1986, are identical to those which give rise to disqualification under section 3 of the CDDA 1986, namely a disqualification order may be made against a person who has persistently breached those provisions of the companies legislation which require any return, account or other document to be filed with, delivered or sent, or notice of any matter to be given to the Registrar of Companies. As with section 3, the maximum period of disqualification under section 5 is five years. The

---

[29] This is a criminal offence and, accordingly, a person's "fraudulent" activities will need to be established in line with the criminal standard of proof, i.e. beyond any reasonable doubt.
[30] An officer includes a person who acts as a shadow director, CDDA 1986, s.4(2).

difference between section 3 and section 5 is that under the former provision, the imposition of a disqualification order may be made by a court which has a jurisdiction to wind up a company, whereas under section 5, the ability to impose a disqualification order is restricted to the court of summary conviction at which a person was found guilty of an offence which went to establish a finding of a persistent breach of the companies legislation, in relation to the return, filing, etc. of relevant documents.

7.4 Other types of disqualification

7.4.1 *Disqualification following a DTI investigation (section 8 CDDA 1986)*

Section 8 of the CDDA 1986 stipulates that a person may be disqualified[31] as a result of an application by the Secretary of State for the Department of Trade and Industry(DTI); the application will arise following a DTI investigation of a company in which the said person acted as a director.[32] In order to disqualify a person under section 8, it must be shown that the director was unfit to be concerned in the management of a company. The maximum period of disqualification under section 8 is fifteen years. In considering whether to impose a disqualification order under section 8, the court in its assessment of whether a director was unfit, must take into account the relevant matters set out in Part 1 of Schedule 1 to the CDDA 1986 (discussed at p.162).[33] The matters mentioned in Part 1 of Schedule 1 are appropriate to the determination of whether a person's conduct as a director or shadow director

---

[31] As the imposition of a disqualification order under the CDDA 1986, s.8 is determined in a like manner to the CDDA 1986, s.6, i.e. on the basis of a director's unfit conduct, it is somewhat peculiar that s.8, unlike s.6, does not carry a mandatory period of disqualification. However, it may be possible to explain this apparent lacuna on the basis that a director of a solvent company may be subject to proceedings under s.8 but not s.6. In relation to a director of a solvent company, the public interest may be adversely affected by imposing a disqualification order in so far as the order may be prejudicial to the interests of the company as a whole.

[32] Following *Re Rex Williams Leisure plc* [1993] BCLC 568, a report compiled by investigator under CA 1985, s.447 is not to be regarded as hearsay evidence. Further, in so far as proceedings under the CDDA 1986 are civil proceedings, evidence which is compelled in accordance with an investigation under CA 1985, s.432, may be used in subsequent disqualification proceedings; the use of compelled evidence in this situation is not contrary to art. 6(1) of the European Convention of Human Rights, see *R v. Secretary of State, ex parte McCormick* [1998] BCC 379. However, the use of compelled evidence would, in respect of subsequent criminal proceedings be contrary to art. 6(1) see, *Saunders v. UK* [1997] BCC 872.

[33] See, for example, *Re Samuel Sherman plc* [1991] BCC 699.

of a solvent or insolvent company makes him unfit to be concerned in the management of a company. Part 2 of Schedule 1 (discussed further at p.163) is also applicable to the determination of a director's unfitness to act in the management of a company, but only in a situation where a director acted in the management of an insolvent company.

7.4.2 *Disqualification for fraudulent/wrongful trading (section 10 CDDA 1986)*

Where the court finds that a person is liable to make a contribution to a company's assets under section 213 of the Insolvency Act 1986 (fraudulent trading) or section 214 of the Insolvency Act 1986 (wrongful trading), the court may of its own volition make a disqualification order against that person under section 10 of the CDDA 1986. The maximum period of disqualification under section 10 is fifteen years. In so far as section 10 is applicable to fraudulent trading, it should be stressed that this provision is not relevant to the criminal offence of fraudulent trading (which is dealt with under section 4 of the CDDA 1986). Accordingly, whilst section 4 is applicable to a person who would appear to have been guilty of fraudulent trading in connection with a solvent or insolvent company, section 10 will only be applicable to a person who is liable (in the civil as opposed to criminal sense) for fraudulent (or wrongful trading) in connection with the management of the affairs of an insolvent company.

7.4.3 *Disqualification of undischarged bankrupts (section 11 CDDA 1986)*

Section 11 of the CDDA 1986 provides that except with the leave of the court,[34] it is an offence for a person who is an undischarged bankrupt to act as a director, or take part in (directly or indirectly) or be concerned in, the promotion, formation or management of a company. It is no defence to an action under section 11 for a person to allege that at the time of his relevant involvement in the activities of a company he was under a reasonable but mistakenly held belief that he had been discharged from a bankruptcy order.

---

[34] There are very few reported cases in which a discussion of the matters affecting the court's discretion to grant leave have been considered. However, see, *Re McQuillan* (1989) 5 BCC 137, a decision of the Northern Ireland High Court, and by analogy, see, *Re Alit Pty Ltd* [1968] 2 NSWR 762, a decision of the Supreme Court of New South Wales. The said cases are naturally indicative of a reluctance to grant leave.

The offence is one of strict liability.[35] Where an undischarged bankrupt acts in contravention of section 11, he will, in accordance with section 15 of the CDDA 1986, be made jointly and severally liable for the debts incurred by the company during the period in which he was involved in its management. He will share this liability with the company and any other person who, whether under section 15 or otherwise, was liable for the company's debts during the requisite period.

7.4.4 *Disqualification resulting from a failure to comply with payment under a county court administration order (section 12 CDDA 1986)*

A person who fails to make a payment which is required under Part VI of the County Courts Act 1984, (relating to an administration order) may, in accordance with section 429 of the Insolvency Act 1986, have the administration order revoked and may also be made subject to a disqualification order under section 12 of the CDDA 1986. Under section 12, the maximum period of disqualification is two years.

---

[35] So held, by the Court of Appeal (Criminal Division) in *R v. Brockley* [1994] 1 BCLC 606.

Chapter 8

DISQUALIFICATION FOR UNFIT CONDUCT IN THE MANAGEMENT OF AN INSOLVENT COMPANY (section 6 CDDA 1986)

8.1 Introduction

The statutory history of section 6 of the CDDA 1986 may be traced to section 9 of the Insolvency Act 1976, a provision which was consolidated into section 300 of the Companies Act 1985. Prior to the enactment of the CDDA 1986, section 300 of the Companies Act 1985 provided that a person who was, or who had been, a director of at least two companies, both of which had been placed into insolvent liquidation within a five-year period, could be made subject to a disqualification order where his conduct of either company made him unfit to be concerned in the future management of a company. Under section 300, the court's power to impose a disqualification order was, as with other types of disqualification proceedings, a discretionary one.

In 1982, the Report of the Review Committee on Insolvency Law (The Cork Report)[1] recommended that section 9 of the Insolvency Act 1976, (later to become section 300 of the Companies Act 1985) should be reformed to provide a more stringent regime for controlling the activities of delinquent directors.[2] The Cork Report proposed the following amendments to section 9:[3]

(a) section 9 should apply where a director's conduct was established to be unfit in relation to any insolvent company and not (as under section 9) at least two insolvent companies;

---

[1] Cmnd. 8558.

[2] This recommendation was endorsed by the White Paper, "A Revised Framework for Insolvency Law" (Cmnd. 9175).

[3] Cmnd. 8558, at para. 1818.

(b) the courts should no longer have a discretion to impose a disqualification order in circumstances where it had been established that a director of an insolvent company had been a party to the wrongful trading of the company or, that in any other respect, the director's conduct made him unfit to be concerned in the management of a company;

(c) the duration of a disqualification order should be for a minimum of two years up to a maximum of fifteen years; and finally

(d) it should be open to a liquidator or, with the leave of the court, a creditor of the company, to make an application for a disqualification order.

On 28 April 1986, the Insolvency Act 1985 was passed. The 1985 Act sought to reform section 9 of the Insolvency Act (section 300 of the Companies Act 1985) in line with the spirit of the proposals advanced by the Cork Report.[4] On 29 December 1986, section 12 of the Insolvency Act 1985 became section 6 of the CDDA 1986.

8.2 Section 6 of the CDDA 1986

Section 6(1) of the CDDA 1986 provides that it is the duty of the court to make a disqualification order against any person in a case where:

(a) that person is or has been a director of a company which has at any time become insolvent (whether while the person was a director or subsequently); and

(b) that person's conduct as a director of the company (either taken alone or taken together with the person's conduct as a director of another company or companies) makes the person unfit to be concerned in the management of a company.[5]

---

[4] A proposal which sought to provide a means for the automatic disqualification of a director of any company which had been made subject to a compulsory winding up order (subject to a defence of having acted in the best interests of the company's creditors) was originally incorporated into the Insolvency Bill 1985. However, during the passage of the Bill through Parliament, this proposal was rejected by the House of Lords. The said proposal would have been a draconian measure because its enactment would have sought to penalise directors of a failed company on an unsubstantiated assumption that they had been a party to some form of misconduct.

[5] The Cork Report's recommendation that disqualification should be mandatory following a finding that a director had been privy to wrongful trading, was not incorporated into IA 1995, s.12 (now CDDA 1986, s.6). This is understandable in the sense that an instance of wrongful trading may be insufficient to warrant it being labelled as unfit conduct.

Under section 6(4) of the CDDA 1986, the minimum period of disqualification following a contravention of section 6(1), is two years. The maximum period for disqualification under section 6 is fifteen years.[6]

In accordance with section 7(1) of the CDDA 1986, the justification for commencing disqualification proceedings under section 6 is to protect the public interest from the unfit conduct of delinquent directors.[7] The following statement, taken from the judgment of Henry LJ in *Re Grayan Building Services Ltd*,[8] aptly illustrates the purpose of the provision. His Lordship remarked,

"The concept of limited liability and the sophistication of our corporate law offers great privileges and great opportunities for those who wish to trade under that regime. But the corporate environment carries with it the discipline that those who avail themselves of those privileges must accept the standards laid down and abide by the regulatory rules and disciplines in place to protect creditors and shareholders.... The Parliamentary intention to improve managerial safeguards and standards for the long term good of employees, creditors and investors is clear. Those who fail to reach those standards and whose failure contributes to others losing money will often be plausible and capable of inspiring initial trust, often later regretted. Those attributes may make them attractive witnesses. But as section 6 makes clear, the court's focus should be on their conduct — on the offence rather than the offender".[9]

8.3 Factors which are relevant to a section 6 application

8.3.1 *An insolvent company*

An insolvent company is defined in broad terms by section 6(2) of the CDDA 1986 as either:

---

[6] This was in accordance with the proposal of the Cork Report.

[7] Disqualification orders under s.6 have risen annually following the introduction of the CDDA 1986. The Department of Trade and Industry 1996 year-end statistics (published on 7 February 1997) show that the total number of disqualification orders against unfit directors in 1996 was 946, an increase of 49% over the 1995 figure of 633. The increase in orders has occurred despite the fact that there was a reduction of 7.4% in the number of insolvent liquidations between 1995 and 1996. In 1995 there were 14,536 liquidations, whereas in 1996 there were 13,461 liquidations. The 1997 final year figures confirm a decline in the number of liquidations and an increase in disqualifications.

[8] [1995] BCC 554.

[9] *Ibid.*, at p.577.

(a) a company which goes into liquidation at a time when its assets are insufficient for the payment of its debts and other liabilities and the expenses of the winding up;[10]

(b) where an administration order is made in relation to a company; or

(c) where an administrative receiver is appointed to the company.

8.3.2 *Conduct in relation to other companies*

Section 6(1)(b) of the CDDA 1986 provides that the court shall impose a disqualification order against a director of an insolvent company where,

"... his conduct as a director of that company (either taken alone or taken together with his conduct as a director of any other company or companies) makes him unfit to be concerned in the management of a company".

In accordance with section 6(1)(b), and for the purpose of determining whether a director's conduct was unfit in relation to the management of a company, the nature of a director's conduct in relation to any other company will obviously be irrelevant where that conduct was of a satisfactory nature. Similarly, where a director's conduct in relation to the lead company was of a satisfactory nature, then unfit conduct in relation to any other company will also be considered irrelevant to the outcome of the disqualification proceedings.

Prior to the Court of Appeal's decision in *Re County Farm Inns Ltd — Secretary of State v. Ivens*,[11] the courts' interpretation of section 6(1)(b), had been one whereby a director's misconduct in the affairs of another company had to be of a type which was the same as or similar in nature to the director's misconduct in relation to his management of the lead

---

[10] In relation to the construction of s.6(2)(a), in *Re Gower Enterprises Ltd* [1995] BCLC 107, it was held that the asset figure should be calculated on the basis of ignoring any interest payable on debts owed to the company following its liquidation. However, it was stated that any interest owing on debts prior to liquidation should be included in the sum of the company's assets. In relation to corporate liabilities, it was held that winding up expenses must be calculated on the basis of what the court perceived to be reasonable winding up expenses, having regard to the 1986 Insolvency rules and regulations. Further, it was established that in ascertaining the liabilities of a company the amount of any statutory interest payable under IA 1986, s.189 should be ignored.

[11] [1997] BCC 801. The Court of Appeal approved the decision of Judge Weeks QC (sitting as a judge of the High Court [1997] BCC 396).

company. For example, in *Re Goodwin Warren Control Systems plc*[12] Chadwick J commented that,

> "There must in my view be some nexus between the conduct in relation to the other companies and the conduct in relation to the insolvent company.... In my view, where the position is that conduct in relation to other companies is quite independent of the conduct in relation to the insolvent company, it is not to be taken into account for the purposes of the decision which the court has to make under section 6(1)(b)".[13]

However, following the Court of Appeal's decision in *Re County Farm Inns Ltd — Secretary of State v. Ivens*, it is now clear that any impropriety in relation to the conduct of another company may be advanced to support a finding of unfitness in relation to the director's misconduct in respect of the lead company. Morritt LJ, in giving the judgment of the Court of Appeal, fully endorsed the construction of section 6(1)(b) as advanced by the first instance judgment of Judge Weeks QC.[14] Judge Weeks QC in construing section 6(1)(b) stated,

> "...there is no requirement to be inferred from the wording of section 6(1)(b) that the conduct has to be the same or similar in the other companies to that alleged in the lead company. The reason for this conclusion on my part is very simply that, in relation to the lead company, very different types of misconduct can be taken into account and accumulated to reach a decision that the director is unfit to be concerned in the management of a company. Given that there is some misconduct in relation to the lead company, I see no reason why the acts in relation to the other company or companies have to be of the same or similar nature, and why the same process of aggregation should not be capable of being carried out, remembering, of course, that the other companies are different companies and the acts occurred at different times and in different

---

[12] [1993] BCLC 80. Also see the judgment of Jules Sher QC (sitting as a deputy High Court judge) in *Re Diamond Computer Systems Ltd* [1997] 1 BCLC 174, in which the view expressed by Chadwick J in *Goodwin Warren Control Systems Ltd* was unequivocally endorsed.

[13] *Ibid.*, at p.92. This passage had been cited with approval by Morritt LJ in *Re Pamstock Ltd* [1996] BCC 341. However, it is worthy to note that Morritt LJ, in giving the leading judgment of the Court of Appeal in *Re County Farm Inns Ltd*, stated that in *Re Pamstock Ltd* it had, in fact, been unnecessary for the Court of Appeal to express a view on the correctness or otherwise of the observations made by Chadwick J in *Goodwin Warren Control Systems plc*.

[14] [1997] BCC 396.

circumstances, so they may have different probative force. However, I do not accept the proposition that the acts alleged in relation to the other companies have to be either the same or similar acts".[15]

Morritt LJ further emphasised that while section 6 required the lead company to be insolvent, it was unnecessary, in respect of section 6(2)(b), that another company in which the director's conduct was called into question, should also be insolvent. Therefore, providing a director's conduct in relation to any other company was of a type which complied with section 9 and Schedule 1 of the CDDA 1986,[16] then that conduct could be taken into account for the purpose of determining a director's fitness to be concerned in the management of a company.[17]

In considering whether the conduct of the affairs of another company may be taken into account, the court must also have regard to section 22(2)(b) of the CDDA 1986. Section 22(2)(b) provides that for the purpose of section 6(1)(b) "another company" will be one which, " . . . may be wound up under Part V of the Insolvency Act 1986". Accordingly, where for example, a company is registered in a foreign jurisdiction, that is the company is not governed by the Insolvency Act 1986, a director's conduct in relation to that company will be irrelevant in respect of section 6(2)(b).

However, following the judgment of Knox J in *Re Dominion International Group plc*,[18] it is interesting to note that where a person holds a directorship in both a holding company and its subsidiary and the subsidiary is registered as a foreign company, the director's conduct of the affairs of the subsidiary company may, notwithstanding the section 22(2)(b) definition, still be taken into account in the context of its effect on the affairs of the holding company. In *Re Dominion International Group plc*, it was held that a director had breached his duty to the holding company in so far as he had adversely affected the interests of the holding company by improperly disposing of an asset which belonged to the subsidiary company. Knox J explained his finding in the following manner,

"I do not accept that it is right to categorise activities as necessarily belonging exclusively to the directorship of the company whose asset is being dealt with. I do accept that there may very well be many cases where

---

[15] *Ibid.,* at p.399.
[16] Discusssed at p.162.
[17] In accordance with CDDA 1986, s.7(2), an application under s.6 must, in relation to the lead company, be made within two years of the day on which the company became insolvent.
[18] [1996] 1 BCLC 572.

that will be the correct analysis of the activities of a director of a subsidiary company even if he is also a director of the subsidiary company's holding company. But equally, where an individual who is a director of both takes steps which seriously affect the interests of both companies, it strikes me as artificial to ignore his duties as a director of one of the two companies and attribute his actions solely to the directorship of the company whose asset is dealt with. Put baldly, the question is whether a director of a subsidiary company, is in breach of his fiduciary duty to the holding company, if he improperly gets rid of an asset of significant value to the subsidiary. It is clear that conduct inflicts harm on the holding company because it reduces the value of its investment in the subsidiary. In my view a director in such a position is in breach of his duty to both the holding company and the subsidiary".[19]

At first sight, the explanation advanced by Knox J represents a welcome and common sense approach to the question of whether a director's conduct of a foreign subsidiary may be relevant in considering the director's conduct in relation to the holding company (the lead company). Nevertheless, the logical conclusion of this explanation results in the holding company and its subsidiary being treated as one single economic entity, an appearance which may have the effect of distorting the separate corporate identity of the subsidiary company. Further, although Knox J justified his finding on the basis that the director's conduct in the affairs of the subsidiary reduced the value of the holding company's investment in the subsidiary, the director's misconduct in respect of the subsidiary company could not be described as conduct in relation to the affairs of the holding company, albeit that such conduct impliedly and adversely affected the holding company. In accordance with a literal interpretation of section 6(2)(b), it is respectfully submitted that there is an obvious difficulty in seeking to contend that a director's conduct in relation to a subsidiary company may be duplicated as conduct performed in his capacity as a director of the holding company.

8.3.3 *Defining the actions of a director*

The definition of a company director is contained in section 22(4) of the CDDA 1986 and provides that a director is any person occupying the position of director, by whatever name called (an exact copy of section 741 of the Companies Act 1985). The definition of a company director is therefore couched in very general terms. Accordingly, a person who is not formally appointed to a company's board of directors, but who nevertheless acts in the

---

[19] *Ibid.* at p.634.

capacity as a director of the company (a *de facto* director) is capable of being construed to be a director of a company for the purpose of section 22(4).

Although it is possible to contend that in accordance with a literal construction of section 6, the term "director" should be restricted to the activities of a *de jure* director, in so far as unlike, for example, section 14 of the CDDA 1986,[20] the wording of section 6 does not invoke liability in the case of "any person who was purporting to act in the capacity of a director", such an argument has been rejected in at least two decided cases.[21] Indeed, if section 6 was, in this respect, construed in a like manner to section 14, the effect would be to usurp Parliament's perceived intention of penalising all persons, however labelled, who were clearly unfit to be concerned in the future management of a company's affairs. In addition, although there is an obvious logic in the comparison made between the wording of section 6 and the corresponding wording of section 14, the apparent logic may be misplaced, because unlike section 6, section 14 is exclusively a penal provision. It would be expected in relation to a criminal sanction that the criminal liability of any particular class of person would need to be specifically and methodically spelt out (as it is in section 14).

In evaluating whether a person acted as a *de facto* director, the court must consider the degree of involvement and control which that person exerted in the conduct of a company's affairs. In cases where a company's affairs have been conducted without a formally appointed board of directors, the assertion that a person or persons acted in the capacity of a *de facto* director is patently obvious.[22] However, in cases where the affairs of a company were, *prima facie*, under the guardianship of a validly appointed and active board of directors, the evaluation of control which will be deemed necessary to equate a person's activities with those of a *de facto* director may be especially difficult. This problem will be particularly prevalent in cases where a person acting in a professional capacity is appointed by a company to advise on matters connected to the internal and/or external management of the company.

The courts have struggled to define the nature and degree of control which is necessary to identify a person as a *de facto* director. Furthermore, in many cases the determination of a *de facto* director has proceeded without a

---

[20] Section 14 imposes criminal liability against a company which acts in contravention of a disqualification order. Liability is also invoked against any director or other officer of the company or any such person who was purporting to act in any such capacity who consented to, or was negligent in, allowing the company to contravene the order.

[21] See, *Re Lo-Line Electric Motors Ltd* [1988] Ch 477, at p.489 and more recently *Re Richborough Furniture* [1996] 1 BCLC 507, at p.523.

[22] See, for example, *Re Lo-Line Electric Motors Ltd* [1988] Ch 477.

detailed consideration of any formal guidelines to determine the character of the position. Unfortunately, where formal guidelines have been formulated, they have not always been of a uniform nature. This disparity in the formal test to identify the disposition of a *de facto* director may be illustrated by comparing two decided cases, namely *Re Richborough Furniture*[23] and *Re Hydrodam (Corby) Ltd*.[24]

In *Re Richborough Furniture*, it was alleged that M had acted as a director of a small quasi partnership type company. M advised the company in a consultancy capacity; the consultancy agency, in which M was a partner, controlled a third of the company's issued share capital. At the time the company became insolvent it had two formally appointed directors, Z and S. Z was less active in conducting the affairs of the company than S, although Z was also a partner in the consultancy agency. Purportedly, as a consultant of the company, M was empowered by the company's board to involve himself in its financial matters and in doing so was, for example, accorded a discretion in deciding upon which of the company's creditors would be paid. Although M was never given a completely free role in the financial affairs of the company, he was, at least in S's opinion, fulfilling the role of the company's financial director. Indeed, at the suggestion of the company's former managing director, when signing three company letters, M represented himself as the company's business development director.

As an undischarged bankrupt, M was precluded from holding office as a company director and following the advice of his solicitor, he subsequently refrained from signing further company letters in the guise of the company's business development director. Nevertheless, creditors with whom M dealt had also assumed that M's capacity, in acting on behalf of the company, was at a level beyond that of a senior employee. However, in concluding that M had not acted as a director of the company, Timothy Lloyd QC, sitting as a deputy High Court judge, remarked that,

"... the reliance placed on him [M] in this area by Mr Stokes [S] could have led an outsider to assume that they were on an equal footing. But I do not think that this impression received by outsiders, not borne out by the reality of the internal arrangements in the company, makes him a director".[25]

Timothy Lloyd QC considered that a person would be properly described as a *de facto* director where, in the words of the learned judge, there was,

---

[23] [1996] 1 BCLC 507.

[24] [1994] 2 BCLC 180.

[25] *Supra*, n.23 at p.526.

"...clear evidence that he had been either the sole person directing the affairs of the company (or acting with others all equally lacking in a valid appointment...) or, if there were others who were true directors, that he was acting on an equal footing with the others in directing the affairs of the company".[26]

By contrast, in *Re Hydrodam (Corby) Ltd*, a case which was concerned with the construction of section 214 of the Insolvency Act 1986, Millet J, defined a *de facto* director[27] in the following way,

"A *de facto* director is a person who assumes to act as a director. He is held out as a director by the company, and claims and purports to be a director, although never actually or validly appointed as such. To establish that a person was a *de facto* director of a company it is necessary to plead and prove that he undertook functions in relation to the company which could properly be discharged only by a director. It is not sufficient to show that he was concerned in the management of the company's affairs or undertook tasks in relation to its business which can properly be performed by a manager below board level".[28]

In comparing the respective definitions, it is to be observed that in *Re Richborough Furniture*, the determination of a *de facto* director was, in terms of the evidence required to substantiate that finding, more restrictive than the definition applied in *Re Hydrodam (Corby) Ltd*. In accordance with the definition advanced in *Re Richborough Furniture*, a person may *prima facie* fail to be defined as a *de facto* director where, despite performing functions akin to those of a company director, such functions were at a less substantive level than the management activities of, either a person exercising a dominant influence over the affairs of a company or, alternatively, the management activities of the company's formally appointed directors.

It is respectfully submitted that the validity of the definition advanced in *Re Richborough Furniture* is questionable, although more recently it has been accepted by both Evans-Lombe J in *Secretary of State v. Laing*[29] and Judge Weeks QC in *Secretary of State v. Hickling*.[30] The criticism of the definition is

---

[26] *Ibid.*, at p.524.

[27] This case was primarily concerned with the question of whether a director of a holding company could be identified as either a *de facto* or shadow director of the holding company's subsidiary. On the facts of the case, it was held that he could not be. However, the holding company was found to have acted in the capacity of a shadow director.

[28] *Supra*, n.24, at p.183.

[29] [1996] 2 BCLC 324.

[30] [1996] BCC 678.

as follows. First, in its assumption that a person is to be regarded as a *de facto* director where that person acts with an absolute responsibility in directing the affairs of the company, regardless of never having been formally appointed to the company's board, the definition is, without further explanation, too closely aligned to that of a shadow director. Further, the second part of the definition proceeds on the basis that as a genus, company directors contribute equally in the conduct of a company's affairs. This is an erroneous assumption. For example, ordinarily it may be presumed that a non-executive director will not be involved in the managerial affairs of a company to the same extent as an executive director. However, notwithstanding that a non-executive director's contribution to the management affairs of a company may be less substantive than the contribution of an executive director, it is clear that a non-executive director may still be made the subject of a disqualification order.[31] Accordingly, the determination of whether a person acted as a director of a company should not be measured solely on the premise of whether he contributes more or less to the administration of a company's affairs than the company's other directors. If a person performs management tasks properly associated with the functions of a company director, then surely the activities of that person are those of a director.

Notwithstanding the above criticism, it is to be observed that following the decisions of Judge Cooke in *Secretary of State for Trade and Industry v. Elms* (16 January 1997, unreported) and Jacob J in *Secretary of State v. Tjolle*,[32] a more lucid explanation of the definition advanced in *Re Richborough Furniture* has been put forward to illustrate the equal footing test advanced by Lloyd J. In *Secretary of State v. Tjolle*, Jacob J quoted with approval, the following passage taken from the judgment of Judge Cook:

"At the forefront of the test I think I have to go on to consider by way of further analysis what Lloyd J meant by 'on an equal footing'. As to one, it seems to me clear that this cannot be limited simply to statutory functions and to my mind it would mean and include any one or more of the following: directing others, putting it very compendiously, committing the company to major obligations, and thirdly, (really I think what we are concerned with here) taking part in an equally based collective decision process at board level, i.e. at the level of a director in effect with a foot in the board room. As to Lloyd J's test, I think it is very much on the lines of that third test to which I have just referred. It is not I think in any way a question of equality of power but equality of ability to participate in the

---

[31] See, for example, *Re Continental Assurance Co of London plc* [1997] BCLC 48.
[32] [1998] BCLC 333.

notional board room. Is he somebody who is simply advising and, as it were, withdrawing having advised, or somebody who joins the other directors, de facto or de jure, in decisions which affect the future of the company?"

Indeed given the above explanation of the "equal footing test" it is in some respects possible to equate that explanation with the definition of a *de facto* director as advanced by Millet J in *Re Hydrodam (Corby) Ltd*. Under the revised equal footing test and the test advanced by Millet J, a person will act as a *de facto* director providing his contribution to the management of a company is concerned with matters which portray an obvious relationship with the functions one would normally expect to be undertaken by a director of a company. However, in so far as the approach adopted by Millet J in *Re Hydrodam (Corby) Ltd* calls for a finding that a company must hold out a person as having acted as one of its directors, the test advanced by Millet J, has been subject to some criticism. For example, in *Re Moorgate Metals Ltd* [33] Warner J remarked that the expression "held out" should not, as it might possibly be taken to imply, be interpreted to mean that a *de facto* director must be someone to whom the label "director" had been expressly attached.[34] It should also be observed that similar cautionary remarks were expressed by Timothy Lloyd QC, in *Re Richborough Furniture Ltd*.[35]

Nevertheless, despite such cautionary comments, it is suggested that a *de facto* director can aptly be described in terms of a person having been held out by a company as one of its directors. Although the concept of "holding out" implies that a person would only act as a *de facto* director following a representation from the company to confirm him in that capacity, the said representation may simply be intimated from the company's acquiescence in the performance of a person's managerial functions.[36] Consequently, a company may, by implication, represent that a person has an authority to act as a director notwithstanding the absence of any formal or positive affirmation of that status.

8.3.4 *The shadow director*

Somewhat surprisingly, the judicial consideration of the distinction between a *de facto* director and a shadow director has received little attention in the reported cases. Moreover, in some cases, the distinction has appeared quite

---

[33] [1995] 1 BCLC 503.
[34] *Ibid.*, at p.517.
[35] [1996] 1 BCLC 507, at p.522.
[36] By analogy, see, for example, *Freeman & Lockyer v. Buckhurst Properties* [1964] 2 QB 480.

irrelevant.[37] Yet, clearly, the evidence required to establish that a person acted as a *de facto* director will be less substantive than that which would justify a person being labelled a shadow director.[38] Whereas a shadow director is defined in terms of a person exerting a dominant and controlling influence over the company's affairs, the verification of a person acting in the capacity of a *de facto* director is less stringent in respect of the degree of control which he will be expected to exert over a company's affairs.

Although the classification of the type of directorship which is held by a person in relation to the management of a company should be irrelevant for the purposes of calculating the length of any disqualification period, the definitions attributed to a *de facto* and shadow director are, theoretically, quite separate. However, in practice, their distinguishing characteristics may not be that well defined.[39] A shadow director may occasionally experience a need to step from the shadow to resolve corporate issues, thereby identifying himself as active in the conduct of the company's external affairs. When stepping from the shadow, his conduct will be more akin to that of a *de facto* director. Accordingly, it is submitted that a person may occasionally act in a dual capacity, as both a shadow and *de facto* director.

8.4 Conduct of an unfit nature

To establish a director's culpability in respect of section 6 of the CDDA 1986, it is necessary to prove that the director's conduct in the management of a company(ies) is such as to make him unfit to be concerned in the future management of a company. At first sight, section 6 suggests that a director's capacity to act in the future management of a company is the essential yardstick by which a court should determine whether or not to impose a disqualification order. Indeed, if this assumption was correct, a court would

---

[37] For example, in *Re Tasiban (No. 3)* [1993] BCLC 297, the Court of Appeal, affirming the decision of Vinelott J ([1991] BCLC 792), made no attempt in analysing the facts of the case to distinguish between a person's involvement in the management of a company as a *de facto* or a shadow director. Instead, the court was quite satisfied to conclude that the evidence of the case was sufficient to establish that the person acted as either a *de facto* director or a shadow director.

[38] The difficulty in attempting to distinguish between the activities of a professional advisor and shadow director may be especially troublesome. To establish that a professional advisor acted as a shadow director one must first prove that the advisor exerted an influence over the company's affairs which was in a manner far exceeding his advisory status. It would appear that the advice and actions tendered by an advisor should be viewed with objectivity; such actions should be compared with those of a person of the same professional status and occupying a similar advisory role, see *Re Tasiban (No. 3), ibid*.

[39] See, for example, *Re Tasiban (No. 3), ibid*.

primarily be obliged to consider a director's potential to conduct the future affairs of a company in a proper manner; albeit that to a degree, such a potential would inevitably be influenced by the director's past conduct. However, following a finding of a director's unfit conduct, the imposition of a disqualification order under section 6, is mandatory and, accordingly, the section would appear to restrict the court's consideration of whether a director possessed a potential to reform his past misconduct. Therefore, to what extent, if any, may a court consider evidence which may indicate that a director's future conduct is unlikely to be prejudicial to the public interest?

In *Re Polly Peck International plc*,[40] Lindsay J opined that as the language of section 6(1)(b) was in the present tense (makes him unfit) a director's past conduct must be of a type which would satisfy the court of his present and also future unfitness to act in the management of a company. Consequently, in applying the reasoning adopted by Lindsay J, it would appear feasible to contend that notwithstanding the extent of a director's past misconduct, the circumstances of a case may be indicative of a finding that a director would be unlikely to repeat his past misdemeanours in the future management of a company, in which case, it is possible that he should escape a disqualification order. In support of this contention, Lindsay J gave an example of a director who, despite an otherwise exemplary record, may, as a result of a period of very real and worrying domestic pressures, have conducted the affairs of a company in an unfit manner. In such circumstances, Lindsay J considered that the director's past misconduct in the management of a company could be viewed in the light of extenuating circumstances, thereby allowing the court to conclude that on a balance of probabilities it was highly unlikely that the director should be considered unfit to be involved in the future management of a company. Nevertheless, Lindsay J pointed out that the courts should be cautious if not cynical about a respondent's potential to reform.

However, in contrast to the approach adopted by Lindsay J in *Re Polly Peck International plc*, the Court of Appeal in *Secretary of State v. Gray*[41] applied a far more restrictive interpretation to the extent by which a director's potential to reform his past misconduct could ever be considered relevant to the determination of his unfitness to act in the future management of a company. Hoffmann LJ, in delivering the leading judgment of the court, made it clear that under section 6, the courts were obliged to make a disqualification order in circumstances where it was established that a director's past conduct was of an unfit nature; a conclusion which was not to be interfered with by considering a director's potential to reform his past indiscretions. Hoffmann

---

[40] [1994] 1 BCLC 574, at p.583.
[41] [1995] 1 BCLC 276.

LJ approved a statement, taken from the judgment of Vinelott J in *Re Pamstock Ltd.*[42] Vinelott J stated of the respondent in that case,

"The respondent seemed to me (so far as I can judge from the evidence before me) to be a man who today is capable of discharging his duties as a director honestly and diligently. However, . . . I am required to have tunnel vision and to consider whether in relation to Pamstock the respondent's conduct fell short of the minimum standard which the court today requires to be observed by the director of a company which enjoys the privilege of limited liability . . . even though the misconduct may have occurred some years ago and even though the court may be satisfied that the respondent has since shown himself capable of behaving responsibly".[43]

Although Hoffmann LJ conceded that extenuating circumstances may affect the court's consideration of whether a director's past conduct had reached an appropriate standard of unfitness to justify disqualification, his lordship stressed that any decision to impose a disqualification order should not be influenced by considering a director's capacity to reform his past activities.

In harmony with the views expressed by Hoffmann LJ, it is submitted that although section 6(2)(b) is expressed in the present tense, a director's potential to reform his future conduct should not be considered relevant to determining the outcome of disqualification proceedings under section 6. Under section 6, the imposition of a disqualification order is, following proof of a director's unfitness, mandatory. Unlike the predecessor to section 6, namely, section 300 of the Companies Act 1985, the court is not possessed of a general discretion to consider the likelihood of a director's ability to refrain from committing any future malpractice in the exercise of his managerial responsibilities.[44] Indeed, had the court such a discretion, the interpretation of section 6 could be plagued by inconsistency because the perception of a director's unfitness would inevitably be subjected to a speculative and therefore imperfect calculation of a director's capacity to reform his past conduct.

For the purposes of section 6, the court, in assessing whether a director is unfit to act in the management of a company, should, in accordance with

[42] [1994] 1 BCLC 716.

[43] *Ibid.,* at p.737.

[44] The courts, in interpreting s.300, were apt to exercise a discretion in favour of not imposing a disqualification order, despite having found that a director's past misconduct was of an unfit nature, in circumstances where there was positive evidence indicating that a director was successfully involved in the management of another company, see, for example, *Churchill Hotel (Plymouth) Ltd* [1988] BCLC 341.

section 9 of the CDDA 1986, have particular regard to the matters set out in both Part 1 and Part 2 of Schedule 1 to the CDDA 1986. However, as section 9 directs the court to have *particular regard* to the matters contained in Schedule 1, as opposed to confining the court to the matters mentioned in Schedule 1, conduct giving rise to a finding of unfitness may still be found in circumstances which are not directly governed by the Schedule. The matters mentioned in Part 1 of Schedule 1 require the court to consider whether the director, against which a disqualification order is sought, was responsible for:

(1) Any misfeasance or breach of any fiduciary or other duty in relation to the company.

(2) Any misapplication or retention by the director of, or any conduct by the director giving rise to an obligation to account for, any money or property of the company.[45]

(3) The extent of a director's responsibility for the company entering into any transaction liable to be set aside under Part XVI of the Insolvency Act (provisions against debt avoidance).

(4) The extent of a director's responsibility for any failure by the company to comply with any of the following provisions of the Companies Act 1985, namely,

    (a) section 221 (companies to keep accounting records);

    (b) section 222 (where and for how long records are to be kept);

    (c) section 228 (register of directors and secretaries);

    (d) section 352 (obligation to keep and enter up register of members);

    (e) section 353 (location of register of members);

    (f) section 363 (duty of company to make annual returns); and

    (h) sections 399 and 415 (company's duty to register charges which it creates).

It should be noted that former paragraph (g) (time for completion of annual returns (section 365) was removed from the above headings of relevant matters by the Companies Act 1989, section 139(4)).[46]

(5) The extent of the director's responsibility for any failure by the directors of the company to comply with

    (a) section 226 or section 227 (duty to prepare annual accounts), or;

    (b) section 233 (approval and signature of accounts).

---

[45] See, for example, *Re Looe Fish Ltd* [1993] BCLC 1160, where a director was disqualified under the CDDA 1986, s.8 following the allotment of shares to himself and a supporter. The shares were allotted for the purpose of maintaining his control over the company's affairs.

[46] SI 1990/1707.

The matters mentioned in Part 2 of Schedule 1 (where a company has become insolvent) are as follows

(6) The extent of the director's responsibility for the causes of the company becoming insolvent.

(7) The extent of the director's responsibility for any failure by the company to supply any goods or services which have been paid for (in whole or in part).

(8) The extent of the director's responsibility for the company entering into any transaction or giving any preference, being a transaction or preference —
   (a) liable to be set aside under section 127 or sections 238-240, of the Insolvency Act 1986; or
   (b) challengeable under section 242 or 243 of the Insolvency Act 1986 (or any rule of law in Scotland).

(9) The extent of the director's responsibility for any failure by the directors of the company to comply with section 98 of the Insolvency Act 1986 (duty to call creditors meeting in creditors voluntary winding up).

(10) Any failure by the director to comply with any obligation imposed on him by, or under any of the following provisions of the Insolvency Act 1986 —
   (a) section 22 (company's statement of affairs in administration);
   (b) section 47 (statement of affairs to administrative receiver);
   (c) section 66 (statement of affairs in Scottish receivership);
   (d) section 99 (directors' duty to attend meeting; statement of affairs in creditors' voluntary winding up);
   (e) section 131 (statement of affairs in winding up by the court);
   (f) section 234 (duty of any one with company property to deliver it up);
   (g) section 235 (duty to co-operate with liquidator, etc.).

In considering the matters mentioned in Schedule 1, the courts must, on a balance of probabilities, be satisfied that the nature of a director's conduct was sufficiently serious to justify his disqualification. The need to establish that a director's conduct was of a type which constituted a serious failure to have regard to a matter or matters mentioned in Schedule 1, or other matters related to a director's involvement in the managerial activities of a company, may be explained on the premise that the effect of a disqualification order may dramatically infringe upon the commercial liberty of a director in relation to his ability to pursue employment in the management of a company. Indeed, although disqualification proceedings are governed by the civil law, the courts have adopted a tendency to afford the respondent the benefit of any reasonable doubt in the course of the proceedings. For example, in *Re CU Fittings Ltd*,[47] Hoffmann J, in concluding that the conduct of the respondent did not fall within section 6, stated,

> "It may be that in January, or even earlier, a dispassionate mind would have reached the conclusion that the company was doomed. But directors immersed in the day to day task of trying to keep their business afloat cannot be expected to have wholly dispassionate minds. They tend to cling to hope".[48]

Accordingly, the courts have expressed an unwillingness to impose disqualification orders in situations whereby the fault element attached to a director's act or omission was attributable to business practices of an improper but nevertheless naive and imprudent standard. Indeed, in the majority of cases, the courts have emphasised that to justify the imposition of a disqualification order, a director's misconduct will need to be established at a level which is harmful to the public interest, whereby it conveys a clear exploitation of the privileges attributable to the limited liability status of a company. In the majority, if not all cases, the said exploitation will be exhibited by evidence of a wanton disregard and abuse of creditor interests, a director's recklessness or gross negligence in the management of a company, or an obvious and serious (if not persistent) failure to comply with provisions of the companies legislation.

The general approach of the courts to determining the question of a director's potential unfitness for the purposes of section 6 may be neatly summarised by a passage taken from the judgment of Browne-Wilkinson V-C, in *Re Lo-Line Electric Motors Ltd & Ors*[49] (albeit that this case was considered under section 300 of the Companies Act 1985). Browne-Wilkinson VC stated that,

> "The primary purpose of the section is not to punish the individual but to protect the public against the future conduct of companies by persons whose past records as directors of insolvent companies have shown them to be a danger to creditors and others. Therefore the power is not fundamentally penal. But if the power to disqualify is exercised, disqualification does involve a substantial interference with

---

[47] [1989] BCLC 556.
[48] *Ibid.*, at p.559.
[49] [1988] BCLC 698.

the freedom of the individual. It follows that the rights of the individual must be fully protected. Ordinary commercial misjudgement is in itself not sufficient to justify disqualification. In the normal case, the conduct complained of must display a lack of commercial probity although I have no doubt that in an extreme case of gross negligence or total incompetence disqualification could be appropriate".[50]

In *Re Sevenoaks Stationers (Retail) Ltd*,[51] the first case in which the Court of Appeal was asked to consider the appropriateness of a disqualification order under section 6, the court, in approving the above statement of Browne-Wilkinson VC, emphasised that a disqualification order should only be made where there was conclusive proof of conduct which established that a director's actions amounted to commercially culpable behaviour of a type viewed as constituting a threat to the commercial community. In seeking to equate commercially culpable behaviour with conduct of an unfit nature, the Court of Appeal also gave its approval to a statement taken from the judgment of Peter Gibson J, in *Re Bath Glass Ltd*.[52] In this case, Peter Gibson J stated that a director's unfitness would be established where,

"...a director has been guilty of a serious failure or serious failures, whether deliberately or through incompetence to perform those duties of directors which are attendant on the privilege of trading through companies with limited liability".[53]

The ability of a court to label a particular course of business malpractice as conduct constituting commercially culpable behaviour will obviously depend upon the individual circumstances and facts of a given case. It is therefore impossible to prescribe a minimum standard of misconduct to which the label "unfit conduct" can be equated. Indeed, in *Re Sevenoaks Stationers (Retail) Ltd*, the Court of Appeal noted that the true question to be tried in section 6 proceedings was a question of fact. Dillon LJ expressed the nature of this question as one which,

"...used to be pejoratively described in the Chancery Division as 'a jury question'".[54]

---

[50] *Ibid.*, at p.703.
[51] [1991] Ch 164.
[52] [1988] BCLC 329.
[53] *Ibid.*, at p.333.
[54] *Supra*, n.51, at p.176.

Accordingly, it would be inappropriate to attempt to formulate a precise and definite classification of specific instances of misconduct which may or may not warrant the court's imposition of a disqualification order under section 6. However, notwithstanding the improbable task of attempting to label specific instances of conduct as that which is of an unfit nature, it is possible to provide guidance, by way of case law examples, of the type of business conduct which may or may not be regarded as firm (albeit refutable) evidence of unfit conduct.[55] In so doing, it must be stressed that in determining the outcome of section 6 proceedings, the crucial factor to which the court will apply itself will be the seriousness of the conduct and not necessarily the type of conduct in question. The seriousness of a particular course of conduct will be measured in accordance with its perceived prejudicial effect on the public interest. The public interest will be measured in general terms but will undoubtedly include the interests of, for example, corporate creditors, the company's customers,[56] its employees, and company shareholders.

It is also interesting to note that in the majority of cases dealing with disqualification orders under section 6, it is rare to find proceedings which are commenced on the basis of just one count of alleged misconduct. Whilst it is possible for a court to disqualify a director on the premise of one complaint of misconduct, or to indicate that a specific complaint, taken from a number of complaints of misconduct, was sufficient to justify disqualification, it is more common to find that a director's unfitness will be established in relation to a series of delinquent acts.

8.5 Conduct typically relevant to disqualification

The question of whether a director's conduct was of an unfit nature will always be one of fact, to be determined from the individual circumstances of any given case. Other than where a director conducted the affairs of a company in a manner which is established to be of a serious and fraudulent nature, it is impossible to predict with any degree of certainty whether a director's conduct may be properly labelled as unfit conduct. However, notwithstanding the difficulty in defining the concept of unfit conduct, it is tentatively submitted that the following categories of conduct may be used as

---

[55] See, Dine "Disqualification of Directors" (1991) 12 Co Law 6.
[56] For an example of a case in which the court had to consider the effect of conduct in relation to the interests of a company's clients, see *Re CSTC Ltd* [1995] BCC 175. The misconduct in this case involved, amongst other matters, a misapplication and management of funds which were supposed to have been held on behalf of the company's clients. See also, *Secretary of State v. Van Hengel* [1995] 1 BCLC 545.

common examples from which a finding of director's unfitness to act in the management of a company may ordinarily be established.

8.5.1 *The persistent failure to comply with a statutory provision(s)*

Where a director fails (without due excuse) to comply with a requirement of the companies legislation, then *prima facie*, the director's activities will provide evidence of conduct which is of an imprudent nature. However, imprudent conduct will not in itself be conclusive of a finding of a director's unfitness to act in the management of a company. Accordingly, it is unlikely (save in exceptional cases, discussed below) that the courts will ever entertain disqualifying a director where the subject matter of a complaint is concerned with an isolated failure to comply with a statutory obligation. For example, where a director fails to file the company's annual accounts and that failure does not constitute a persistent breach of the company's accounting procedures, it is unlikely that non compliance with the statutory accounting procedures will justify the imposition of a disqualification order.[57] However, where a director persistently infringes statutory obligations,[58] for example, where a director fails to file accounts and returns in a manner which, by analogy with section 3 of the CDDA 1986, constitutes a persistent breach of the accounting requirements, then, in such circumstances, the courts will be more apt to quantify the breach to be of a sufficiently serious nature to justify making a disqualification order.[59] In *Secretary of State v. Ettinger, Re Swift 736 Ltd*,[60] Nicholls V-C remarked that,

> "Isolated lapses in filing documents are one thing and may be excusable. Not so persistent lapses which show overall a blatant disregard for this important aspect of accountability. Such lapses are serious and cannot be condoned even though, and it is right to have this firmly in mind, they need not involve any dishonest intent. . . . It may be that, despite the disqualification provisions having been in operation for some years, there is still a lingering feeling in some quarters that a failure to file annual accounts and so forth is a venial sin. If this is still so, the sooner the attitude is corrected the better it will be. Judicial observations to this effect have been made before, but they bear repetition".[61]

---

[57] See, for example, *Re ECM (Europe) Electronics* [1992] BCLC 814, *Re Wimbledon Village Restaurant Ltd* [1994] BCC 753.

[58] See, for example, *Secretary of State v. Arif* [1996] BCC 586.

[59] See, for example, *Re Cladrose* [1990] BCLC 204.

[60] [1993] BCLC 896.

[61] *Ibid.*, at p.900.

However, it should be noted that in some instances the consequences of a breach of a statutory provision may be perceived to be particularly detrimental to the public interest, to the extent that once breached, the contravention will inevitably be regarded as cogent evidence of a director's unfit conduct. A possible example of such a provision is in respect of a contravention of section 216 of the Insolvency Act 1986.[62] Section 216 precludes a director of a company in liquidation from becoming involved (for a period of five years) in the management of another company which seeks to adopt the name or a name closely associated with the insolvent company.[63] The seriousness of this form of misconduct will vary but in some cases it may be particularly detrimental to corporate creditors. The potential harm which this misconduct could cause was alluded to by Browne-Wilkinson V-C in *Re Travel Mondial (UK) Ltd*.[64] His lordship remarked that such misconduct was,

"... exactly the kind of behaviour by directors that is most to be deplored in that it is the use of the fabric of a limited company to deprive creditors of their money and simply to change cloak in which that is done from one company to the next. It is in my judgement a serious case of unfitness to be a director".[65]

8.5.2 *A breach of fiduciary duty*

A director occupies a fiduciary position in the company in which he holds office. In the case of a solvent company, a director's fiduciary duties will primarily be owed to the company's shareholding body. However, where a company becomes insolvent, the interests of corporate creditors will overshadow those of the company's shareholders with the result that the fiduciary duties of a director will be predominantly owed to the company's creditors.[66] As the degree of seriousness attributed to a director's misconduct must, for the purposes of disqualification under section 6, be such that the director's conduct was of commercially culpable behaviour, the fault element attached to the director's conduct may often be expected to exceed that which

---

[62] CA 1985, s.221 is another example of a statutory provision which, if contravened, may provide cogent evidence of unfit conduct. Section 221 is concerned with a company's obligation to keep internal accounting records. A failure to keep proper accounting records may result in a failure to appreciate the company's dire financial position, see, for example, *Re Firedart Ltd* [1994] 2 BCLC 340, *Re Park Properties Ltd* [1997] 2 BCLC 530. A further example is likely to include a breach of IA 1986, s.213 (fraudulent trading).

[63] This situation is sometimes referred to as the "Phoenix Syndrome", see Chapter 5.

[64] [1991] BCLC 120. See also, *Re Keypak Home Care Ltd (No. 2)* [1990] BCLC 440.

[65] *Ibid.*, at p.123.

[66] Discussed further in Chapter 1.

would substantiate a breach of fiduciary duty. Certainly, the imposition of a disqualification order would seem most inappropriate in instances where a complaint was concerned with a technical breach of duty or where the consequences of the breach of duty had but a marginal effect upon the company's financial position.[67] For example, where directors of a company improperly use corporate funds for the purpose of paying themselves excessive salaries, such an impropriety would not, unless the remuneration award was unduly excessive and totally out of all proportion to the company's financial standing,[68] be viewed to be of an unfit nature.[69]

In relation to disqualification proceedings under section 6, the courts will be particularly concerned with the effect of a breach of a director's fiduciary duty, where its effect is to prevent the repayment of corporate debts. Therefore, a director's breach of fiduciary duty may be equated with unfit conduct where it causes a company to fall into an insolvent state or where the breach exasperates a company's already insolvent position.[70]

8.5.3 *Reckless/negligent conduct which exceeds mere business folly*

Although conduct which is attributable to an act of mere commercial misjudgement or business folly will normally be discarded in the calculation of the appropriate standard by which a director's conduct may be properly construed to be of an unfit nature, such folly may be considered particularly relevant in circumstances where the consequences of the commercial misjudgement were of a reckless nature or where it exhibited the hallmarks of gross commercial incompetence. Therefore, where, for example, instances of business folly could have been reasonably avoided or minimised by a director seeking or following professional advice, the courts may consider the effect of the director's misjudgement in not obtaining, or following such advice, as indicative of a folly which was sufficiently serious to support a finding of the director's unfitness.

For example, in *Re GSAR Realisations Ltd*,[71] a director (S) was disqualified under section 6, following a finding that he had allowed a company to continue to trade in an insolvent state; S had, in effect, been guilty of wrongful

---

[67] See, for example, *Re Time Utilising Business* [1990] BCLC 568.

[68] See, for example, *Re CSTC Ltd* [1995] BCC 173, *Secretary of State v. Van Hengel* [1995] BCLC 545, *Re Dominion International Group plc (No. 2)* [1996] 1 BCLC 572, *Secretary of State v. Cleland* [1997] 1 BCLC 437, *Secretary of State v. Lubrani* [1997] 2 BCLC 115.

[69] See, for example, *Re Keypack Homecare Ltd (No. 2)* [1990] BCC 117.

[70] See, for example, *Secretary of State v. Lubrani* [1997] 2 BCLC 115.

[71] [1993] BCLC 409.

trading.[72] The court regarded the act of wrongful trading as sufficiently serious to justify the imposition of a disqualification order on the premise that S had completely ignored the recommendations of a report compiled by a firm of accountants. The firm of accountants, following a request from the company's principal creditor, had been commissioned by the company to offer guidance on how best the company might resolve its commercial difficulties. The report found the company's financial position to be very fragile but nevertheless recommended that the company's bank (the principal creditor) would be in a far more perilous position were the company to cease to be a going concern. Accordingly, the report suggested that the bank should, in an attempt to save the company, increase the company's overdraft facility.

Unfortunately, S chose to disregard the underlying finding of the report, namely that the company's financial position was in a critical state, and foolishly interpreted the bank's decision to increase the company's overdraft facility as being supportive of his own misconceived belief that the report had been incorrect to conclude that the company's financial stability was precarious. As a direct result of S's failure to observe the recommendations of the report and less than a year after the report had been finalised, the principal creditor was obliged to appoint an administrative receiver. In imposing a disqualification order for a period of three years, Ferris J remarked,

"... I have reached the conclusion that Mr Smith's [S] conduct... in relation to the charge of causing the company to trade after it became insolvent does demonstrate his unfitness to be concerned in the management of a company... Mr Smith's treatment of creditors... and his failure to accept in full the conclusions of the Hacker Young [the accountants] report manifest, in my judgement, a degree of indifference to his duties which constitutes unfitness.... In taking this line Mr Smith was, in my view, guilty of significantly more than commercial misjudgement. To my mind he was obstinately and unjustifiably backing his own assessment of the company's position and largely ignoring the assessment made by Hacker Young".[73]

Likewise, in *Re Hitco 2000 Ltd*,[74] the respondent, the sole director of a company, was disqualified under section 6 for a period of two

---

[72] See Chapter 4.
[73] *Supra*, n.71 at p.422.
[74] [1995] 2 BCLC 63. This case involved an appeal in relation to a decision of the county court in which the trial judge had refused to make a disqualification order under s.6.

years,[75] following misconduct which portrayed an obvious failure to acquaint himself with the financial affairs of the company. The respondent, who had been ignorant of the company's true financial position, had allowed the company to trade whilst it had been in an insolvent state. The respondent admitted that he would have failed to understand all the financial information had it been in his possession. In effect, this admission served to provide evidence of the respondent's recklessness in allowing the company to conduct its business affairs without employing a person properly qualified in the administration of the company's financial matters.[76]

8.5.4 *Commercial incompetence*

Although the courts may be reluctant to impose a disqualification order under section 6 where a director's culpability cannot be equated with an intentional or reckless act of mismanagement,[77] it is possible for a disqualification order to be imposed in circumstances where a director exhibits a marked degree of commercial incompetence.[78] In determining whether a director's conduct was of a commercially incompetent nature it is, once again, important to distinguish commercial incompetence from conduct exhibiting the hallmarks of mere business folly.[79] Commercial incompetence will be established where a director's standard of behaviour is, in relation to the circumstances of any given case, objectively determined to be of a standard which is significantly below a standard of behaviour one would reasonably expect to be exhibited by a company director.

In calculating the appropriate standard of behaviour against which a director's behaviour should be measured, the court will also take into account a director's level of skill and experience and the nature and type of company in which he held office. Accordingly, where, as in the case of *Re Continental Assurance Co Ltd*,[80] a senior employee of a bank (B) was

---

[75] However, it should be noted that the court indicated a willingness to entertain an application by the director for leave to take part in the management of another company. The court would entertain such an application providing the director ensured that, in respect of the other company, adequate financial controls were put in place.

[76] See also, *Re New Generation Engineers Ltd* [1993] BCLC 435.

[77] See, for example, the judgment of Sir Nicholas Browne-Wikinson V-C in *Re Lo-Line Electric Motors Ltd* [1988] Ch 477, at p.486.

[78] See the comments of Dillon LJ in *Re Sevenoaks Stationers Ltd* [1991] Ch 164, at p.184. See also *Re Park Properties Ltd* [1997] 2 BCLC 530.

[79] See Finch "Disqualification of Directors: A Plea for Competence" (1990) 53 MLR 385.

[80] [1997] BCLC 48. See also, *Re Linvale Ltd* [1993] BCLC 654. The test is an objective one and is comparable to the objective test employed in respect of both IA 1986, s.212 (see Chapter 2) and IA 1986, s.214 IA 1986 (see Chapter 4).

appointed to hold a non executive directorship in a company (Y) which had secured a substantial loan from B, one would have expected the director to have kept himself up to date with the financial affairs of the company. In *Re Continental Assurance Co Ltd*, the said director, who was also appointed to a non executive directorship in the company's subsidiary (C), failed to appreciate that C was lending money to Y, in order that Y could service its indebtedness to B. The loan transactions were used to finance share acquisitions contrary to section 151 of the Companies Act 1985.[81] In disqualifying the director for a period of three years, Chadwick J, commenting on the director's conduct, observed that,

"Those dealing with the client company are entitled to expect that external directors appointed on the basis of their apparent expertise will exercise the competence required by the Companies Act 1985 in relation to the affairs of the company of which they have accepted office as directors. The competence required by the 1985 Act extends, at the least, to a requirement that a director who is a corporate financier should be prepared to read and understand the statutory accounts of the holding company of the company of which he is a director — *a fortiori*, where he is a director also of that holding company — and satisfy himself that transactions between holding company and subsidiary are properly reflected in the statutory accounts of the subsidiary".[82]

In deciding whether a director's commercial incompetence was of a sufficiently serious nature to justify his disqualification under section 6, the court will, naturally, consider the extent of the prejudicial effect of the conduct.[83] Where, for example, a director's commercial incompetence results in a failure to keep proper accounting records and such a failure conceals the fact that a company was trading in an insolvent state, the consequences of the negligent conduct may be so prejudicial to the interests of corporate creditors that it justifies the court in imposing a disqualification order.[84]

As noted in the case of *Re Continental Assurance Co Ltd*, commercial incompetence giving rise to the imposition of a disqualification order under section 6 may be found in a situation where a director of a company abandons

---

[81] CA 1985, s.151 provides that it is unlawful for a company to give financial assistance to persons who are acquiring the company's own shares.

[82] *Supra*, n.80, at p.58.

[83] See, for example, *Re CSTC Ltd* [1995] BCC 175, where the interests of a company's customers was a paramount consideration.

[84] See, for example, *Re D D J Matthews (Joinery Design) Ltd & Anor* [1988] BCC 513, *Re City Investment Centres Ltd* [1992] BCLC 956, *Re Burnham Marketing Services Ltd* [1993] BCC 518, *Secretary of State for Trade & Industry v. Arif* [1997] 1 BCLC 34.

his responsibilities and duties to the company by failing to involve himself in the performance of managerial tasks which he would otherwise have been reasonably expected to perform. Accordingly, a person who holds office as a director must ordinarily involve himself in managerial tasks associated with the proper functioning of the company. A director who neglects such responsibilities or allows them to be improperly performed by others, may be made the subject of a disqualification order.[85]

Although, as will be observed, the courts have been somewhat inconsistent in their approach to the seriousness to be attached to a director's failure to involve himself in a company's managerial affairs, the decision of Neuberger J in *Re Park House Properties Ltd*[86] provides an apt illustration of the courts reluctance to ignore what may be described as an absolute failure of a director to involve himself in the managerial affairs of the company. In *Re Park House Properties Ltd*, a family controlled company was dominated by C, who acted as the company's managing director. The company's other three directors, C's two children and his wife, acted as non-executive directors but failed to involve themselves in the management of the company's affairs and indeed turned a blind eye to the irresponsible manner in which C allowed the company to trade. The three non-executive directors relied on C's experience and honesty and were content in the knowledge that the company employed an able and honest bookkeeper and that in financial matters C was apt to consult and follow the advice of the company's accountant. In effect, the three directors completely divorced themselves from the affairs of the company and showed no inclination to act as the company's appointed directors. As a consequence of this failure, Neuberger J observed that,

"As a matter of principle, it appears to me that it cannot be right that a director of a company involved in activities which justify a disqualification order against the director responsible for those activities can escape liability simply by saying that he knew nothing about what was going on. The court must enquire whether in the circumstances the failure to discover what was going on was attributable to ignorance born of a culpable failure to make enquiries or, where inquiries were made, of culpable failure to consider or appeciate the results of those enquiries: if such culpability is established then the court would have to go on to decide whether, in all the circumstances, the culpability was sufficient to justify the conclusion that

---

[85] Although the failure to perform managerial duties may give rise to the imposition of a disqualification order, the duration of the order will commonly be set at the minimum period of two years.

[86] [1997] 2 BCLC 530.

the conduct of the person concerned was such as to make him unfit to be concerned in the management of a company".[87]

In concluding that the directors' neglect justified the imposition of disqualification orders (in each case for a period of two years) Neuberger J stated that,

"The law imposes statutory and fiduciary duties on directors of companies, and even where, as here, the respondents recieved no payment, and any advice given to Mr Carter (C) would have been unlikely to have been acted on, they cannot escape from those duties. The three respondents' complete inactivity in relation to, and complete uninvolvement with, the runnning of the company, the financial problems of the company, the preparation and filing of accounts, and the decision to spend a substantial sum on the construction of the extension, seem to me to lead to the conclusion that, in the absence of special circumstances, they are unfit".[88]

Similarly, in *Re A & C Group Services Ltd*,[89] O, a director and majority shareholder of the company had, prior to suffering a period of ill-health, been actively involved in the management of the company's affairs. The company had been solvent during O's guardianship of its affairs. However, following O's illness, the fortunes of the company declined. In an attempt to halt the decline, another director (T) was appointed to the company's board. In appointing T, O believed (mistakenly, as it transpired) that T would instigate a buy out of the company's shares. As a direct result of O's illness, T, was in effect, given the day to day responsibility of running the company's affairs. Unfortunately, and indeed as a direct consequence of T's appointment, the company's fortunes declined to the extent that within a year of T's appointment, the company became insolvent. The company was subse-quently wound up with debts of over £413,000. T was disqualified for a period of six years for eight separate counts of misconduct. O was disqualified for two years.

The court disqualified O for a period of two years, on the basis that O should, at the very least, have been in a position to question T's managerial activities. O continued to act as a director of the company during the period of T's mismanagement of the company's affairs and from his contact with the company's solicitors and accountants had indeed expressed reservations about the company's financial position. In effect, O had failed to involve

---

[87] *Ibid.*, at p.554.
[88] *Ibid.*, at p.555-6.
[89] [1993] BCLC 1297.

himself in the management of the company's affairs at a time when he should have realised that intervention was necessary. Accordingly, O, having been aware of the company's financial difficulties, was obliged to shoulder his share of responsibility for the mismanagement of the company's affairs.

However, by contrast to the decisions in *Re A & C Group Services Ltd* and *Re Parkhouse Properties Ltd*, it should be noted that, in other cases, directors have escaped disqualification orders despite the fact that they have failed to involve themselves in the management of the company's affairs. The ability to so avoid a disqualification order may arise even in circumstances where, but for the director's breach of duty of care, serious corporate problems may have been mitigated, or indeed avoided. For example, in *Re Austinsuite*,[90] Vinelott J imposed disqualification orders against three directors of a company, (the three directors had been actively involved in the mismanagement of the company's financial activities) but refused, albeit with some hesitation, to impose a disqualification order against a fourth director of the company. The fourth director (S) had primarily been concerned with the manufacturing side of the company's business as opposed to the administration of the company's financial affairs.

In *Re Austinsuite* the company had traded at a time when it was insolvent and in doing so had incurred massive debts. As a member of the company's board, S had been in breach of his duty to the company in so far as he had failed to involve himself in the day to day management of its activities. He had, in effect, "turned a blind eye" to the financial chaos to which the company was privy and in doing so had acquiesced in the mismanagement of the company's affairs. However, in concluding that S should not be disqualified, Vinelott J opined that, for the purposes of section 6, a director's commercial misjudgement should not, without evidence of a lack of commercial probity, justify disqualification. The learned judge remarked that,

"In his own field Mr Stokes(S) was conscientious and hard-working and was throughout, I think, motivated by feelings of loyalty to the workforce. He should have pressed . . . for fuller disclosure of the company's financial position and should not have been as willing as he was then . . . to accept . . . that arrangements to raise working capital were in hand. However, I have come to the conclusion that, while he fell short of his duties as a director, his conduct was not such that would be justified in finding that he has shown himself unfit to be a director".[91]

---

[90] [1992] BCLC 1047.
[91] *Ibid.*, at pp.1065-6.

Further to the decision in *Re Austinsuite*, it should be noted that, in *Re Cladrose Ltd*,[92] Harman J held that it was possible for a director to evade a disqualification order, despite having breached his duty of care to the company, in circumstances where the director relied upon the skill and experience of a professional adviser. In *Re Cladrose*, the director in question was accused of persistently failing to ensure that the three companies with which he had been involved, provided annual returns and lodged accounts. The director explained this failure on the premise that he had relied upon the skill and experience of a qualified accountant. The court accepted this explanation, notwithstanding the fact that the said accountant had also been a director of the said three companies.[93]

Likewise, in *Re Wimbledon Village Restaurant Ltd*,[94] Michael Hart QC, sitting as a deputy High Court judge, found that W, a director of Wimbledon Village Restaurant Ltd, a company which had been put into creditors' voluntary liquidation with debts of over £327,000, should not be subjected to a disqualification order because W had never played an active part in the management of the company. W had become a director of the company as a means of protecting her own position as the unlimited guarantor of the company's overdraft. Michael Hart QC held that W had been entitled to rely on the skill and experience of the company's other two directors.

8.5.5 *Crown debts*

When considering a director's unfitness to act in the management of a company, the degree of importance to be attached to a company's non payment of Crown debts has often been the subject of some controversy. The controversy has centred around whether a company's inability to repay Crown debts should be viewed to be a more serious misdemeanour than a company's inability to repay ordinary trade creditors. The principal point of distinction between trade debts and Crown debts being that the Crown is a involuntary creditor of a company, whereas a trade creditor extends credit facilities to a company on a voluntary basis.

Crown debts incorporate debts by way of taxes, for example, VAT, and moneys payable to the state in the form of PAYE and National Insurance contributions. The non payment of Crown debts affects the public purse in so far as the failure to discharge Crown debts diminishes the pool of funds

---

[92] [1992] BCLC 204.

[93] It should be noted that the accountant was, however, made the subject of a disqualification order.

[94] [1994] BCC 753.

available for state expenditure.[95] At one time it was also contended[96] that the non payment of Crown debts, in the form of PAYE and National Insurance contributions, would have had a prejudicial effect on the interests of company employees. However, in *Re Sevenoaks Stationers (Retail) Ltd*,[97] the Court of Appeal dismissed this contention as one based upon the mistaken assumption that the Crown would not be responsible for carrying the burden of an employer's failure to collect and deliver contributions which were due to the Crown.

Notwithstanding a body of case law which lends support to the view that the non payment of Crown debts should be considered to be a more serious form of misconduct than the non payment of trade creditors,[98] it must be noted that in *Re Sevenoaks Stationers (Retail) Ltd*, the Court of Appeal opposed the contention that the non payment of Crown debts should automatically be taken to be of a more serious nature than the non payment of other corporate debts. Accordingly, the Court of Appeal declared that the crucial factor in assessing the seriousness of any debt was the nature of the debt and the company's culpability in relation to its non payment. In its assessment of the non payment of Crown debts, the Court of Appeal favoured the approach adopted by Hoffmann J in *Re Dawson Print Group Ltd*.[99] Here, the learned judge, commenting upon the relative importance of the Crown as an involuntary creditor stated that,

"...the Commissioners of Customs and Excise have chosen to appoint traders to be tax collectors on their behalf with the attendant risk. That risk is, to some extent, compensated by the preference which they have on insolvency. There is, as yet, no obligation on traders to keep such moneys in a separate bank account as there might be if they were really trust moneys. They are simply a debt owed by the company to the Revenue or the Customs and Excise. I cannot accept that failure to pay these debts is regarded in the commercial world generally as such a

---

[95] In *Re Wedgecroft Ltd* (7 March 1986, unreported) and *Re Cladrose Ltd* [1990] BCLC 204, Harman J regarded Crown debts as "quasi-trust" moneys, i.e. moneys which should be specifically held by a company for the Crown.

[96] See, for example, the comments of Harman J in *Re Cladrose Ltd*, *ibid.*, at pp.210-211.

[97] [1991] Ch 164.

[98] See also, *Re Lo-Line Electric Motors Ltd* [1988] Ch 477, where (at p.487) Nicholas Browne-Wilkinson V-C, commenting upon the seriousness of the non payment of Crown debts remarked that, "Although the Crown debts are not strictly trust moneys, ... I consider the use of the moneys which should have been paid to the Crown to finance a continuation of an insolvent company's business more culpable than the failure to pay commercial debts".

[99] [1987] BCLC 601.

breach of commercial morality that it enquires in itself a conclusion that the directors concerned are unfit to be involved in the management of a company".[100]

Although the Court of Appeal's decision in *Re Sevenoaks* emphasised that the non payment of Crown debts should not be viewed as evidence of any automatic assumption of a director's unfitness to act in the management of a company, but rather that their non payment should simply be viewed in a like manner to a company's non payment of ordinary trade creditors, the Court of Appeal did however provide an exception. The court stated that where a company chose to pay trade creditors who were pressing for the repayment of their debts ahead of passive creditors, (the Crown) then in such circumstances the non payment of the passive creditor should be viewed as a serious form of misconduct.[101] Likewise, the Court of Appeal concluded that a director who had expended corporate funds which were specifically kept for the purpose of discharging Crown debts,[102] should be presumed to have acted in an unfair and culpable manner.

8.6 Conduct falling outside the ambit of section 6

Where a court perceives that a director's imprudent conduct was undertaken without any form of malice or serious neglect, then such conduct will not justify the application of section 6.[103] For example, in *Re Bath Glass Ltd*,[104] Peter Gibson J concluded that two directors who had been a party to the company's wrongful trading (over a period of two years) should not be disqualified under section 6, because while their misconduct had been imprudent, it had not been undertaken with an intention to benefit themselves at the expense of the company's creditors. This finding as to the directors' honesty in the conduct of the company's affairs was substantiated, in part, by their willingness to make a firm financial commitment to the company by, for example, taking shares in the company in return for repaying the company's overdraft. In addition, the two directors had sought to act upon professional advice, had drawn up regular and meticulous (albeit inaccurate) business

---

[100] *Ibid.*, at pp.604-5.

[101] This reasoning was recently adopted by Neuberger J in *Re Verby Print for Advertising Ltd* [1998] 2 BCLC 23.

[102] See, for example, *Re Stanford Services Ltd* [1987] BCLC 607.

[103] However, it must be noted that conduct which is without any form of malice may still be regarded as conduct of an unfit nature, i.e. where it amounts to recklessness or gross negligence (discussed above).

[104] [1988] BCLC 329.

plans and genuinely and reasonably believed that the company would be able to trade itself out of its difficulties.[105]

Other than where a director of an insolvent company honestly and reasonably believed that the company was capable of trading itself out of its financial difficulties, a director's continued involvement in the affairs of the insolvent company will provide *prima facie* evidence of his unfit conduct. However, in such a case the presumption that his conduct was of an unfit nature may be overturned. For example, in accordance with the decision of Chadwick J in *Secretary of State v. Gash*,[106] a director of an insolvent company, who continues to hold office, despite realising the folly of existing corporate policy, may escape any charge of having acted in an unfit manner if it can be established that he objected to and took no part in, or had no responsibility for, the deployment of the ill-fated policy. Nevertheless, notwithstanding the decision in *Secretary of State v. Gash*, it is respectfully suggested that where a director is unable to influence corporate policy, with the result that the company continues to pursue its trading activities without recourse to the interests of its creditors, it may, in such circumstances, be more prudent for the director to resign his directorship so as to disassociate himself from any involvement in the affairs of the insolvent company.

The case of *Re Looe Fish*[107] provides a further example of the courts' desire to differentiate between, on the one hand, conduct of a serious nature meriting the imposition of a disqualification order and, on the other, conduct which, whilst imprudent, was not of a commercially culpable standard.[108] The case involved two separate instances of corporate misconduct on the part of the respondent. The first type of malpractice was a contravention of section 143 of the Companies Act 1985; namely the unauthorised return of capital to shareholders. The second malpractice was the allotment of shares for an improper purpose; the shares having been issued to ensure that the respondent retained control of the company.

In considering the breach of section 143 of the Companies Act 1985, Jonathan Parker J found that the respondent honestly believed (albeit mistakenly) that the company had the power to re-purchase its shares; a belief reinforced by the failure of the company's professional advisors to question

---

[105] On one occasion, the directors also failed to file the company's accounts. As this failure had only occurred in one financial year and had, in relation to the submission of accounts for the year in question, been subsequently corrected, it could not, when viewed in isolation, be regarded as serious misconduct.

[106] [1997] 1 BCLC 341.

[107] [1993] BCLC 1160.

[108] This case was concerned with disqualification proceedings pursuant to the CDDA 1986, s.8, under which it is also necessary for the court to establish a director's unfit conduct.

past re-purchases of capital. Therefore, taken in isolation, the contravention of section 143 was not of a sufficiently serious nature to substantiate an allegation of the respondent's unfitness to act in the future management of a company. However, the second instance of misconduct, namely, the issue of shares for an improper purpose, was of a more serious nature. The respondent manipulated his powers as a director of the company to benefit his own personal interests and in doing so the interests of the company as a whole were disregarded. According to the learned judge, the respondent had, in relation to this second instance of commercial misjudgement, displayed a "clear lack of commercial probity".[109]

8.7 Determining the length of the disqualification period

Where, under section 6, the court finds a director to be unfit to be concerned in the future management of a company, it will be obliged to impose a disqualification order. In accordance with section 6(4) of the CDDA 1986, the length of a disqualification order must be for a minimum of two years, the maximum period of disqualification being fifteen years. In determining the length of a disqualification period, the court must be mindful of the seriousness and extent of a director's misconduct and will also take into account the director's position within the management structure of the company. For example, where a director holds a senior executive position, or otherwise has a capacity to dictate a company's operations, it may ordinarily be presumed, in accordance with his position of responsibility, that the extent of his culpability (and the duration of any disqualification order) will be more pronounced than for officers of the company who exerted less influence in the management of the company's affairs.[110]

Where a director's misconduct involves dishonest conduct, it is more logical to assume that the disqualification period will be of a greater duration than had the misconduct been of a reckless or negligent manner.[111] In disqualification proceedings involving a serious degree of dishonesty or fraud,

---

[109] *Ibid.*, at p.1172.
[110] See, for example, *Re Peppermint Park Ltd* [1998] BCC 23, *Secretary of State for Trade & Industry v. Baker* (unreported 29 July 1997).
[111] See, for example, *Re Goodwin Warren Control Systems* [1993] BCLC 80. Here, it is interesting to compare the disqualification periods imposed against two directors of a company. One director was disqualified for six years because his misconduct involved a deliberate and self serving deception. The other director was disqualified for a period of three years on the basis that his conduct represented an inadequate response to difficult circumstances, it did not however involve a planned course of wrongdoings.

it is quite normal for the disqualification period to be set at a minimum of six years. This type of disqualification period may be imposed against a director who was responsible for fraudulent or dishonest conduct even in circumstances where the director had subsequently improved his conduct in respect of the management of another company. For example, in *Re T & D Services*,[112] a director was disqualified for a period of ten years, because prior to becoming involved in a successful enterprise, the director had shown a serious want of probity in relation to four other companies, in which he held directorships.

As disqualification periods are set by the judiciary in accordance with their perception of the relative seriousness of proved instances of unfit conduct, there is an obvious danger that disqualification periods may prove to be of an inconsistent nature. In *Re Sevenoaks (Retail) Ltd*,[113] the Court of Appeal, in an attempt to alleviate the potential for inconsistency, gave the following guidelines for setting disqualification periods:[114]

(1) The top bracket of disqualification for periods of over ten years should be reserved for particularly serious cases. Disqualification in this bracket could include those cases where a director who had previously been disqualified was the subject of a further disqualification order.

(2) The middle bracket of disqualification for a period between six to ten years should apply in serious cases but cases which did not merit the attention of the top bracket of disqualification.

(3) The minimum bracket of two to five years should be applied in cases where a director was found to be unfit to be concerned in the management of a company, but it was nevertheless established that the misconduct was not of a particularly serious nature.

In *Re Sevenoaks*, the director, a chartered accountant, had misconducted the businesses of five trading companies over a period of five years with the

---

[112] [1990] BCC 592.

[113] [1991] Ch 164.

[114] In giving the judgment of the Court of Appeal, Dillon LJ commented upon statistics which conveyed an obvious inconsistency in the judicial approach to disqualification periods and more so in respect of the approach as between the High Court and the County Court. The said statistics showed that in 1989, of 115 disqualifications made in the High Court under s.6, only one director had been disqualified for a period of more than five years, whereas of 123 orders made in County Courts, 18 involved disqualification for more than five years. In the first six months of 1990, of 79 disqualification orders made in the High Court under s.6, only four imposed disqualification periods for more than five years, whereas, out of 96 such orders made in the County Courts, 18 orders had been imposed for a period of more than five years.

result that the total net deficiency as regards company creditors was estimated to be some £559,000; this figure included a sum of £116,000 in respect of the non payment of Crown debts. The director conducted the businesses in a manner which amounted to commercially culpable behaviour. At first instance,[115] Harman J disqualified the director for a period of seven years. On appeal, the disqualification period was reduced to five years, thereby relegating it, in relation to the Court of Appeal's own guidelines, to within the lowest disqualification bracket. The Court of Appeal reduced the disqualification period on the basis that at first instance, Harman J had taken into account matters which he ought not to have considered. For example, Harman J had found that an allegation relating to a failure to keep proper accounting records had been made out against all five companies when in fact the evidence of the case pointed to the allegation having been made out against only one of the said companies.

Notwithstanding that some form of guidance in relation to appropriate disqualification periods would be beneficial to the lower courts, in reality, the Court of Appeal's guidelines are of little assistance. In effect, they amount to little more than common-sense generalisations. Indeed, at best they may be regarded as but a reminder to the lower courts of the need to adopt a greater degree of consistency in the imposition of disqualification periods. Other than for the Court of Appeal's example of when the first and most serious bracket of disqualification should apply, and the example provided by the disqualification period set in *Re Sevenoaks*, the guidelines are seriously devoid of examples from which the lower courts can draw some positive form of guidance. Although the imposition of a disqualification period will always be dependent upon the individual facts of a case, it is a pity that the court did not attempt to provide hypothetical examples (or case examples) of conduct which would be applicable to each of the three brackets. However, despite the fact that the Court of Appeal's guidelines serve little practical purpose, it must nevertheless be noted that it is commonplace to find reference to the guidelines within the judgments of the lower courts.

8.7.1 *The court's power to increase a disqualification period*

An appellate court may exercise a discretionary power to increase a disqualification period. For example, in *Secretary of State for Trade and Industry v. McTighe and Ega*,[116] the judge at first instance imposed disqualification periods against two directors, one director was disqualified for eight years, the other for a period of four years. On appeal, the

---

[115] [1990] BCLC 668.
[116] [1997] BCC 224.

disqualification periods were increased to twelve years and eight years respectively. Although the Court of Appeal conceded that a period of disqualification should ordinarily be decided according to the discretion of the judge in hearing of the initial application, the court held that an appellate court could not ignore an error of principle as to the manner by which a disqualification period was calculated.[117] In this case, the error had arisen as a result of the trial judge's failure to correlate the seriousness of the substantiated allegations within the correct bracket periods formulated in *Re Sevenoaks*.[118]

8.7.2 *Overturning a finding that a director's conduct failed to justify the imposition of a disqualification order*

For an appellate court to overturn a decision of a lower court in respect of a finding that a director's conduct was not of a serious enough nature to warrant the imposition of a disqualification order, the appellate court will be required to either dispute the factual findings of the lower court or, alternatively, will be obliged to disturb the conclusions of the lower court in relation to its assessment of whether the factual evidence merited the imposition of a disqualification order. In so far as the question of unfitness is akin to a "jury question",[119] an appellate court will be wary of disturbing a first instance decision. Further, unlike a hearing of first instance, the appellate court will not have the benefit of oral evidence and, therefore, will be unable to assess the personal demeanour and character of the director who is the subject of the proceedings.[120]

However, where the factual evidence of a case is not in dispute and the question of a director's fitness to act in the management of a company is, in reality, one to be determined on the basis of whether or not the technical requirements of section 6 have been met, then in such circumstances, a judge of first instance may not always be infallible in reaching a conclusion that the evidence presented in the course of the trial fell below a standard which merited the imposition of a disqualification order.

Re Grayan Building Services Ltd[121] was the first case in which the Court of

---

[117] See also, *Re Swift Ltd* [1993] BCLC 896.

[118] The substantiated allegations included the sale of the business of another company on deferred terms and without security, the payment of excessive remuneration, the failure to co-operate with the liquidator and official receiver in relation to the liquidation, the misappropriation of corporate assets, and the non-payment of Crown debts.

[119] *Per* Dillon LJ in *Re Sevenoaks Stationers (Retail) Ltd* [1991] Ch 164, at p.176.

[120] See, for example, the comments of Jules Sher QC, sitting as a deputy High Court judge, in *Re Hitco 2000 Ltd* [1995] BCC 161, at p.163.

[121] [1995] BCC 554.

Appeal were called upon to adjudicate on the correctness of a finding in which a director's conduct was adjudged to be of a standard which did not merit the necessity of a disqualification order under section 6. In this case, proceedings had been invoked against two directors. In the High Court, Arden J accepted that the two respondents had traded the company whilst it was insolvent, had failed to keep proper accounting records in accordance with section 221 of the Companies Act 1985, had failed in one year to file accounts in compliance with section 242(4) of the Companies Act 1985, and finally, had allowed two preferential payments to be made contrary to section 239 of the Insolvency Act 1986. Nevertheless, the learned judge found that, for the purposes of section 6, the respondents' conduct was not of an unfit nature.

Arden J explained her decision on the basis that although the respondents had been in breach of sections 221 and 242(4), the contravention was not of a sufficient gravity to establish a finding of unfitness. Of the preferential payments, Arden J held that as the liquidator had already pursued preference proceedings against the directors, it therefore followed that they had paid a sufficient penalty for the contravention of section 239. According to the learned judge, their conduct in respect of the past preferences could not be subsequently described as unfit conduct. In respect of trading the company whilst insolvent, the learned judge found that whilst the respondents had erred in their decision to allow the company to continue to trade, their error had been induced by a false, albeit at the time, reasonable expectation that the company would be able to trade itself out of its financial difficulties.

In overturning the decision of Arden J and disqualifying each director for a period of two years, the Court of Appeal found that the learned judge had erred in her assessment of the weight to be attached to the preference proceedings. The Court of Appeal forcefully disagreed with the approach taken by Arden J[122] in respect of the judge's finding that the successful pursuit of the preference claims would enable the preferential payments to be discarded in the determination of whether the directors conduct was of an unfit nature.[123] It is also to be noted that the court questioned the leniency of the test adopted by Arden J in relation to the allegation that the directors had been trading the company whilst in an insolvent state.[124]

---

[122] See the comments of Hoffmann LJ, *ibid.*, at p.576.

[123] Although the Court of Appeal in *Re Grayan Building Services Ltd* expressly rejected the idea that the successful recovery by the office holder of proceeds related to the preferences should result in such preferences not being considered in relation to the determination of the s.6 proceedings, it should be noted that a finding of a preference will not always result in the automatic assumption that a director's conduct was of an unfit nature, see, for example, *Re New Generation Engineers Ltd* [1993] BCLC 434.

[124] *Supra*, n.122.

8.8 Mitigation

In considering the length of a disqualification period or, in respect of section 17 of the CDDA 1986,[125] whether the court should grant leave to a person who has been made subject to a disqualification order, the courts are permitted to take account of mitigating factors.[126] The significance and effect of a mitigating factor will be dependent upon issues relating to the justice of an individual case. In considering the justice issue, the court must attempt to balance the respective interests of the respondent against the seriousness of the unfit conduct and its perceived threat to the public interest.

8.8.1 *Conduct in the course of disqualification proceedings*

A director's conduct in the actual course of the disqualification proceedings may, in appropriate circumstances, act as a mitigating factor if, for example, his conduct during the disqualification process enables the court to deal with the proceedings in a more efficient manner. Accordingly, by co-operating with the liquidator,[127] or as a result of admitting his responsibility for the alleged acts of misconduct,[128] it may be possible for a director to escape what would otherwise have amounted to a heftier disqualification period.

A further example of a mitigating factor which may exist in the context of the conduct of disqualification proceedings would be in a situation where there was a substantial delay in the proceedings, a delay which was caused as a result of a fault on the part of the Secretary of State or Official Receiver; the effect of which was to put the respondent director in jeopardy.[129] However, other than where a delay in disqualification proceedings is of a type to justify the court in staying proceedings,[130] the courts will be reluctant to accede to any argument that the delay merits a reduction in the disqualification period. The aforementioned approach is justified on the basis that section 6 requires the court to make an order where it is satisfied that a director's past conduct was of an unfit nature; logically, it would appear quite irrelevant that the date of the trial was some time after the instigation of the alleged misconduct.[131]

---

[125] Discussed at p.190.

[126] In *Re Sevenoaks Stationers (Retail) Ltd*, Dillon LJ stated that, "Matters of mitigation can of course be taken into account in favour of the director in fixing the period of disqualification". *Supra*, n.113, at p.177.

[127] See, for example, *Re Cargo Agency Ltd* [1992] BCLC 686.

[128] See, for example, *Re A & C Group Services Ltd* [1993] BCLC 1297.

[129] See, for example, the comments of Hoffmann LJ in *Re Grayan Building Services Ltd* [1995] BCC 554, at p.577.

[130] Discussed in Chapter 9, at p.220.

[131] See, for example, *Secretary of State v. Arif* [1996] BCC 586.

8.8.2 *The age of the director*

In at least one reported case, namely, *Re Melcast (Wolverhampton) Ltd*,[132] the age of a director was, of itself, considered to be a mitigating factor in the court's decision to impose a more lenient disqualification period than the nature of the director's conduct would ordinarily have warranted. In this case, Harman J disqualified a director, aged 68, for a period of seven years. The learned judge commented that the director's misconduct would, but for his age, have warranted a disqualification period of ten years. Harman J justified the leniency of the disqualification period on the basis that in protecting the public interest it was sufficient that the director be disqualified up until he reached the age of 75. The learned judge considered that at the age of 75, it was unlikely that the director would ever again be concerned in the management of a company. The lenient treatment of the director (Mr Boyd), was explained, in the following manner,

> "...he was...a person of such gross irresponsibility in his financial conduct that the public should be kept away from the risk of Mr Boyd's deprivations for a really substantial time. On the other hand he is a man of 68 rising 69 and the probability of his having much further say in connection with companies is small. Since I am not here to punish Mr Boyd but to protect the public for the future that must be a mitigating factor because the risk is much less".[133]

Although it is unlikely that a director of a company will ordinarily exceed 75 years of age, it is of course, quite possible for a person to act in the capacity of a company director at that age, and indeed beyond that age.[134] Accordingly, and with respect to the views expressed by Harman J, it does appear questionable whether the learned judge was correct to modify a disqualification period on the strength of what, in effect, was a presumption that the age of 75 would be a conclusive cut off point as to the respondent's desire or capacity to be concerned in the future management of a company.

By contrast to the approach adopted by Harman J in *Re Melcast (Wolverhampton) Ltd*, it is to be noted that in *Re Moorgate Metals Ltd*,[135] Warner J concluded that the age of the respondent director (in *Re Moorgate* the respondent was 70 years old) should not be considered as a mitigating

---

[132] [1991] BCLC 288.

[133] *Ibid.*, at p.298.

[134] However in accordance with CA 1985, s.293(1), a director of a public company or a director of one of its subsidiaries must retire at the age of 70, unless he continues to hold office with the approval of the general meeting.

[135] [1995] 1 BCLC 503. It is to be noted that *Re Melcast (Wolverhampton) Ltd* was not cited in the course of the proceedings.

factor in determining the length of the disqualification period. In *Re Moorgate*, the director was disqualified for a period of ten years. Warner J commented on the relevance of the director's age in the following terms,

"...I realise also that when the period of disqualification ends Mr Rawlinson will be 80. That does not, however, seem to me to be a reason for reducing the period".[136]

In relation to the age of a director being considered relevant to the calculation of a disqualification period, it is submitted that the approach adopted by Warner J is to be preferred to that taken by Harman J. The age of a director is a far too inconclusive and uncertain tool to be used in the calculation of a disqualification period. For example, at what specific age should a director be considered "over the hill"? Surely, in all cases, the disqualification period to be imposed by the court should be the one which most appropriately reflects the seriousness of the director's conduct, a matter which should be decided irrespective of the director's age.

8.8.3 *The state of health of a director*

Although it is suggested that the age of a director should not, of itself, be regarded as a mitigating factor in favour of a reduction in the disqualification period, it should be noted that a director's age may be a relevant consideration in a situation where the director is suffering from very poor health. For example, where it is established that as a result of a serious illness a director has a short life expectancy, a scenario which may be more apt in the case of a director of advanced years, then in such a case it would seem inappropriate to impose an excessive disqualification order. There would seem little point in imposing a long disqualification order against a person who is physically or mentally incapable of repeating his past misconduct.[137]

8.8.4 *The loss of a director's personal wealth*

A director who is to be disqualified may, in terms of the calculation of the disqualification period to be imposed, hope to be afforded some leniency

---

[136] *Ibid.*, at p.520.

[137] See, *Re Polly Peck International plc (No. 2)* [1994] 1 BCLC 574. Although this case was concerned with an application under CDDA s.7(2), i.e. for leave for the Secretary of State to bring proceedings out of time, as opposed to the determination of the length of a disqualification period, one of the factors which the court considered relevant in refusing the application under s.7(2) was the ill health and age of three of the four respondent directors; two of the said three directors were over 70 years old, the other was 60.

where prior to the collapse of the company, he sought to expend, or put at risk, his own personal funds in an attempt to secure the company's financial well being. The director's personal losses may be justified as a mitigating factor in the sense that such funds were voluntarily provided to aid the company's financial position. Indeed, as a result of the loss of a director's personal funds the court may consider that the director has, to some extent, already been penalised for his misconduct of the company's affairs.[138]

Nevertheless, it is arguable that as the purpose of the CDDA 1986 is to protect the public interest and more especially the commercial community from the future activities of incompetent directors, that any personal losses incurred by a director as a result of a company's failure should only be considered as a mitigating factor where the funds were used to reduce the burden of the company's debt and not, as is usually the case, where the funds were ploughed back to finance the company's failing trading activities. Indeed, the courts may not be willing to consider a director's personal loss as a justifiable ground for a reduction in the disqualification period in circumstances where the loss was sustained other than to benefit the collective interests of the company's creditors. For example, in *Re Firedart*,[139] Arden J refused to accept, as a matter of mitigation, the fact that the respondent director had personally guaranteed the company's overdraft, and in addition, had provided security over his own property to the bank. The learned judge found that the provision of the guarantee and security for the company's debts benefited only one of the company's creditors, namely the bank. As the company was grossly undercapitalised, Arden J considered that the respondent should have raised funds on the strength of his personal security, funds which could then have been injected into the company in return for an issue of share capital. The provision of capital would at least have provided the company's general pool of creditors with some realistic buffer following the company's decline into an insolvent state.

8.8.5 *Reliance on professional advice*

Although it may be possible for a director to escape the imposition of a disqualification order where the conduct of the company's affairs was

---

[138] See, for example, *Re Pamstock Ltd* [1994] 1 BCLC 716. Also see, *Re Swift 736 Ltd* [1993] BCLC 1, however note that on appeal [1993] BCLC 896, the director's disqualification period was increased from three to five years. Although the Court of Appeal recognised that the director had suffered personal losses the court took the view that at the original hearing, Hoffmann J, in considering the seriousness of the misconduct involved, had been far too lenient in the determination of the disqualification period.

[139] [1994] 2 BCLC 340.

attributable to his reliance on the skill and expertise of a professional advisor,[140] it is suggested that it is more probable that in such circumstances the reliance factor would be more aptly used to mitigate the length of the disqualification period.

8.8.6 *A director's success in the management of another company*

Where a director is found to have conducted the affairs of a company in a manner which justifies the court in imposing a disqualification order, the director will not, in so far as disqualification under section 6 is mandatory, be able to escape the consequences of the order by claiming that it should be nullified as a result of his favourable conduct in respect his management of another company. Nevertheless, the court may, as a matter of mitigation, take into account a director's conduct in the management of another company,[141] or may grant leave to the director in accordance with section 17 of the CDDA 1986.

8.9 An application for leave to act (section 17 CDDA 1986)

A court is obliged to make a disqualification order under section 6 where a director's conduct in the management of a company was of an unfit nature. Nevertheless, in some circumstances the court may be reluctant to fetter the future management activities of the director, especially where a director is successfully involved in the management of another company. In such a case the imposition of a disqualification order may adversely affect the interests of the successful company, causing prejudice to the company's employees and creditors. Accordingly, in such cases, the imposition of a disqualification order may cause more harm than good.

A possible solution to the mandatory effect of a disqualification order is to be found in the court's power to grant leave to a director to continue to act in the management of a nominated company(ies). This power is alluded to by section 1 of the CDDA 1986; the procedure for obtaining leave to act is contained within section 17 of the CDDA 1986. Section 17(1) provides that,

As regards the court to which application must be made for leave under a disqualification order, the following applies—

---

[140] See, for example, *Re Mcnulty's Interchange* [1989] BCLC 709, at p.712, *Re Cladrose* [1990] BCLC 204, at p.208, *Re Park Properties Ltd* [1997] 2 BCLC 530, at p.542.
[141] See, for example, *Re Pamstock Ltd* [1994] 1 BCLC 716.

(a) where the application is for leave to promote or form a company, it is any court with jurisdiction to wind up companies, and

(b) where the application is for leave to be a liquidator, administrator or director of, or otherwise to take part in the management of a company, or to be a receiver or manager of a company's property, it is any court having jurisdiction to wind up that company.

On a literal construction of section 17(1), it would appear implicit that the provision is invoked to enable a director (or other specified office holder) to apply to have an existing period of disqualification suspended, thereby enabling him to continue his managerial activities in another company. As such, section 17 appears to presume that the application for leave incorporates a distinct legal procedure from the procedure which governs proceedings under section 6. This presumption is confirmed by the wording of section 17(2), which states that either the Secretary of State, the Official Receiver (or the liquidator[142]) responsible for instigating disqualification proceedings must appear at a hearing concerned with the application for leave. At the hearing to consider the leave application, the Secretary of State, Official Receiver or liquidator, may call to the attention of the court any matter which appears relevant to the application and may also give evidence and call witnesses.

However, and notwithstanding the apparent intention of section 17, it is commonplace for the leave issue to be raised during the actual disqualification proceedings. Indeed, in *Secretary of State v. Worth*,[143] the Court of Appeal considered this to be a preferred practice. The court concluded that if a director was to be granted leave to continue to act in the management of another company, then it would be imperative that there would be as little a time lapse as possible to interrupt his involvement in the management of the other company. In addition, the Court of Appeal pointed out that in a practical sense, the time and preparation involved in a separate application for leave would inevitably result in the incursion of a higher level of costs than would otherwise have been the case had the application been dealt with at the time of the initial disqualification proceedings.

The practical effect of a grant of leave is the creation of a modified type of disqualification order, whereby a director is disqualified following a finding of his unfitness to act in the management of a company, but is nevertheless allowed to continue in the management of another company (or companies),

---

[142] A liquidator is not allowed to apply to instigate proceedings under s.6, although he may instigate proceedings under the CDDA 1986, ss.2-5.

[143] [1994] 2 BCLC 113.

as specified by the terms of the order. The director, is in effect, given a "second chance" in respect of the specified company on the premise that his involvement in the management of that company is considered to be in the public interest. While the adoption of a modified order may be considered justifiable in the sense that it protects the interests of the employees and creditors of the specified company, in reality, the nature of the order would appear to be quite contradictory to the required mandatory effect of section 6.

As the modified order is a practice which impliedly permits a director, with a dubious past history in the management of a company(ies) to, in part, escape the consequences of his past indiscretions, the adoption of the modified order must be applied with caution. Obviously, when considering whether to grant leave the court must ponder the likelihood of a director re-offending.[144] In an attempt to minimise the possibility of a director exploiting the modified order, the order will normally be made subject to specific conditions; notwithstanding that neither section 1 or section 17 provide the courts with a capacity to grant leave subject to such specific conditions.[145] For example, in *Re Gibson Davies Ltd*,[146] Sir Mervyn Davies, upheld an appeal by a director against the dismissal of an application for leave under section 17, but did so only on the understanding that the modified order would be made subject to nine conditions. The said conditions specified, *inter alia*, that the director should give an undertaking that he would set up proper financial controls in respect of the company's financial affairs, that he would restrict his own ability to obtain financial benefits from the company and that he would also be responsible for making proper accounting returns to the Registrar of Companies. Similarly, in *Re Majestic Recording Studios*,[147] a director was disqualified for five years but was allowed to continue to act as a director of a specified company, subject to an undertaking concerned with the director's involvement in the financial control and administration of the company's affairs. The principal condition attached to the section 17 order was that the specified company was required to appoint a further director to its board. The order specified that the director had to be approved by the court and further

---

[144] See the comments of Hoffmann LJ in *Re Grayan* [1995] BCC 554, at p.574.

[145] It would appear that the court may vary the conditions following an application by the respondent, see, for example, *Re Brian Sheridan Cars Ltd* [1995] BCC 1035.

[146] [1995] BCC 11.

[147] [1989] BCLC 1, a case heard under CA 1985, s.300. See also, *Re Lo-Line Electric Motors Ltd & Ors* (1988) 4 BCC 414, *Re Chartmore* [1990] BCLC 673, *Secretary of State v. Palfreman* [1995] 2 BCLC 301.

that he had to be a qualified chartered accountant.[148] The importance of determining whether there is a justifiable need to grant leave under section 17 was recently highlighted by the decision of Rattee J in *Secretary of State v. Barnett*.[149] In this case, the respondent, having been disqualified from acting as a director for a period of four years, sought leave to continue to act as a director of a specified company. The respondent had been disqualified as a result of instances of wrongful trading in respect of two previous companies. In effect, the specified company carried on the same business (a restaurant business) as the two defunct companies in which the respondent had acted as a director.[150] The respondent contended that in determining whether to grant leave the court should look to the needs of the specified company, the interests of which should, it was alleged, be divorced as a separate legal entity, from those of the respondent. In looking at the needs of the company, it was contended that as the respondent was the brain and driving force of the business, it followed that its continued survival was dependant upon him remaining as one of its directors. It was alleged that without the respondent as a director, the company's business would cease, resulting in prejudice to creditors and the loss of 14 jobs.

Although the respondent offered the court specific undertakings to prevent any repeat of his failings as a director of the two previous companies in which he had been involved, Rattee J refused to grant leave under section 17. In refusing leave, Rattee J came to the conclusion that, notwithstanding the specified company's status as a separate legal entity, the reality of the matter was that it would be unrealistic to distinguish the company's needs from those of the respondent, in so far as together with his wife, the respondent wholly owned and controlled the business. As the said business was in its third corporate incarnation and given the fact that the business, now in the guise of the specified company, was, as with the previous companies, grossly undercapitalised, Rattee J concluded that it was inappropriate for the court to protect the respondent's ability to continue to run the business with the advantage of a limited liability status and lower charges to tax. Rattee J accepted the argument advanced by the Secretary of State, namely, that the

---

[148] It should be noted that in *Re Cargo Agency Ltd* [1992] BCLC 686, Harman J refused to grant the applicant leave to act as a director of a specified company. Leave was refused on the premise that the applicant had not been appointed to a directorship of the specified company and therefore there was no immediate need to grant the application under s.17. However, a modified type of order was made in so far as the director was allowed to continue to be engaged as a general manager of the company.

[149] [1998] 2 BCLC 64.

[150] In carrying on the business under the same trade name "Mao Tai" as the previous two companies, the respondent, as a director of the specified company, was clearly acting in contravention of IA 1986, s.216; a point which was not lost on Rattee J.

business could be continued by the respondent as a sole trader or, alternatively, continued with his wife, as a partnership concern.[151]

Although the decision of Rattee J in *Secretary of State v. Barnett* may, in a liberal sense, be considered too be harsh, given that there had, for example, never been any suggestion that the respondent conducted any of the three companies in a fraudulent manner, it is submitted that the strict approach taken by the learned judge, is to be applauded. Once imposed, a disqualification order should not, in terms of its intention of protecting the public interest, be readily overturned unless there is cogent evidence to indicate that the benefit of granting leave under section 17 was a benefit couched in terms of the public interest as opposed to the interests of an individual applicant. Although the reasoning adopted by Rattee J, in respect of the "corporate entity" argument may, in a technical sense, be flawed,[152] the court's ability to lift the corporate veil, the effect of which is to treat a company and its human constituents as a single body as opposed to two distinct entities, is one which may often be born out of a necessity to provide justice and provide sense to the economic realities of a situation.

Finally, it should be observed that while a period of delay in disqualification proceedings cannot ordinarily (without proof of prejudice) be taken into account as a mitigating factor in relation to the length of a disqualification order, that nevertheless, it may be taken into account in respect of the court's decision in respect of granting leave under section 17.[153]

---

[151] This acceptance was subject to leave being granted under IA 1986, s.216(3).

[152] Under the common law, the ability of the courts to disturb the corporate veil is severely restricted, the justice of a situation is not ordinarily regarded as a justification for the veil to be lifted, see, for example, the recent decision of the Court of Appeal in *Ord v. Belhaven Pubs Ltd* [1998] BCC 607.

[153] See, for example, *Secretary of State v. Arif* [1996] BCC 586.

Chapter 9

PROCEDURAL AND EVIDENTIAL MATTERS PERTINENT TO THE CDDA 1986

9.1 Introduction

An in depth study into the disqualification of company directors would be incomplete without some specific and detailed consideration of the law governing the procedural and evidential matters which affect the disqualification process. This chapter is devoted to such matters, with particular reference to section 6 of the CDDA 1986. Procedural and evidential matters in respect of section 6 have generated an expanding volume of case law.

9.2 Proceedings under section 6

9.2.1 *Commencement of proceedings*

Section 7(1) of the CDDA 1986 specifies that, if it appears to the Secretary of State to be expedient in the public interest that a disqualification order under section 6 should be made against any person, an application for the making of such an order against that person may be made—

(a) by the Secretary of State; or
(b) if the Secretary of State so directs in the case of a person who is or has been a director of a company which is being wound up by the court in England and Wales, by the Official Receiver.

Accordingly, in respect of section 7(1)(b), where a director is subject to disqualification proceedings and the company in which he held office has already been wound up, the application should be made by the Secretary of State. However, following the decision of the Court of Appeal in *Re NP Engineering & Security Products Ltd*,[1] (reversing the first instance decision of

---

[1] [1998] 2 BCLC 208.

Harman J)[2] where such proceedings are mistakenly instigated by the official receiver, the proceedings may, in accordance with RSC Ord. 15, r.6(2), be continued by the Secretary of State, providing that the continuation of proceedings is deemed to be in the public interest.

In accordance with section 6(3)(a) of the CDDA 1986, the relevant court in which disqualification proceedings should be commenced against a director, in a situation where a company is being wound up by the court, is the court in which the company is being wound up.[3] The correct court is determined by reference to the date on which the disqualification application was first made.[4] Where disqualification proceedings are commenced in the wrong court, for example the County Court instead of the High Court, the proceedings may, if it is in the public interest, be transferred to the correct court.[5] Where a person who is, or who has been a director of a company which is being wound up voluntarily, then in accordance with section 6(3)(b), the relevant court will be any court having the jurisdiction to wind up the company.[6] In relation to disqualification proceedings involving a company which is made subject to an administration order, then the relevant court will

---

[2] [1995] 2 BCLC 585. Harman J considered that in such a case the official receiver would have no *locus standi* to instigate proceedings.

[3] The IA 1986, s.117 provides that the High Court has jurisdiction to wind up any company registered in England and Wales. However, where the amount of a company's paid up share capital, or capital which is credited as paid up, does not exceed £120,000, then the County Court of the district in which the company's registered office is situated will have a concurrent jurisdiction, with the High Court, to wind up the company.

[4] In accordance with CDDA 1986, s.6(3)(a), the relevant court in which a company is being wound up remains the relevant court for the purposes of disqualification proceedings, notwithstanding that, prior to the disqualification proceedings, the company had already been made the subject of a winding up order, see *Re The Working Project Ltd* [1995] 1 BCLC 226.

[5] See, for example, *Re NP Engineering & Security Products Ltd, supra,* n.1.

[6] See, *Re Lichfield Freight Terminal Ltd* [1997] BCC 11. In this case, it was contended by the respondent that the Birmingham County Court did not have the jurisdiction to hear disqualification proceedings brought against him in a situation where the company in which he had acted as a director had been wound up in the Walsall County Court. The respondent argued that s.6(3)(b) should be construed in a like manner to CDDA 1986, s.6(3)(a) & (c) so as to preclude disqualification proceedings being commenced in the court other than where the voluntary winding up order was made. This argument was rejected by Neuberger J on the premise that at the time when the disqualification proceedings were brought the court which had jurisdiction to wind up the company was the Birmingham County Court because that was the County Court which would have had the jurisdiction to wind up the company if a petition had been presented at the date the application to disqualify was made (the company which had originally been registered in the Walsall district had subsequently been re-registered in the Birmingham district). As the company's registered office had been within the Birmingham district for the six months prior to the application (in accordance with IA 1986, s.117(6)) the wording of s.6(3)(b) allowed any court to hear disqualification proceedings where that court had the jurisdiction to order a voluntary winding up order to be made against a company.

be the court in which the administration order was made. In any other case, for example, where an administrative receiver has been appointed to a company, or, where an application for the disqualification of a director is commenced after the dissolution of a company, then the relevant court will be, by virtue of section 6(3)(d), the High Court or, in Scotland, the Court of Session.

9.2.2 *The summons*

The Insolvent Companies (Disqualification of Unfit Directors) Proceedings Rules 1987[7] apply to applications for disqualification orders made by the Secretary of State or the Official Receiver.[8] Rule 2 of the 1987 Disqualification Rules specifies that where an application for a disqualification order is made in the High Court, it must be made by originating summons. Where an application for disqualification is made in the county court, it is to be made by an originating application. The Rules of the Supreme Court or County Court Rules apply accordingly, except where the rules provide otherwise.

Following the issue of the summons, a date will be set for the first hearing; this date must be not less than eight weeks from the date of the summons. The evidence in support of a summons must be filed when the application is issued. The evidence in answer of the summons must be filed within 28 days of service of the summons. The evidence in reply must then be filed within 14 days.

Rule 3.1 of the Disqualification Rules 1987 provides that,

"There shall, at the time when the summons is issued, be filed in court evidence in support of the application for a disqualification order; and copies of the evidence shall be served with the summons on the respondent".

Rule 3.2 of the Disqualification Rules 1987 provides that,

"The evidence shall be by one or more affidavits, except where the applicant is the Official Receiver, in which case it may be in the form of a written report (with or without affidavits by other persons) which shall be treated as if it had been verified by affidavit by him and shall be prima facie evidence of any matter contained in it".

---

[7] SI 1987/2023. Hereafter referred to as the Disqualification Rules 1987.
[8] The Disqualification Rules also apply to an application by the Secretary of State under the CDDA, s.8.

In the context of an Official Receiver's report, it should be noted that in *Re City Investment Centres Ltd*,[9] Morritt J held that third party statements which are contained in separate documents but which are annexed to the report, will not preclude the said documents from being treated as evidence of the matters of the complaint. This will be the case notwithstanding that if the report was to be treated as an affidavit, the documents would be inadmissible unless appropriate notices had been served under the Civil Evidence Act 1968. Morritt J, explained the matter in the following way,

"The addition of the words ['prima facie evidence of any matter contained in it'], were obviously intended to confer on the report an evidential status in addition to that which an affidavit would have. The words 'any matter' are entirely general and do not warrant any restriction to statements which would have been admissible under the Civil Evidence Act 1968 if the requisite notices had been served. In assessing the weight to be attached particular matter the court will no doubt consider the source of the Official Receiver's information as well as any other relevance and all the circumstances".[10]

Rule 3.3 of the Disqualification Rules 1987, states that,

"There shall in the affidavit or affidavits or (as the case may be) the official receiver's report be included a statement of the matters by reference to which the respondent is alleged to be unfit to be concerned in the management of a company".

As the courts will be concerned with an investigation of serious allegations of misconduct when considering applications under section 6, *prima facie* it would appear logical to assume that documentary evidence which fails to contribute to a finding of a director's commercial culpability should not, ordinarily, be placed before the court. In *Re Pamstock Ltd*,[11] Vinelott J suggested that in order to prevent a court from becoming overloaded with irrelevant evidence, complaints of a minor nature should not be included within the statement of matters, but should instead be contained within a separate schedule or addendum. Accordingly, this so called "irrelevant evidence" would not be viewed as evidence relevant to the subject matter of a complaint. In *Re Pamstock Ltd*, the wealth of evidence relating to a director's alleged misconduct referred to no less than ten separate companies.

---

[9] [1992] BCLC 956.
[10] *Ibid.*, at p.960.
[11] [1994] 1 BCLC 716.

Notwithstanding the great bulk of evidence brought against the director, Vinelott J held that the only relevant evidence to substantiate the director's unfitness was conduct in respect of his activities in just one of the said ten companies (the director's activities in respect of *Pamstock Ltd*).[12] According to the learned judge, those matters of complaint which were advanced in *Re Pamstock Ltd* and which were concerned with allegations of misconduct in relation to the director's involvement in the other nine companies, were matters which should have been reserved to a schedule or addendum. Without more, the learned judge found that the said complaints (in relation to the nine other companies) would have been too insignificant to justify the imposition of a disqualification order.

However, it is important to note that following the decision of the Court of Appeal in *Re Sevenoaks Stationers (Retail) Ltd*,[13] a disqualification period will only be fixed by reference to matters properly alleged against the director and not (as occurred in part, in the *Sevenoaks* case) on the basis of charges which were never made in the statement of complaint but which happened to be made out in the evidence given in the course of the disqualification proceedings.[14] Therefore, it would appear logical to assume that the applicant, in the majority of cases, will advance documentary evidence of a potentially non serious nature on the premise that while such evidence may not be of a particularly damning nature, it may, nevertheless, when combined with more cogent evidence, be of a type which could tip the scales in favour of the court making a disqualification order.

9.2.3 *Period of notice*

In accordance with section 16(1) of the CDDA 1986, the Secretary of State or, where applicable, the Official Receiver, "shall", when intending to apply for a disqualification order to be made by the court having jurisdiction to wind up a company, give not less than ten days' notice of that intention to the person against whom the order is sought. The person against whom the disqualification order is sought may, at the hearing of the application, appear and give evidence or call witnesses.

---

[12] In relation to the case of *Re Pamstock Ltd*, evidence of the director's misconduct included delays in the filing of accounts and returns, and the non payment of Crown debts. However, the principal justification for finding that the director's conduct was of an unfit nature was that the company had continued to trade whilst in an insolvent state, a state of affairs which had been directly attributable to the director's failure to devise an adequate system of management for the company.

[13] [1991] BCLC 325.

[14] See, for example, *Re Hitco 2000 Ltd* [1995] 2 BCLC 63, at p.69.

In applying a literal interpretation to the wording of section 16(1), one would assume that as the section prescribes that the applicant "shall" give a notice period of not less than ten days, then the said notice period must be viewed in terms of a mandatory requirement. Indeed, in *Re Jaymar Management Ltd*,[15] Harman J held that where a notice period did not satisfy the "not less than ten days" requirement, then the application should be struck out. In calculating the ten days requirement, Harman J held that the period of ten days was to be calculated exclusive of both the day on which the notice of intention was given and of the day on which the proceedings were issued. Accordingly, where, as a result of a failure to give the prescribed ten day notice, the two year period for the commencement of disqualification proceedings expired, (as occurred in *Re Jaymar*) then the applicant, if he wished to continue the proceedings, would, in accordance with section 7(2) of the CDDA 1986, be required to rely on an application for leave to commence proceedings out of time.[16]

Although the decision of Harman J in *Re Jaymar* was followed at first instance by Mummery J in *Cedac Ltd*,[17] the decision in that latter case was subsequently reversed by the Court of Appeal.[18] The Court of Appeal (Nourse LJ dissenting) held that it could not accept that non compliance with the ten day notice period in section 16(1) should result in the defective act being declared a nullity in circumstances where the breach of the provision resulted in a procedural wrong of but a trivial nature; the breach having caused the respondent no substantive prejudice. The Court of Appeal justified its decision on the basis that non compliance with the terms of the provision would, in the majority of cases, merely result in the suspension of the disqualification proceedings; in most cases the applicant would simply re-apply under section 16(1)[19] or, in a case where the application was out of time (beyond the two year period prescribed by section 7(2)) the applicant would be able to seek the court's leave to have the application heard. As such, the majority of the court were of the view that the suspension of the proceedings would confer no practical benefit to the disqualification process.

9.2.4 *The evidence in support of an application under section 6 CDDA 1986*

The evidence in support of an application for a disqualification order should, in accordance with Rule 3 of the Disqualification Rules 1987, be filed in court

---

[15] [1990] BCLC 617.

[16] Section 7(2) is discussed at p.201.

[17] [1990] BCC 555.

[18] *Re Cedac Ltd Secretary of State for Trade and Industry v. Langridge* [1991] BCC 148.

[19] Discussed at p.197.

and copies served on the respondent at the time when the summons is issued. Where the application is made by the official receiver, it may take the form of a written report as opposed to an affidavit; the report is considered *prima facie* evidence of any matter contained therein. The evidence in support of the application, be it by affidavit(s) or contained in the official receiver's report, must state the reasons by which the respondent's conduct is adjudged to have been unfit for the purposes of section 6.[20] Rule 5 of the Disqualification Rules 1987, specifies that the service of the summons and the respondents acknowledgement of service should be completed and returned to the court within 14 days from the date of the original service. The acknowledgement should indicate if the respondent intends to resist the terms of the application and whether or not he wishes to adduce mitigating factors for the purpose of pursuing a claim to reduce the period of disqualification. A respondent may resist the terms of the application on the premise:

(1) that he was not a director or shadow director of the company at the relevant time; or

(2) that his conduct was not of the type alleged, or that the alleged conduct does not make him unfit to be involved in the future management of a company.

Under Rule 6 of the Disqualification Rules 1987, the respondent has 28 days from the date of service of the summons to file any affidavit evidence in opposition to the application. If the applicant then wishes to file further evidence in response to the respondent's evidence it should be filed within 14 days from the receipt of a copy of the respondent's evidence. In *Re Rex Williams plc*,[21] the Court of Appeal held that the effect of rule 6 was that in circumstances where a respondent wished evidence to be taken into consideration, then such evidence had to be in the form of affidavits filed under rule 6, and that additional oral evidence in chief at the trial would only be allowed at the discretion of the court. It is to be observed that in respect of disqualification proceedings and in accordance with RSC Ord. 38, r.2(3), the court may order the cross examination of the deponents of affidavits. The failure of a particular deponent to attend court to give evidence may,

---

[20] See, *Re Sutton Glassworks Ltd* [1997] 1 BCLC 26 in which Chadwick J noted that where an applicant had not set out part of his case with sufficient clarity then in such circumstances it would be appropriate to strike out those parts of the applicant's evidence. Chadwick J recognised that in some cases this could lead to the striking out of the application in its entirety.

[21] [1994] 4 All ER 27.

at the court's discretion, result in that deponent's affidavit being deemed inadmissible.[22]

9.2.5 *The applicant's report*

Under section 6, the information which forms the basis of an application to disqualify a director will be contained within a report which, depending upon the type of insolvency proceedings, will be compiled by either the official receiver, the liquidator, the administrative receiver or the administrator of a company. In accordance with section 7(3), the compilation of the report is an obligatory requirement where the nature of a director's mismanagement of a company's affairs appears to correspond to the conditions set out in section 6(1). However, it must be stressed that whilst the views expressed in the report are influential to the determination of whether proceedings should be commenced against a director, they are not in any way to be regarded as conclusive of that matter, in so far as the decision to commence proceedings is exclusively vested in the Secretary of State.[23] Although a report which is made to the Secretary of State, pursuant to section 7(3), will ordinarily be crucial, albeit not conclusive to any subsequent disqualification proceedings, it is to be presumed that the report will be regarded as privileged information.[24] However, a contrary conclusion was reached by Sir Richard Scott V-C in *Re Barings plc*.[25] Here, Sir Richard Scott V-C held that notwithstanding that such a report was likely to be relied upon by the Secretary of State in the preparation of his case, its disclosure would not ordinarily offend the principle that communications between the Secretary of State and his legal advisers, relating to the institution or prosecution of disqualification proceedings, should be protected against disclosure.

---

[22] See *Re Dominion International Group plc* [1995] 1 BCLC 570.

[23] See, for example, *Re Pinemoor Ltd* [1997] BCC 708, *Re Park House Properties Ltd* [1997] 2 BCLC 530. In this latter case, the liquidator had originally recommended that disqualification proceedings be commenced against three non-executive directors of the company. In his evidence, the liquidator changed his mind explaining that he had sworn his affidavit under some time pressure. After the liquidator admitted his error, the three respondents sought to have the proceedings against them dismissed. However, notwithstanding the liquidator's change of heart, the Secretary of State was of the opinion that proceedings should continue. Neuberger J ruled that proceedings should continue on the premise that the triggering event for the bringing of proceedings was the Secretary of State's opinion as to whether it was expedient in the public interest to commence proceedings; the views of the liquidator were deemed to be irrelevant (see, *ibid.*, at p.535). This case is discussed further in Chapter 8, at p.173.

[24] See *Secretary of State v. Sananes* [1994] BCC 375.

[25] [1998] 1 BCLC 16.

In accordance with section 7(4) and in response to the contents of the report, the Secretary of State or the official receiver may request further information from the liquidator, administrator or administrative receiver of the company, or the former liquidator, administrator or administrative receiver of the company in relation to a person's conduct as a director. For example, books, papers and other records relevant to a person's conduct as a director may be called for. Where the Secretary of State or the official receiver's request for documents is not met, an order may, depending upon the discretion of the court, be obtained to compel the production of the requested documents.[26]

Although, in practice, the respondent will be given access to the documents which are relied upon in the affidavits sworn in support of the disqualification proceedings,[27] documents in the custody of the liquidator, administrator or administrative receiver of the company, or the former liquidator, administrator or administrative receiver of the company are not to be regarded as within the Secretary of State's power for the purposes of discovery. The discovery and inspection of documents provided by RSC Ord. 24, r.2 is not applicable because the Secretary of State does not have an absolute right to the possession of the documents. The Secretary of State's ability to take possession of any document in the custody of the liquidator, administrator or administrative receiver of the company, or the former liquidator, administrator or administrative receiver of the company is not an absolute right as it is dependent upon the court's discretion to order possession under reg. 6(2) of the Insolvent Companies (Reports on Conduct of Directors) Rules 1996.[28] Accordingly, the Secretary of State is not responsible to the respondent for collating, labelling or copying documents held in the custody of the liquidator, administrator or administrative receiver of the company, or the former liquidator, administrator or administrative receiver of the company.[29] However, where the official receiver is responsible for instigating disqualification proceedings, that is, in a case where a company is being wound up by the court, then in relation to the said company, the official receiver will

---

[26] See reg. 6(2) of the Insolvent Companies (Reports on Conduct of Directors) Rules 1996 (SI 1996/1909). Note that under reg. 6(3) the court's order may provide that all the costs of, and incidental to, the application will be borne by the person to whom the order is directed.

[27] Despite the fact that a specified document(s) may have been referred to in evidence presented by the Secretary of State, the court may order that the production of the document(s) be refused in circumstances where the document(s) in question is considered unnecessary for the purpose of disposing of the matter fairly, or for saving costs, see *Re Polly Peck International plc v. Nadir (No. 3)* [1994] 1 BCLC 661.

[28] (SI 1996/1909).

[29] See, *Re Lombard Shipping and Forwarding Ltd* [1992] BCC 700.

already have custody of all documents relevant to the disqualification proceedings and as such the respondent may be entitled to its discovery in accordance with RSC Ord. 24, r.2.

9.2.6 *Leave for the extension of the period of application*

Section 7(2) of the CDDA 1986 provides that other than where the court grants leave for the extension of the period in which an application for disqualification is to be made, an application to disqualify a person under section 6 may not be made more than two years after the day on which the company, in which the person acted as a director, became insolvent. In accordance with section 6(2) a company becomes insolvent when it is put into liquidation, administration or administrative receivership. Following the Court of Appeal's decision in *Re Tasiban Ltd*,[30] the two year period prescribed in section 7(2) runs from the happening of the first of the events mentioned in section 6(2). For example, where an administrative receiver is appointed to a company but is subsequently replaced by the official receiver, the official receiver will not be permitted to proceed with an application under the terms of section 7(2), if that application was commenced more than two years after the appointment of the administrative receiver; it may therefore be quite irrelevant that the application was commenced within two years of the appointment of the official receiver.[31]

Although the procedure for granting leave under section 7(2) is not contained in the CDDA 1986 or the Disqualification Rules 1987, the courts have not construed section 7(2) as a limitation provision. Therefore, a failure to comply with an application for proceedings within the prescribed time period does not automatically give rise to the proceedings being time barred. Indeed, section 7(2) provides that the two year period applies "other than where the court grants leave". The justification for allowing applications beyond the two year period is obvious in the sense that the lapse of the two year period should not be viewed as an automatic escape route to evade the disqualification process. The protection of the public interest is the vital consideration in determining any application and the expiry of the prescribed two year period should not distort that consideration.

In *Probe Data Systems (No. 3)*,[32] the Court of Appeal concluded that when considering an application under section 7(2), the court should be mindful of

---

[30] [1990] BCC 318; approving the decision of Peter Gibson J (1989) 5 BCC 729.
[31] See, *Re Tasiban Ltd, ibid.*
[32] [1992] BCLC 405. See also, *Secretary of State v. Cleland* [1997] 1 BCLC 437, *Secretary of State v. Morrall* [1996] BCC 229.

the length of the delay in commencing proceedings and any explanation advanced by the Secretary of State in respect of the delay. Further, the court should consider the strength of the case against the respondent and the degree of prejudice which might be suffered by the respondent as a result of the delay. However, it is important to note that a delay in the application will not, of itself, be regarded as a sufficient justification for the court to refuse an application for leave. Accordingly, a lengthy delay or/and an unsatisfactory reason for the delay in commencing proceedings may not, in the light of overwhelming evidence against a director, be accepted as a sufficient justification to refuse an application for leave.[33] Indeed, other than where the application is, in all probability, likely to fail,[34] the courts will readily grant leave.

In the absence of specific statutory guidelines, the courts have sought to identify an appropriate procedure for an application for leave. In *Re Probe Data Systems Ltd (No. 2)*[35] Millet J, after considering and rejecting leave procedures under RSC Ord. 11, r.1, and the Family Provision Act 1966, found that the most appropriate procedure for an application for leave under section 7(2) would be for the applicant to apply in the first instance ex parte to the registrar. Millet J considered that where the registrar viewed the application to be *prima facie* appropriate, then directions should be given to the applicant to serve the respondent with the summons or other application and evidence in support. The respondent would then, if he so wished, be entitled to argue that leave should not be granted; in such a case the burden of proof would remain with the applicant.

However, in *Re Crestjoy Products Ltd*,[36] Harman J applied a different procedure.[37] Harman J considered that the procedure adopted by Millet J in *Re Probe Data Systems* was too cumbersome, to the extent that he viewed it to be unnecessary for the Secretary of State to be asked to present the application on the premise that it would only proceed where it was *prima facie* considered to be appropriate. Harman J was of the opinion that the Secretary of State would not seek an application for leave other than in an

---

[33] This has been confirmed by the Court of Appeal in *Re Copecrest Ltd* [1993] BCC 844, and more recently in *Secretary of State for Trade and Industry v. Davies* [1997] BCC 235. A lengthy delay will not be accepted as sufficient justification to defeat the application in circumstances where, for example, the delay did not materially affect the respondent's ability to defend himself, see, for example, *Re Blackspur Group plc* [1996] BCC 835.

[34] See the comments of Balcombe LJ in *Re Tasiban (No. 3)* [1992] BCC 358, at p.362.

[35] [1990] BCLC 574.

[36] [1990] BCLC 677.

[37] The procedure adopted by Harman J was based upon the leave procedure under the Leasehold Property (Repairs) Act 1938 (as amended by the Landlord and Tenant Act 1954).

appropriate case. The learned judge considered the correct procedure to be as follows:

"The Secretary of State should issue an originating summons for leave, serving it and making good before the judge (possibly before the registrar) with the respondent to the summons for leave present, following which, if leave was granted, the disqualification summons would then be issued. Either way the originating summons for leave to issue proceedings for disqualification will have been disposed of ".[38]

The procedures applied by both Millet J in *Re Probe Data Systems* and Harman J in *Re Crestjoy Products Ltd* have subsequently been accepted for the purpose of an application for leave under section 7(2).[39] However, applications have normally followed the procedure advanced in *Re Crestjoy Products Ltd*; this is not surprising in the sense that in terms of the public interest, this procedure is more efficient and less time consuming.

9.3 Disqualification orders made in the absence of the respondent

In accordance with rule 8(1) of the Disqualification Rules 1987, the court may impose a disqualification order against a respondent, irrespective of whether he appears at trial and notwithstanding that he has failed to file evidence in compliance with rule 6 of the Disqualification Rules or complete and return the Acknowledgement of Service. However, under rule 8(2) of the Disqualification Rules 1987, any disqualification order made in the absence of the respondent may be set aside or varied by the court on such terms as it thinks just. As yet it is somewhat unclear as to the precise manner in which the courts will exercise the discretion under rule 8(2), although in *Re Electronic Messaging plc, Official Receiver v. Wilson*,[40] Chadwick J held that rule 8(2) should be construed in a like manner to RSC Ord. 35, r.2; in so far as the substance of both rules were very similar. In *Shocked v. Goldschmidt*,[41] the Court of Appeal advanced propositions in relation to the approach to be

---

[38] [1990] BCLC 677, at 680.

[39] Indeed, the courts are likely to strike out an application other than where it is framed in accordance with the procedures adopted in the said two cases, see, for example, *Re Westmid Packing Ltd* [1995] BCC 203.

[40] At the time of writing, this case was unreported, it was heard on the 17 July 1996 and is discussed at length by Mithani in (1996) 18 *Insolvency Lawyer* 2.

[41] (1994) *The Times*, 4 November.

taken by the courts in applying RSC Ord. 35, r.2. For example, it was stated that a respondent would normally be bound by the court's decision where he had failed to avail himself of the opportunity of appearing at the hearing in circumstances where his absence was deliberate as opposed to accidental, or where, irrespective of the reason for the respondent's failure to attend the hearing, any re-trial would involve a consideration of matters of fact which the court had already investigated.

9.4 Disqualification proceedings by way of summary procedure (the *Carecraft* procedure)

In circumstances where the facts relating to a director's conduct are not disputed and where both the Secretary of State and the respondent are willing to allow the case to be dealt with on the understanding that a disqualification order be made for a period falling within one of the brackets specified in *Re Sevenoaks Stationers (Retail) Ltd*,[42] then disqualification proceedings may be dealt with by a summary form of procedure. This procedure was first sanctioned by Ferris J in *Re Carecraft Construction Co Ltd*.[43] Following the *Practice Direction No. 2 of 1995*,[44] whenever a *Carecraft* application is made, the applicant must:

(a) except in simple cases where the circumstances do not merit it or when the court otherwise directs, submit a written statement containing in respect of each respondent any material facts which (for the purposes of the application) are either agreed or not opposed (by either party); and

(b) specify in the written statement or, a separate document, the period of disqualification which the parties will invite the court to make or the bracket (ie 2-5 years; 6-10 years; 11-15 years) into which they will submit that the case falls.

In *Secretary of State v. Rogers*,[45] the summary procedure was approved by the Court of Appeal, albeit that it was made subject to some technical qualifications. Although the Court of Appeal welcomed the objective of the summary procedure, because where applicable, it would inevitably save the court and the parties involved in the proceedings the time and expense that

---

[42] [1991] Ch 164.
[43] [1994] 1 WLR 172.
[44] Issued by Sir Richard Scott V-C [1996] 1 All ER 442.
[45] [1996] 2 BCLC 513.

would have otherwise been incurred had the application proceeded to a full trial, the court was reluctant to remove a judge's discretion to overturn the findings of an agreement entered into between a director and the Secretary of State in respect of the agreed facts of a case and an agreed disqualification period. Whilst the Court of Appeal considered it unlikely that a judge would ever wish to interfere with such an agreement, it felt that it would be inappropriate to sanction a judge, on the basis of a pre-trial agreement, to always be obliged to concur with the findings of the agreement. Nevertheless, the Court of Appeal held that where the *Carecraft* procedure had been adopted, it would be wrong for a judge to pursue allegations other than those contained in the agreed facts. For example, in *Secretary of State v. Rogers* the Court of Appeal found that the trial judge had been wrong to speculate on whether, if disputed facts had been heard (here the disputed facts related to the director's honesty) in conjunction with the agreed facts, then a finding as to the seriousness of the director's conduct may have been affected.

As it is important for a court, in applying the *Carecraft* procedure, to restrict itself to the alleged statement of facts, it is to be observed that it is imperative that any facts which are advanced by the applicant should be precise in the sense that they should leave no room for any form of speculative interpretation. Accordingly, where, for example, a director's conduct was of a dishonest nature, it would be inappropriate for the agreed statement of facts to allege that the director knew or ought to have known of the impropriety of his conduct. This statement would be far too ambiguous for the court to conclude that the director's admission of misconduct was based upon the acceptance that his conduct had been of a dishonest nature.[46]

9.4.1 *Disqualification by way of a formal undertaking*

The advantage of a procedure whereby a director is capable of being precluded from taking part in the future management of a company[47] without the necessity of the court having to impose a disqualification order would, in the light of an ever expanding number of pending disqualification cases, ease the pressure upon the courts and, as such, advance the *Carecraft* procedure in a most logical way. Indeed, in *Secretary of State v. Rogers*,[48] Sir Richard Scott V-C, reiterated his belief,[49] first pronounced in *Practice Direction No. 2*

---

[46] See, *Re P S Banarser & Co (Products) Ltd* [1997] BCC 425.
[47] To include the other restrictions set out in the CDDA 1986, s.1(1).
[48] *Supra*, n.45.
[49] *Ibid.*, at p.518.
[50] [1996] 1 All ER 442.

of 1985,[50] that, in circumstances where both the Secretary of State and the respondent agreed that the respondent's conduct warranted a prescribed period of disqualification, it would be sensible if the period of disqualification could be imposed by a formal undertaking, as opposed to a court order.

In so far as the DTI's Insolvency Service's Disqualification Unit[51] must cope with an ever expanding case load (for example, as of 31 March 1997, DTI statistics showed that approximately 1,100 cases, involving 2,160 respondents were awaiting prosecution), the creation of a scheme which would permit the disqualification of a director without the necessity of a court hearing may be the only viable solution to prevent a collapse in the disqualification system. Further, in so far as such a scheme would diminish the amount of cases which proceeded to court, it would also reduce the costs incurred in the prosecution of disqualification cases.

However, notwithstanding that a system which sanctioned disqualification by means of a formal undertaking would, undoubtedly, ease the pressure on both the Insolvency Service and the judicial system, the acceptance of such a procedure may be open to criticism on the basis that it would be contrary to the public interest to have matters relating to the accountability of unfit company directors, dealt with in a manner absent of judicial scrutiny. Although the *Carecraft* procedure is, in itself, little more than a judicial "rubber stamping" of an agreement reached between the Secretary of State and the respondent director, it does at least maintain the role of the court as the guardian of justice and the protector of the public interest. Indeed, it is possible (albeit unlikely) for a court to overturn the terms of a *Carecraft* agreement.

In addition, a procedure which permitted formal undertakings could also be criticised on the premise that, in terms of the public interest factor, it may not be perceived as a sufficiently effective deterrent in comparison to a court imposed disqualification order. For example, it could be argued that the adverse publicity surrounding a court hearing and the cost associated with the disqualification process are factors which may serve to deter others from engaging in serious corporate malpractice. Moreover, should a director who has been privy to serious commercial misconduct be allowed to escape the public humiliation of a court hearing?

Despite the above criticisms, the introduction of a statutory procedure to permit the use of formal undertakings could, if used in well defined circumstances, be of great advantage in those cases where the public interest would not be served by having a formal court hearing. Indeed, it does appear

---

[51] The administration of corporate insolvency in England and Wales is carried out by the Insolvency Service as an Executive Agency of the Department of Trade and Industry (DTI).

logical to conclude that the Insolvency Service, the judiciary and the courts time would be more efficiently taken up in relation to the prosecution of cases in which there was a real dispute to be tried. Accordingly, an obvious example of where the use of formal undertakings would be beneficial would be in relation to cases where a director, having admitted he was a party to commercially culpable behaviour, agreed to a life long abstention from acting in any of the capacities prescribed by section 1(1) of the CDDA 1986.

Notwithstanding that the formal undertaking procedure is, as yet, devoid of any statutory recognition,[52] the courts have, in three reported cases,[53] already stayed disqualification proceedings following a respondent's undertaking to refrain from acting in the future management of a company. In the said cases, the judicial acceptance of a formal undertaking was justified because the ill health and age of the directors in question warranted a conclusion that it was highly improbable that they would ever again act in the management of a company. However, it is important to note that the actions were stayed and not dismissed, that is, it remained open to the Secretary of State to apply for the stay to be lifted if, for example, it was subsequently discovered that the terms of the undertaking had been broken. In the most recent of the aforementioned cases, namely, *Secretary of State for Trade and Industry v. Cleland*,[54] Lloyd J stayed disqualification proceedings against one of three respondent directors on the basis that the director in question, who was 60 years old, had suffered serious medical problems to the extent that he had been advised never to work again. Indeed, as a result of the medical advice the director had sought early retirement and as such felt able to assure the court that he had no intention of ever seeking future employment as a part of the management of a company.

Following the decision of the Court of Appeal in *Secretary of State v. Davies*,[55] it may now be said that the validity of a judicial procedure which recognises formal undertakings as an alternative option to the imposition of a

---

[52] On February 11 1998, the Minister for Competition and Consumer Affairs announced that legislation would be passed to introduce a statutory procedure regulating formal undertakings. However, given the constraints of Parliamentary time, it is impossible to predict when such legislation will be enacted.

[53] See, *Re Homes Assured Corporation plc* [1996] BCC 297, *Re Company X Ltd* (unreported) and *Secretary of State v. Cleland* [1997] BCC 473.

[54] *Ibid*.

[55] [1998] BCC 11. The Court of Appeal confirmed the first instance judgment of Rattee J [1997] 1 WLR 710. Rattee J refused to agree to stay disqualification proceedings by way of a formal undertaking on the premise that an undertaking did not (at present) have the effect of a disqualification order. Further, the learned judge was able to distinguish those cases in which an undertaking had previously been given on the basis that in *Davies*, the director was not suffering any form of ill-health.

disqualification order will only be permitted in a situation where a director is willing to agree to make a full admission to the effect that his misconduct was of a commercially culpable nature (it is to be noted that full admissions were not made in any of the three cases noted above).

In *Secretary of State v. Davies*, the appellant's undertakings were intended to reflect an order under section 1 of the CDDA 1986, save that they exceeded the terms of such an order, in the sense that the duration of the undertaking was to be for the lifetime of the appellant. The appellant also offered to pay the costs of the Secretary of State's proceedings up to the date on which the undertakings had been offered. The appellant contended that, given his undertakings, it would be an abuse of process of the court for the Secretary of State to continue disqualification proceedings at a substantial cost to the public purse.

In refusing to accept the appellant's undertakings, Mummery LJ, (delivering the judgment of the court) held that, although the ultimate object of the CDDA 1986 was the protection of the public interest, the means by which that object was to be achieved was embodied in a carefully structured, detailed statutory scheme and, accordingly, to give effect to the type of undertaking on offer, would have been quite contrary to the spirit of that scheme, which provided that the imposition of a disqualification order was dependent upon a factual finding that a respondent's conduct was of an unfit nature. In this case, the appellant had purported to offer undertakings without any admission of the facts. Further, Mummery LJ noted that this case could be distinguished from previous cases in which undertakings had been accepted on the premise that the appellant had failed to adduce any evidence of his state of health or of any other exceptional matters which may have persuaded the Secretary of State that it was not expedient to continue with the proceedings.

In addition, his lordship observed that, the factual basis for making disqualification orders, whether in the contested context or in the summary uncontested procedure (sanctioned in *Re Carecraft Construction Co Ltd*), ensured that orders, determined on findings or admissions of unfitness, had a real deterrent effect and, in that way, afforded public protection against the threat of persons who were unfit to enjoy the privileges of limited liability. Mummery LJ approved the comments of Ferris J in *Re Carecraft Construction Co Ltd*,[56] where the learned judge stated,

"In disqualification proceedings . . . there is no scope for the parties to reach an agreement and then ask the court to embody their agreement in a

---

[56] [1994] 1 WLR 172.

consent order. The court itself has to be satisfied, after having regard to the prescribed matters and other facts which appear to be material, that the respondent is unfit to be concerned in the management of a company; and the court itself must decide the period of disqualification if it decides to make a disqualification order".[57]

Furthermore, Mummery LJ noted that the CDDA 1986 did not, in relation to undertakings, expressly provide the court with a discretion to apply common law and equitable remedies to restrain future misconduct (injunction or undertaking in lieu of injunction), to punish for disregard of restraints imposed by court order (contempt powers of imprisonment or fine), to compensate for past loss unlawfully inflicted (damages) or to restore benefits unjustly acquired (restitution). His lordship went on to observe that,

"The Secretary of State has reasonable grounds for adopting the position that adherence to the statutory scheme is in the interest of the promotion of good regulation: the possibility of contempt proceedings for breach of an undertaking is unlikely to have a deterrent effect equivalent to a charge and trial of a criminal offence of breach of a disqualification order; there is no statutory procedure for the policing and variation of, or for the grant of leave to act under, an undertaking; even if an extra-statutory procedure could be devised, it would be difficult to operate in the absence of findings or admissions of fact made at the time when the undertaking was given; the 'indebtedness undertaking' to the court cannot provide the same degree of protection for creditors as the statutory protection in s.15(1)(b) of the 1986 Act; there is no statutory authority for the entry of undertakings on the register of disqualification orders".[58]

Although Mummery LJ concluded that the appellant's undertaking was inappropriate for the purposes of complying with the current statutory procedure as represented by the CDDA 1986, it is pertinent to note that his lordship considered that the appellant's real dispute was with Parliament, in so far as Parliament had failed to provide the legislative machinery for consent undertakings as a means to summarily disposing of cases against directors who were unwilling to contest the proceedings or to concede any of the allegations made against them. In relation to legislative reform, it is interesting to observe the comments of Rattee J, who at first instance, had stated,

---

[57] *Ibid.*, at p.181.
[58] *Supra*, n.55, at p.14.

"I would recommend...that the Secretary of State give consideration to the possibility of introducing amending legislation, under which an agreement between a director and the Secretary of State, or the official receiver, as to the disqualification period to be applied to the director, be given the same effect as a court order imposing the disqualification period. If the director is willing to bar himself from acting as a director for a period that the Secretary of State, or official receiver, regards as being sufficient to protect the public interest, I do not see why time and money should be expended by the insistence on bringing the case before the court. It would, of course, be necessary to provide for these agreements, of the sort that I have described, to be entered on a suitable register at Companies House, and for a breach by the director of any such agreement to attract the same criminal sanctions as a breach of a court imposed disqualification order attracts. Legislation could provide easily for this. A very great advantage, in the procedure of the sort that I have described, would be the saving of costs. The Department of Trade and Industry, very naturally, seeks (and usually obtains) an order for its legal costs to be paid by the director against whom a disqualification order has been made. If the summary *Re Carecraft* procedure is used, the costs, though less than in a disputed case, may still be substantial. I would hazard a guess that in a number of cases a director may contest the disqualification proceedings in order to postpone, for as long as possible, his liability to meet an order for costs that he may have no easy means of paying".[59]

9.5 The ability to strike out disqualification proceedings

9.5.1 *For want of prosecution*

For a respondent to succeed in having disqualification proceedings struck out for want of prosecution, it must be established that he suffered serious prejudice as a consequence of periods of inordinate and inexcusable delay in the course of the proceedings.[60] Whether a period of delay is inordinate and inexcusable will be a matter for the court's discretion, although it is clear from the decided cases[61] that the Secretary of State will need to be especially

---

[59] *Ibid*.

[60] This requirement is applicable to civil proceedings, a fact confirmed by the House of Lords in *Birkett v. James* [1978] AC 297.

[61] See, for example, *Re Noble Trees Ltd* [1993] BCLC 1185, *Official Receiver v. B Ltd* [1994] 2 BCLC 1.

diligent where, following a substantial delay in the commencement of proceedings (proceedings should be commenced within two years of the company's insolvency, see section 7(2) of the CDDA 1986) the prosecution of the action is subject to further delay.[62]

In accordance with civil law procedures, serious prejudice will be established in the conventional sense where, a delay in the proceedings results in a negation of the respondent's expectation of a fair trial, or alternatively, where the delay results in some other form of prejudice which is of a sufficiently serious nature to justify the curtailment of proceedings. Although a delay in the pendency of proceedings is likely to cause a respondent anxiety, and uncertainty, the courts will not ordinarily classify this type of prejudice as being of a sufficiently serious nature to justify the proceedings being struck out.[63]

Despite the fact that an inordinate delay in progressing the proceedings may result in witnesses being unable to accurately recollect events pertinent to the trial of the proceedings, the courts have, somewhat surprisingly, been reluctant to hold that this type of prejudice will damper the respondent's ability to attain a fair trial, nevertheless they have been willing to find that prejudice of this type may be of a sufficiently serious nature to justify the proceedings being struck out. Indeed, the courts' identification of serious prejudice is predominantly restricted to instances whereby a delay in proceedings adversely affected the respondent in respect of the efficiency of the proceedings. A further example of circumstances which may, following an inordinate delay in the advancement of proceedings, be likely to give rise to a finding of serious prejudice would be where documents, crucial to the

---

[62] In *Secretary of State for Trade & Industry v. Martin* [1998] BCC 184, at p.187, Judge Weeks QC defined the term "inordinate" to mean materially longer than the time the courts or the profession would regard as acceptable. In the majority of the decided cases, an inordinate period in the delay of the proceedings has been established where, as from the time of the company's insolvency (as defined by CDDA 1986, s.6(2) there was a delay of three to four years (or more) in prosecuting the case. It is to be noted that following the decision of the European Commission of Human Rights in *EDC v. UK* [1988] BCC 370, an inordinate delay in proceedings may be viewed to constitute a violation of art. 6(1) of the European Convention for the protection of Human Rights and Fundamental Freedoms. Article 6(1) provides that in the determination of a person's civil rights and obligations "... everyone is entitled to a ... hearing within a reasonable time". In the instant case there had been a delay of almost seven years. Although it was stated that the proceedings should be assessed in accordance with the complexities of the case and whilst it was acknowledged that the instant case was a particularly complex one, it was held that the period of delay constituted a breach of art. 6(1) in so far as the UK authorities had no persuasive reason for why the delay had occurred.

[63] See, for example, the comments of Lord Griffiths in *Eagil Trust Co Ltd v. Pigott Brown* [1985] 3 All ER 119, at p.124.

preparation of the respondent's case and held by the Secretary of State, were misplaced or lost.[64]

In *Re Manlon Trading Ltd*,[65] Evans-Lombe J sought to extend the conventional approach to determining serious prejudice on the basis that disqualification proceedings affected the public interest and were therefore quite distinct from other civil law matters. Accordingly, he considered that matters other than those represented by the conventional approach should be examined when calculating whether an inordinate and inexcusable delay in the proceedings resulted in serious prejudice. According to the learned judge, serious prejudice was also capable of being established in circumstances where:

(a) following an inordinate and inexcusable delay in the pendency of the proceedings, the respondent's business reputation was seriously and unnecessarily disturbed; or

(b) in a situation where the effect of an inordinate delay in the proceedings rendered the imposition of a disqualification order futile in so far as an expected disqualification period would, had it been imposed, have been for no longer a duration than the period of the delay between the commencement and the trial of the proceedings.

On this latter point, Evans-Lombe J commented that,

"... by contrast with private litigation where the plaintiff's interest in enforcing his private rights against the defendant remains constant, the interest of the public in obtaining the protection of the disqualification order must diminish as time passes from the commencement of the relevant liquidation and certainly from the commencement of the proceedings to disqualify".[66]

The learned judge's extension of the conventional identification of serious prejudice was deemed unacceptable by a majority of the Court of Appeal[67] (Peter Gibson LJ and Beldam LJ), although it is to be observed that the minority view, represented by Staughton LJ, was supportive of the approach adopted by Evans-Lombe J. Although a majority of the court disapproved of

---

[64] Obviously, much will depend upon the importance attached to the reports. In some cases a respondent may be adequately compensated for the loss of reports, etc., by a reduction in the period of his disqualification, see for example, *Re Dexmaster Ltd* [1995] 2 BCLC 430.

[65] [1995] 1 BCLC 84.

[66] *Ibid.*, at p.99.

[67] [1995] 1 BCLC 578.

the manner in which Evans-Lombe J had departed from the conventional approach, they nevertheless accepted that it was possible to modify the conventional approach. The conventional approach was capable of modification in the sense that, following an inordinate and inexcusable delay in the advancement of proceedings, an inherent form of prejudice, in the guise of a director's inability to actively participate in the management of a company, could, in appropriate circumstances, be considered as a subsidiary and mitigating factor in the court's assessment of whether the respondent suffered serious prejudice.[68] However, it is to be stressed that the majority expressed a reluctance to accept that a prolonged delay which resulted in a complaint based solely on the effect of the pendency of proceedings in relation to a director's ability to retain or attain a managerial position would ever justify a finding of serious prejudice. The majority justified this finding on the basis that serious prejudice had to be established to an extent whereby it negated the necessity for a trial, a consideration which would always need to be weighed against the public interest of continuing to pursue the proceedings.

In relation to the contention advanced by Evans-Lombe J, to the effect that a delay in progressing the proceedings was capable of rendering the imposition of a disqualification order futile, the majority of the Court of Appeal considered that such a contention should be fervently rejected. The majority was adamant that in protecting the public interest, it was essential that a director's present unfitness should be determined by a consideration of his past misconduct[69] and further, that the significance of imposing a disqualification order would not diminish as time went by.

The observations of the Court of Appeal in *Re Manlon Trading Ltd* were recently considered by Judge Weeks QC in *Secretary of State for Trade & Industry v. Martin*.[70] From the facts of this case, the learned judge identified five instances of prejudice:

(1) As a result of the delay of some 18 months in the prosecution of the case, the memories of witnesses had faded.

(2) The respondent had been suspended from one position of employment and had been rejected when applying for other positions.

(3) After the date on which the trial of the action should properly have

---

[68] The Court of Appeal confirmed that the disqualification proceedings should be struck out. The majority of the court justified this finding on the basis that, together with the inherent prejudice, the delay in proceedings would have adversely affected the memory of witnesses.

[69] See also, *Secretary of State v. Arif* [1996] BCC 586. However, note that in *Re NP Engineering & Security Products Ltd* [1995] 2 BCLC 593, Harman J found that it would be inappropriate to impose a disqualification order where the period of delay exceeded the expected duration of an order.

[70] [1998] BCC 184.

been commenced, the respondent's bank issued possession proceedings. Further, the respondent, as a consequence of his dire financial position, was forced to obtain loans and sell items of property.

(4) Had the trial proceeded on time the respondent would have been in a position whereby he would have qualified for legal aid, this position had now changed.

(5) Finally, the respondent suffered family problems which were exasperated by the delay.

In accordance with the decision of a majority of the Court of Appeal in *Re Manlon Trading Ltd*, of the five instances of prejudice, clearly only the first two could be considered to support a finding of serious prejudice in the modified conventional sense. However, in so far as the other considerations (although not point 5) related to the economic welfare of the respondent, it is arguable that the learned judge was correct to consider them, providing of course, they were considered as mitigating factors and not issues of substantive prejudice.

In relation to determining whether the proceedings should be continued in terms of the public interest, Judge Weeks QC considered that there were three relevant factors to consider. First, the strength of the case against the respondent, in that there would be little benefit in pursuing the action if it turned out to be a hopeless case. The learned judge considered the evidence of the case to be persuasive although not watertight. Secondly, the seriousness of the charges, because if the allegations of misconduct were very serious then in terms of the public interest there would be a greater need to pursue the proceedings. The learned judge concluded that the respondent would, had the trial proceeded, been subject, at the maximum, to a penalty of five years. Finally, Judge Weeks considered that it was important to consider the public interest in terms of the manner in which the Secretary of State had sought to prosecute the action, in the sense that it was not in the public interest to secure a disqualification order at all costs. The learned judge considered that the Secretary of State had presented the case in a less than proper and objective manner. For example, the Secretary of State had omitted material favourable to the respondent and had made sweeping and unsubstantiated statements about the respondent's alleged misconduct.

On the basis of the evidence before him and in attempting to balance the prejudice factor against public interest considerations, Judge Weeks QC concluded that he should strike out the proceedings. However, notwithstanding the validity of the decision, the method by which it was attained may, in some respects, appear questionable. For example, in relation to the public interest factor, the learned judge sought to consider the strength of the Secretary of State's case and the likely disqualification period which may have been imposed had the proceedings advanced to trial. It is to be noted that while both these considerations were in accordance with those adopted in the first instance decision of Evans-Lombe J in *Re Manlon Trading Ltd* (considerations which were also approved by Staughton LJ), the majority of the Court of Appeal had considered that deliberations of such a nature were inappropriate to the determination of an action to strike out disqualification proceedings.

9.5.2 *Awaiting the outcome of other proceedings*

Although the courts will stay disqualification proceedings in the case of pending criminal proceedings[71] they will not do so where the evidence adduced in support and in defence of disqualification proceedings relates to the subject matter of some other form of civil proceedings. The justification for the courts refusal to await the outcome of other civil proceedings before acceding to hear the disqualification proceedings is explained by the fact that the primary purpose of proceedings is to protect the public interest. Matters in which the protection of the public interest are deemed to be an important consideration outweigh any subsidiary interest an individual may have in respect of some other form of private litigation.[72]

On a slightly different, but nevertheless related point, it is interesting to note that where allegations in the course of disqualification proceedings have been established and the very same allegations also form the substance of other civil proceedings commenced by the disqualified director, then in such circumstances the court may find that the pursuit of the subsequent civil proceedings would constitute an abuse of process. For example, in *Re Thomas Christy Ltd (in liquidation)*,[73] a former director of Thomas Christy Ltd sought an order to reverse the decision of the company's liquidator who had rejected a claim for a debt allegedly owed by the company to the said director. The liquidator also sought a declaration that the director had been guilty of misfeasance under section 212 of the Insolvency Act 1986. Prior to the action under section 212, the director had been disqualified pursuant to section 6 of the CDDA 1986. The matters raised in the disqualification proceedings concerned the director's dishonest use of corporate funds. In the section 212 proceedings, the director alleged he had been unfairly dismissed from office and disputed the assertions of dishonest conduct which had been made out against him in the disqualification proceedings. Jacob J found that the "massive overlap" between the two sets of proceedings was such that it

---

[71] See, for example, *Re Blackspur Group plc* [1995] BCC 835.
[72] See, for example, *Re Rex Williams Leisure plc* [1993] BCLC 568.
[73] [1994] 2 BCLC 527.

would have been an abuse of process to allow any re-litigation concerning the director's service contract and his claim for unfair dismissal. The evidence relating to the unfair dismissal issue was, in all material respects, the same as that which had been advanced in the disqualification proceedings.

9.5.3 *Staying or suspending a disqualification order pending an appeal*

The High Court or Court of Appeal have the power under their inherent appellate jurisdiction[74] to stay or suspend a disqualification order under the CDDA 1986, notwithstanding the fact that the CDDA 1986 makes no specific provision to that effect. This power was confirmed in *Secretary of State v. Bannister*,[75] where the Court of Appeal refused to accept the Secretary of State's argument that Parliament in failing to confer the court with an express power to stay or suspend proceedings, had therefore never intended the power to be available in disqualification proceedings.[76] The Court of Appeal took the contrary view, namely that if Parliament had intended to exclude the power it would have made express provision to that effect within the CDDA 1986. The Court of Appeal favoured this approach notwithstanding the court's ability under section 17 of the CDDA 1986 to alleviate the effect of an order, pending appeal, by giving a person leave to act as a director. The court considered that the grant of leave could, in extreme cases, be insufficient to counter a situation where proceedings in the lower court had been blatantly questionable and where the very existence of the disqualification order was likely to cause irreparable harm to the person against whom it had been made.

It should be noted that although the decision of the Court of Appeal in *Secretary of State v. Bannister* confirms that both the Court of Appeal and High Court have an inherent jurisdiction to stay or suspend a disqualification order pending appeal, it is uncertain and indeed unlikely that the County Court has such a power under the County Courts Act 1984.

---

[74] Under the Supreme Court Act 1981, s.49(3).

[75] [1995] 2 BCLC 271.

[76] The Secretary of State's argument was supported by comparing other forms of legislation which regulate disqualification procedures and which specifically include an express provision to enable the court to stay or suspend a resulting order, see, e.g. Licensing Act 1964, ss.100 and 101, Gaming Act 1968, ss.24 and 25, Road Traffic Offenders Act 1988, ss.37, 39 and 40.

9.6 Conduct which may give rise to other proceedings

Where a court which is involved in hearing a disqualification case finds that a director's conduct was of a type which could have justified other proceedings (other than disqualification proceedings) for irregularities connected to the director's management of a company's affairs,[77] is the court correct to conclude that where such proceedings have not been commenced against the director, then the irregular conduct in question was of a type which obviously fell below an appropriate standard to warrant the proceedings? In which case, if the conduct failed to merit the attention of separate proceedings, would the court be correct to assume that the significance of the conduct should be ignored for the purposes of determining proceedings under section 6?

In seeking to answer the above questions, it is submitted that the court should not ignore instances of misconduct solely on the premise that the misconduct did not form the substance of a distinct and separate action. Indeed, the explanation for an absence of proceedings may be unconnected to the seriousness of the conduct and the likelihood of sustaining a successful action. For example, the liquidator of a company may decide that although the commencement of wrongful trading proceedings would, in all probability, prove to be a successful exercise, that such an action would nevertheless prove futile because of the director's poor financial position and his inability to meet the terms of any order. In addition, although conduct may, when taken in isolation, not be serious enough to warrant separate proceedings, it could nevertheless, when combined with other forms of misconduct, be sufficient to tip the balance in favour of a finding that a director was unfit to act in the management of a company.[78]

---

[77] For example, conduct which involved transactions at an undervalue, preference transactions, misfeasance proceedings or wrongful trading.

[78] In *Re Bath Glass* [1988] BCLC 329, Peter Gibson J formed the opinion that irrespective of whether an action may or may not arise against a director in some other context, the conduct which forms the basis of that other action should not be discarded in the court's assessment of whether a director's overall conduct was of an unfit nature. However, note the decision of Mervyn Davies J in *Re ECM (Europe Electronics) Ltd* [1992] BCLC 814, where the absence of proceedings against the respondent for a preference transaction was held to be interpreted as confirming that the complaint had been unsubstantiated. The preference complaint was therefore considered to be unworthy of consideration in the context of the s.6 proceedings.

9.7 The standard of proof

As a contravention of section 6 does not invoke a penal sanction, the civil standard of proof will be employed to determine whether the evidence of a case justifies the imposition of a disqualification order. Therefore, for the purposes of section 6, a director's unfitness must be established "on a balance of probabilities". The civil standard of proof necessarily involves the confirmation of a director's culpability at a standard which is less onerous than the standard which would be applicable to criminal proceedings. However, as allegations made in the course of disqualification proceedings may involve very serious insinuations of misconduct, the courts have been reluctant to apply a standard of proof based upon evidence which is indicative but not sufficiently conclusive of a director's culpability.[79]

A case example of what may, in its most liberal sense, be termed a restrictive application of the civil standard of proof is *Re Living Images Ltd*.[80] Here, Laddie J, in analysing the standard of proof required for proceedings under section 6, was adamant that a court should not, in determining the nature of a director's conduct, afford him the benefit of any reasonable doubt. However, in rejecting the criminal standard of proof, the learned judge opined that as disqualification proceedings were likely to introduce serious charges of moral condemnation, the courts should be wary of giving credence to allegations affecting a director's moral character, that is, without substantial evidence to confirm their validity. The learned judge also noted that the court should be wary of analysing the facts of a case with the benefit of hindsight.

In accepting that a court must appreciate that allegations concerning the unfitness of a director's conduct should be viewed with great caution, Laddie J indicated that the starting point for any investigation concerning the deficiency of a director's conduct would involve the court in recognising that the evidence against a director must, in terms of its probability, be overwhelming as opposed to marginally indicative of the director's culpability. In effect, therefore, the evidence required would extend the standard of proof beyond one based on a literal construction of the term "balance of probabilities".

Indeed, some case examples have specifically alluded to the standard of proof applicable to section 6 in language compatible to, and on occasions, positively affirmative of, a standard which is appropriate to criminal proceedings. For example, in *Re Swift 736 Ltd*,[81] Hoffmann J construed

---

[79] See, Dine "The Disqualification of Company Directors" (1988) 9 Co Law 213.
[80] [1996] 1 BCLC 348.
[81] [1993] BCLC 1.

section 6 as a penal provision and therefore found that the court, in assessing the evidence of a case, should afford a director the benefit of any reasonable doubt in its perception of the evidence of the case. Likewise, in *Re Polly Peck International plc*,[82] Lindsay J was of the opinion that a director should be given the benefit of any reasonable doubt. In this case, the learned judge, in commenting on the standard of proof required under section 6, remarked that,

"Where a provision, here s.6(1)(b), whilst not wholly or even primarily penal in intent, is none the less plainly quasi-penal in effect, it would, in my view, be wrong of a court, unless constrained to do so, to make the threshold which a complainant has to cross other than, and certainly not lower than, whatever Parliament shall by its language have provided".[83]

The justification for the adoption of a more restrictive standard of proof in relation to section 6 is based upon a natural and justifiable desire to protect a director's moral reputation, in circumstances where the evidence of a case is perhaps indicative but not overwhelming of the exactness of a finding confirming a director's unfitness to participate in the management of a company. However, in some cases, it is submitted that the underlying reason for the distortion in the civil standard of proof may be more aptly explained by the courts' desire to protect the commercial interests of a company's creditors and employees, persons who would otherwise be adversely affected by the disqualification of a company director.

9.8 Evidence in proceedings under section 6

9.8.1 *Hearsay evidence*

In relation to an application for a disqualification order, the court will, in accordance with section 1 of the Civil Evidence Act 1995, accept an affidavit which contains hearsay evidence, albeit that the weight to be attached to the hearsay evidence will be of a lesser degree than had the affidavit been supported by direct evidence. In *Re Rex Williams*,[84] Hoffmann LJ remarked that,

"In a disqualification application, hearsay evidence untested by cross examination of the informant may be insufficient to satisfy the burden of

---

[82] [1994] 1 BCLC 574.

[83] *Ibid.*, at p.581.

[84] [1994] Ch 350. This case concerned disqualification proceedings pursuant to the CDDA 1986, s.8. However, the position is the same for proceedings under the CDDA 1986, s.6, see, *Secretary of Trade v. Ashcroft* [1997] BCC 644.

proof against opposing evidence. It will depend upon the facts and probabilities of each case. Once the Secretary of State knows from the opposing affidavits which material facts are seriously in dispute, he may well be advised to reinforce his case by affidavits from the appropriate informants. But that is no reason why their hearsay evidence... should be inadmissible".[85]

9.8.2 *Evidence as to character*

Under the Rules of the Supreme Court, Ord. 41, r.6, the court may exercise a discretionary power to strike out of any affidavit a matter which is scandalous, irrelevant or otherwise oppressive. In respect of disqualification proceedings, evidence of a director's good and honest character will be caught by this discretionary power in so far as the question of a director's fitness to act in the management of a company is an issue for the court to decide. Indeed, in the context of civil proceedings, other than where character, in the sense of general reputation, is the principal issue of an action, evidence as to a respondent's character will ordinarily be inadmissible. This is to be contrasted to the position in criminal proceedings where the accused may lead evidence of character to attempt to bring himself within the generally held presumption that a person of good character would not commit a crime. Notwithstanding that disqualification proceedings may, in some respects, be likened to criminal proceedings, the courts have maintained that even in cases where a director's honesty is called into question, evidence of a director's general good character cannot be put before the court.[86]

Although the evidence of a third party in relation to matters of opinion will generally be inadmissible, by way of an exception, the opinion of an expert witness may be admissible. However, it should be noted that in accordance with RSC, Ord. 41, r.6, the court may order to be struck out of any affidavit any matter which is scandalous, irrelevant or otherwise oppressive. For example, in *Re Oakfame Construction Ltd*,[87] R Reid QC (sitting as a deputy High Court judge) struck out affidavits sworn by two accountants, acting as so-called expert witnesses. The affidavits were struck out on the grounds that they were irrelevant and oppressive. This matter was so decided on the premise that the accountants' reports (exhibited to their affidavits) consisted mainly of hearsay, advocacy and submissions, rather than what the learned judge perceived to be justifiable expert opinion.

---

[85] *Ibid.*, at p.367. See also, *Secretary of State v. Moffatt* [1996] 2 BCLC 21.

[86] See, for example, *Re Dawes & Henderson (Agencies) Ltd (in liquidation)* [1997] 1 BCLC 329.

[87] [1996] BCC 67. See also, *Re Pinemoor Ltd* [1997] BCC 708.

INDEX

Index compiled by John Jeffries